THE THIRD REICH IN ANTARCTICA

The German Antarctic Expedition

1938 - 39

THE THIRD REICH IN ANTARCTICA

The German Antarctic Expedition 1938-39

by

Cornelia Lüdecke & Colin Summerhayes

BLUNTISHAM BOOKS   ERSKINE PRESS

2012

THE THIRD REICH IN ANTARCTICA
The German Antarctic Expedition
1938-39

First published in 2012 by

The Erskine Press, The White House, Eccles, Norwich, NR16 2PB
WWW.ERSKINE-PRESS.COM
and
Bluntisham Books, Oak House, East Street, Bluntisham, Huntingdon, PE28 3LS
WWW.BLUNTISHAMBOOKS.CO.UK

Text © Cornelia Lüdecke & Colin Summerhayes

ISBN 978 1 85297 103 8

Typeset by Esme Power; Barkers Print & Design
Printed by CPI Group (UK) Ltd, Croydon, CR0 4YY

CONTENTS

Captain Alfred Ritscher

PREFACE

Anyone with enough money can now take a tourist ship to the Antarctic coast, or fly in to the Patriot Hills in the Ellsworth Mountains, southwest of the Weddell Sea, for an adventure holiday on ice. A mere click or two of the mouse will take any computer user to a detailed satellite map of the continent. Four thousand scientists spend large parts of the southern summer months based at one of 60 or so permanent or summer stations run by more than 30 countries on Antarctica or its offshore islands. With comfortable all-weather clothing, global positioning, and instant communications, conditions now are far more conducive to exploration and adventure on the continent than they were when the 3rd German Antarctic Expedition set sail in December 1938, with not even a map of where they were going. It was their job to make one.

The expedition continued a long-standing German interest in Antarctic exploration, which began with the establishment of a German research station on the sub-Antarctic island of South Georgia during the first International Polar Year of 1882-83. In 1898-99, the German Deep Sea Expedition on *Valdivia*, visited Bouvet Island and the waters off Antarctica's Enderby Land. In response to the International Geographical Congress of 1895 making Antarctica the main target for new geographical exploration, the first German Antarctic Expedition (1901-03), was launched under Erich von Drygalski on the *Gauss*. It discovered Kaiser Wilhelm II Land south of Kerguelen. Later, in 1911-12, a second German Antarctic Expedition was launched under Wilhelm Filchner on the *Deutschland*. This expedition entered the Weddell Sea and discovered the Luitpold Coast and the ice shelf later called the Filchner-Ronne Ice Shelf. In 1935, and again in 1937, Hans-Peter Kosack proposed a German Weddell Sea Expedition to continue the tradition, but resources were not available at that time.

Throughout the early exploration of Antarctica little attention had been paid to its Atlantic coast due south of Cape Town. Norwegian whaler Lars Christensen had sponsored expeditions there on the *Norvegia* (1927-31) and the *Thorshaven* (1932-37), which had photographed sections of the coast from the air. South Atlantic whaling also inspired the British, who had begun the *Discovery* investigations (1924-51), a scientific analysis of the conditions of the whale fishery off that same coast. And the German research ship *Meteor* had mapped the oceanography and bathymetry of the South Atlantic as far south as 64°S, south of Bouvet Island in 1925-27.

Inevitably, given the imperial ambitions of the early 1900s, Antarctic investigation and discovery gave rise to territorial claims:- Chile in 1904; Britain in 1908; France and New

Zealand in 1924; Norway in 1929; Australia in 1933. Christensen's investigations had led him to make unofficial claims on the area south of Cape Town, which he named Dronning (Queen) Maud Land. Byrd similarly made unofficial territorial claims on behalf of the USA in the 1930s. Australia's claim made the Germans too think about such possibilities for themselves.

In 1936/37 Germany had joined the whaling nations in the South Atlantic, keen to obtain whale oil without having to use valuable foreign currency reserves needed for rearmament. Its whaling fleet carried out scientific research on ocean conditions to improve understanding of the whales' environment. Considering that, like Britain, it needed a local whaling base, Germany decided to explore the possibility of setting up a supply base on the coast of Dronning Maud Land. In the absence of any formal claim to that coast by Norway, Germany saw an opportunity to claim Antarctic territory there for itself.

The primary drivers for the 3rd German Antarctic Expedition were thus economic and political. Geographical discovery was an essential first step towards occupying the region and setting up a whaling base there. And the expedition could also undertake valuable scientific investigations en route and along the coast. Three areas of scientific research were identified as high priority: first, to use the novel technology of echo-sounding to supplement the study of the topography of the South Atlantic seabed made by the *Meteor* in 1925-27; second, to use the novel technology of balloon-carried radio-sondes to probe the structure of the atmosphere on a north-south transect across the globe; third to use standard physical and biological oceanographic techniques to obtain more information about the characteristics of the whales' environment. In addition a secret visit was a planned to the uninhabited Brazilian islands of Trinidade and Martin Vaz, to assess their suitability as U-Boat bases in the event of war.

In these pages we tell the story of this ambitious and little-known expedition, which set out to map a large piece of Antarctica from the air, and in the process discovered an 800 km long mountain range and previously unsuspected freshwater lakes. The ship's meteorologists produced the data that led to the first section through the lower 20 km of the atmosphere, between 50°N and 80°S. From echo-soundings the geographer mapped the seabed from the equator to the coast at 70°S and deduced that the mid-ocean ridge was most likely volcanic in origin, a novel and plausible suggestion at that time.

Though their skill was great, their technology state-of-the-art and their luck stupendous in finding the coast virtually free of sea ice, their timing was bad. World War II erupted within a few months of their return to Germany. Whereas normally their geographical and scientific discoveries would have been rapidly disseminated world-wide, much of what they found remained unstudied following the death in war of almost half of the scientific party, and the destruction of much original material by bombing. Not until 1958 was a comprehensive collection of results published, as a German contribution to the International Geophysical Year of 1957-58. Even then its appearance in the German language was not conducive to its widespread dissemination and rapid use by others. Furthermore, some small reports were never published - like that on the visit to Trinidade, and the medical report. This book analyses the scientific achievements of the expedition in the light of later research, and provides the first comprehensive review in 70 years of the expedition's accomplishments.

We have written this book to bring this story to light, especially for the benefit of non-German speakers, since almost all of the few publications on the expedition remain solely in that language. We have benefited from the provision of generous access to the private files of the expedition's leader and its geographer, allowing us to lift a veil on the expedition, the official files of which were more or less totally destroyed during World War II. Access to those private files has provided us with authentic insight into the background to the expedition, helped us to give an extensive account of its activities and outcomes, and enabled us to dispel myths about the expedition and its aftermath. This real tale deserves to be told to a wider audience.

I
ORIGINS

CHAPTER 1: SETTING THE SCENE: WHALING - THE ECONOMIC ENGINE FOR ANTARCTIC EXPLORATION

Germany's Scientific Aspirations in Antarctica

The origins of the Third German Antarctic Expedition lie in a unique combination of the aspirations of German scientists to contribute as much as other industrial nations to exploring and understanding the Antarctic environment, and the Nazi Party's drive for self-sufficiency on the road to war.

Germany's early forays into Antarctic exploration were the inspiration of the eminent German scientist Georg von Neumayer (1826-1909), author of an autobiographical book entitled *Auf zum Südpol!* (To the South Pole! [1]). Neumayer had risen to prominence by founding and directing the Flagstaff Observatory for Geophysics, Magnetism and Natural Sciences in Melbourne, Australia, from 1857-64 [2]. Afterwards he returned to Germany to publish the results of his meteorological and magnetic observations. In 1871 he proposed to the International Geographical Congress in Antwerp that there should be an international research study of the still unknown continent of Antarctica. His efforts to find support for a German Antarctic expedition were to no avail, not least because for those with a polar interest Arctic research was easier and cheaper by virtue of proximity. Undeterred, in a lecture on geographical problems within the polar regions, which he delivered in Berlin in 1874, by which time he had become Hydrographer of the German Admiralty, he proposed – again to no avail - studies in both polar zones to resolve certain problems relating to the physics of the Earth. But his luck was about to change.

Quite coincidentally, Neumayer's plans to lead Germany into the Antarctic were forestalled at this very moment by another German, in the shape of Eduard Dallman (1830-96), who was commissioned by the German *Polarschiffahrtsgesellschaft* (Polar Shipping Association) to investigate the commercial potential of Antarctic whale and seal populations. Dallman carried out an expedition to the islands off the Antarctic Peninsula on his ship *Grönland* in 1873-74. Dallmann contributed significantly to knowledge about Antarctica, discovering Bismarck Strait and Neumayer Channel, among others. He is known to have landed on King George Island in the South Shetland Islands. Dallman Bay, between Anvers and Brabant Islands in the Palmer Archipelago is named after him, as is the 'Dallmann Laboratory' operated by the Alfred Wegener Institute for Polar and Marine Research on King George Island.

(From top)
Carl Weyprecht;
Eduard Dallmann;
Georg von Neumayer;
Erich von Drygalski;
Wilhelm Filchner

6

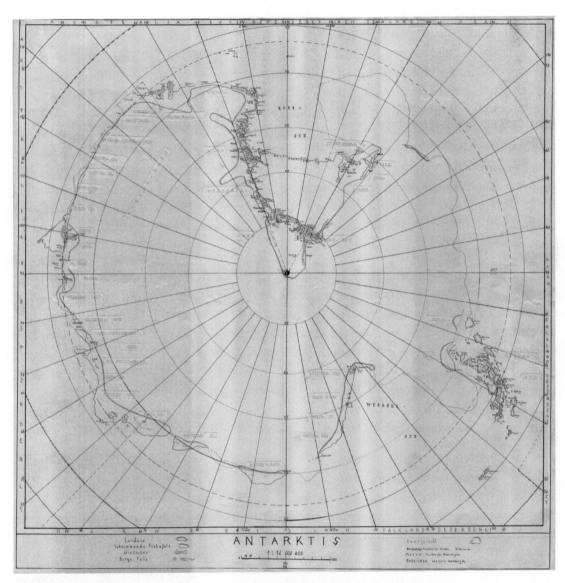

Unpublished map of Antarctica at 1: 10.000.000
scale constructed by Kosack in 1935 in
preparation for his proposed expedition

At about the same time, Carl Weyprecht (1831-81), a young German Lieutenant in the Imperial Austro-Hungarian Navy, was returning from leading the 1872-74 expedition that discovered Franz Josef Land in the high Arctic. He proposed that nations work together to solve a number of major scientific questions in meteorology and magnetism in the Arctic that could only be addressed by co-ordinated simultaneous research [3,4]. His proposal triggered the idea of an International Polar Year, which he duly presented to the International Meteorological Congress of 1879, in Rome. His idea was similar in some respects to that of Neumayer's of 1874, though much more detailed. By then, Neumayer, who had become Director of the *Deutsche Seewarte* (the German Naval Observatory) in 1876, was an influential member of the Meteorological Congress. With Neumayer's support, the Congress launched the process to create the first International Polar Year (IPY) of 1882-83, and, at Neumayer's insistence, included Antarctic stations. Given his position and his Antarctic interests, it is hardly surprising that Neumayer was elected to chair the first meetings of the International Polar Commission - known as the International Polar Conference – which planned the IPY, or that one of the two major IPY research stations in the south was a German one – on South Georgia.

Neumayer's influence continued through the International Geographical Congress of 1895, in London, which made the Antarctic a target for new geographic exploration and spawned many of the European activities we know today as the "Heroic Age" of Antarctic exploration [2,4]. To facilitate German involvement in these activities, a German Commission for South Polar Exploration was established under Neumayer's chairmanship. The Commission readied the First German Antarctic Expedition (1901-03) aboard the *Gauss*, under Erich von Drygalski (1865-1949), which visited the Antarctic coast at about 90°E. Given Neumayer's involvement in these various affairs it is no wonder that his name adorns the German Antarctic Station in Atka Bay in Dronning Maud Land.

In 1897 Neumayer was a member of another Commission that supported promotion of the German Deep Sea Expedition on the *Valdivia*, under Carl Chun (1852-1914), between 1898-99 [5]. The *Valdivia* visited Bouvet, fixed its position accurately, and surveyed the seabed around it, then headed east towards the Antarctic coast of Enderby Land, to carry out a wide range of oceanographic research including deep-sea soundings that showed that the Kerguelen Islands were separated from Antarctica by a deep ocean basin.

In due course a Second German Antarctic Expedition followed, on the *Deutschland*, under Wilhelm Filchner (1877-1957) in 1911-12. Drygalski's expedition was mainly financed by the German Reich: Filchner's, in contrast, was entirely privately organised and funded. Both expeditions focused on scientific and geographic discovery, and made no territorial claims for Germany. Whilst moderately successful in geographic exploration, they did provide a wealth of scientific data.

The 1925-27 German Atlantic Expedition on the *Meteor* visited Bouvet and penetrated as far south as 63° 51'S, 5° 16'E (on 24 February 1926) By now Germany had established a record of visiting the Antarctic region about once every decade, much like the British and the Americans. The next proposal came along in 1935 when Hans-Peter Kosack (1912-76), a young geographer, suggested to Johannes Georgi (1888-1972) of the Deutsche Seewarte that there be a German Weddell Sea Expedition to fill in geographic and glaciological gaps between the work of Filchner in the Weddell Sea, and the work of John Rymill (1905-68), who was then investigating Graham Land on the Antarctic Peninsula in 1934-37 [6].

Kosack also wanted to build on the results of the expeditions of Richard Evelyn Byrd (1888-1957) that took place on and around the Ross Ice Shelf in 1928-30 and 1933-35, and in particular to test the notion that there was a submarine trough connecting the Ross and Weddell Seas and separating East and West Antarctica[7]. Kosack proposed to take aircraft to carry out aerial surveys (like Byrd and Rymill), and to use the latest echosounders à la *Meteor* to map the depths of the Weddell Sea below the sea ice and the ice shelf. Kosack's plan for the German Weddell Sea Expedition did not get enough support from German geographers to enable him to apply for financial assistance, not least because he was young, unknown, and untested in polar exploration [8]. But his plan had sown seeds in peoples' minds.

The Origins of Political Support for Antarctic Exploration

Science by itself, then, was not enough to launch an Antarctic expedition in mid to late 1930s Germany. Support for such a venture only came about as part of the Nazi Party's drive for self-sufficiency on the road to war, and had very little indeed to do with science; the main driver was economic.

Hitler came to power in 1933 in a country suffering badly from the effects of the Great Depression, and still smarting from a sense of injustice over the arrangements for reparations after World War I. Playing strongly to populist expectations he set out three immediate requirements to revitalise the nation. First, Germany had to become a bulwark against the red tide of Bolshevism represented by the Soviet Union and its commitment to communist expansion, which was directly threatening Germany. Fighting Bolshevism called for weapons. Weapons called for raw materials – most of which lay outside Germany and under the control of the United States and the empires of France, Britain, and the Soviet Union. Second, like many Germans he thought that Germany was overpopulated and thus unable to feed itself adequately by increasing its agricultural yield. At the time, like France and Portugal, it was around 80% self-sufficient, hence reliant on imports to make up the difference. Unlike Germany, France had colonies to supply cheap food. In Hitler's mind an expansion of territory was required to provide the needed agricultural land some of which had been German before the Versailles Treaty. That realisation led to the third requirement - given that expansion outside Europe was not an option because it would bring Germany into direct competition with Britain, France and the United States, the territorial expansion had to take place in the east into what Hitler saw as *Lebensraum* - the vast underutilised spaces of Poland and Russia. Expanding east would provide land, food and raw materials, help to eradicate bolshevism, and make Germany once again the great power it was before the Treaty of Versailles, through which Germany lost its colonies and parts of eastern Germany (the Polish Corridor). Hitler's vision embraced a greater Germany incorporating those many Germans living outside the nation's borders, in Austria, Poland and Czechoslovakia. With such an expansion a resurgent Germany could once again take its 'deserved' place at the high table of the nations [9,10]. Expansion to the east was not a novel idea. There is compelling evidence that once the First World War had begun Germany saw occupation of land to the east as one solution to the (largely imaginary) crises of overpopulation and undersupply [11,12,13].

The resurgence that Hitler envisaged, based on a land-grab, demanded massive investments in military hardware to ensure that Germany could take what it wanted and keep it. Resources that might otherwise have gone into expanding industry to create wealth, instead went into expanding industry to generate guns. This was in direct conflict with the Treaty of Versailles, which intended that Germany should not re-arm. But Hitler gambled that the western democracies were too weak to respond to what he planned to do, and that he had the support of the German people many of whom, of all political persuasions, felt that the Treaty was unjust.

Whilst the manufacturing capacity for rearmament existed in Germany, buying the raw materials to build aeroplanes, ships, tanks and guns would cost scarce foreign exchange. The solution was to focus on self-sufficiency – autarchy – in as many realms of the economy as possible, so as to preserve the dwindling store of foreign currency for the purchase of raw materials for weapons [10]. The psychological assumptions underlying the adoption of the goal of food autarchy go back to the near starvation caused by the blockade of Germany in World War I, when around 150 million people in Germany and its occupied territories were suffering from hunger by the winter of 1916-17 [14]. Some 700,000 people starved to death in central Europe during the war, and another 900,000 people after it.

Building self-sufficiency was not something brought in by the Nazi Party; it had been a key to German economic development since the end of the First World War. However, in the Weimar Republic prior to 1933, food self-sufficiency had not been linked to rearmament, whereas in Nazi Germany it was so linked because food supply was seen as a key element of national security.

From 1934 onwards Hitler's Economics Minister, Hjalmar Schacht (1877-1970), applied a so-called New Plan with the motto 'Foreign trade without foreign currency', which prioritized the import of industrial raw materials ultimately destined for rearmament over the import of raw materials required for civilian consumption. The policy was not simply one of guns versus butter. Rearmament provided a means of rebuilding the economy. And if war were successful, in the end guns would bring more butter. Schacht's trade policy was also aimed at achieving some level of independence from the dominant economies of the United States, the British Empire and France, and was connected in turn to the repudiation of Germany's foreign debts to Britain and the USA [15]. In 1933, Germany still owed 19 billion Reichsmark to foreign creditors – at least 8.3 billion of them to the USA – all of which seriously threatened German living standards.

By August-September 1936 Hitler's logic had led him to develop a Four-Year Plan for the German economy. The plan's paramount objective was to develop the German army within a very short period to be the finest army in the world in respect of training, equipment and mobilisation. It called for acceleration in the pace of rearmament through a combination of increased production of domestically available materials like low grade German iron ore, further restriction of non-essential imports like coffee and tea, and substitution of essential imports with synthetic alternatives like ersatz fuel (petroleum created from coal), rubber and fats [10]. This was a plan for war. It called for the German armed forces and the German economy to be fit for war within four years. War would enable Germany to annex the living space and requisition the raw materials it needed to be the leading power in Europe and to eliminate the threat of Bolshevism. Hitler considered wisely that when they realised how fast he was rearming, Germany would very soon find itself in an arms race with Britain, France and Russia. Because he had started first, and in secret, he had a small window of opportunity. Postponing war longer than 1940 would enable those others to catch up, so eliminating the advantage Germany would obtain by getting prepared first. Indeed, it is true to say that the Hurricanes and Spitfires that won the Battle of Britain were built in the 11 months of peace bought by Neville Chamberlain with the appeasement of Munich – the British were rearming too, though not fast enough. Their defence budget rose from 12.5% in 1925 to 15% in 1932 then jumped to 44% in 1938; the corresponding German budget rose from 4% in 1925 to 25% in 1935 then jumped to more than 50% in 1938 [16].

On 4 April 1936, immediately following the remilitarisation of the Rhineland, Hitler appointed Hermann Göring (1893-1946) as special commissioner for foreign exchange and raw materials. His mission was to ensure 'continued military preparation'. On 18 October, Hitler put Göring in charge of implementing the Four-Year Plan. Acceleration was rapid; of the goods and services purchased by the Reich, the Wehrmacht would consume 70% in 1935 and 80% three years later [15]. The Plan would account for 20-25% of all investment in the German economy between 1936 and 1940. It would halve Germany's import bill by creating the capacity to produce raw materials to the tune of 2.3 billion Reichsmark, or roughly 5% of total German industrial production.

The German Fat Plan and the Need for Whale Oil

The part of this economic tale that lay behind the decision to send an expedition to Antarctica is the apparently mundane economic subject of the supply of fats. Since the late nineteenth century Germans had been eating more and more animal fats and protein – largely from German dairy animals, which depended in turn on an abundant supply of imported, high-energy, high-protein animal feeds, particularly vegetable fats from imported oilseed sourced from soya or peanuts among other things. By 1933-34, 30% of calories in the German diet came from fats and about 50% of the fats were imported as oilseed or other fats [14]. These imports imposed a serious burden on German's foreign exchange balance – something the Reichsbank could ill afford [15].

The German Fat Plan, which was devised in the early 1930s and later streamlined by the Nazis, was designed with the aim of enabling Germany to improve the efficiency of its supply of fats in the face of cuts in imported vegetable oils [14]. A government monopoly was created to control the entire market for edible fats including dairy products. This huge, synchronised and coordinated machine for fat production aimed to close 'the fat gap' by making Germany as far as possible independent of imported fats and fat-producing materials - not least because food supplies were considered basic for national defence. Agriculture was reorganised like an army, with the farmer as a private soldier under direct instruction.

The Fat Plan covered milk, cream, butter, cheese, lard, bacon, shortening, margarine, salad oils, soap, detergents, candles, linoleum and paints. It included oils as well as fats, since oils can be converted to fats by hydrogenation. One of the highest-grade sources of fat was whale oil. Whale oil was a prime source for the fats in German margarine, so the demand for whale oil had been rising along with the rising demand for margarine – the supply of butter not being enough to meet the public demand for fats in the diet, while the secret demand for technical fats in the armaments industry was also rising. Whale oil imports increased tenfold between 1924 and 1930, making Germany a leading buyer of whale oil; in some years almost half the world whale oil production was imported. In 1935, 54% of German margarine came from imported whale oil; by 1937 this had been reduced to 30.2%, to reduce the need for foreign exchange [17].

The Fat Plan included a national drive for increased food production. Determined efforts were made to increase agricultural production (including planting flax to supply vegetable oils), to improve the supply of butter, to cut oilseed imports, and to offset a cut in the supply of margarine (which used imported fats) [14]. These developments cut the 'fat' burden on the foreign exchange balance from more than 850 million Reichsmark per year in 1928 to less than 260 million Reichsmark by the mid 1930s [15].

THE MANIFOLD USES OF WHALE PRODUCTS

Whale oil contributed to the economy in a wide variety of ways. When purified, de-odorized, de-coloured and hydrogenated, whale oil could be used as frying and baking fat, as a substitute for lard, and as a raw material for margarine. It was also used in making soaps or detergents; in oiling wool for combing; in preparing vegetable fibres (e.g. flax) for spinning or weaving; for tanning hides, finishing fine leather, and making chamois; for waterproofing leather shoes and harness; as raw material for oil paints and in making oilcloth and linoleum; for lubricating the shafts of axles; or as fuel oil for lamps and stoves. A by-product of soap manufacture was glycerine – raw material for nitro-glycerine. Sperm whale heads provided spermacti, high quality liquid waxes used for lubricating watches, clocks and other sensitive machinery, and in face creams and other cosmetics. Baleen whales also provided whalebone – used from the 12th until the 20th century in a wide array of applications from medieval weaponry and armour to cabinet making and fashion, with corsets, stays, and farthingales being the most well known, as well as in brooms for chimney sweeps. Ambergris (a product from sperm whale intestines) was used in the perfume industry. Whales also provided whale meat, fertiliser, animal feed, hormones (from organs), and vitamin A (from the liver); as well as leather and glue. Military uses included explosives and lubrication of precision instruments[17].

The German Whaling Industry

As the world's biggest customer for whale oil, Germany had a dominant position in the oil market. However the rising demand for such oil, mostly imported from Norway, combined with dwindling foreign currency reserves began to create some economic stress within the Fat Plan. Entering the international competition for Antarctic whale oil under the German flag had been considered a very risky business. But this policy was overthrown in 1935, when Norwegian whaler owners made a bilateral currency clearing agreement dysfunctional by more than doubling their oil prices. In response, that year Germany decided to embark on the risky business of whaling [14,18]. It was recognised that initially the costs of German whale oil production would be high because of having to pay to construct new factory ships and whale catchers, but the advantage was that this would not be a drain on the scarce foreign currency reserves needed for rearmament.

The idea of a sizable whaling fleet flying the swastika flag over hostile Antarctic waters at the end of the world fitted well with the Nazi's political propaganda. The Nazi government's decision to encourage German whaling was thus hailed by the media and a few steadfast whaling lobbyists, and also by seaport-related businesses. The whale oil-consuming industries – the margarine and detergent producers – had to adapt to the new situation and started to build, convert or buy floating factory ships and whale catcher fleets. *Jan Wellem* [19], converted at the Bremer Vulkan yard in Vegesack from a HAPAG tourist cruise steamer to a whaling factory ship, and her eight newly-built *Treff* whale catchers, formed the first modern pelagic whaling fleet under the German flag to set sail for the Antarctic in autumn 1936. She was operated by the *Erste Deutsche Walfang Gesellschaft* (First German Whaling Company, Ltd), a filial company founded by the giant *Henkel* detergent trust. *Jan Wellem* was joined by two whaling fleets under German charter from Norway, C.A. *Larsen* and *Skytteren*, and under the Norwegian flag, but managed by the Hamburger Walfang Kontor (Hamburg Whaling Counting House Ltd) for a consortium of oil millers. For the following season the *Hamburger Walfang Kontor* purchased a Norwegian factory ship with eight catcher boats and renamed her *Südmeer*. The German branch of the British-Dutch *Unilever* trust established the *Unitas Deutsche Walfang-Gesellschaft mbH* (German Whaling Company Ltd) in Hamburg, and built the most modern floating factory of her time, *Unitas*, at the *Deschimag Weser* shipyard in Bremen. With similarly modern whale processing equipment, the newly built floating factory ship *Walter Rau* [20], was commissioned by *Walter Rau Walfang AG*. Rau (1874-1940), proud of being Germany's biggest (business) 'trust-free' margarine producer, had been one of the few entrepreneurs advocating German whaling and had founded a whaling study company in 1934. *Unitas*, *Walter Rau* and *Südmeer* augmented the German whaling fleet in the 1937/38 Antarctic whaling season. The fleet's latest addition, for 1938/39, was *Wikinger* and her eight whale catchers, all purchased from Norway and placed under the management umbrella of the *Hamburger Walfang Kontor*. [21].

Jan Wellem

Thus, within three Antarctic seasons, seven floating factory expeditions would operate for the German account, five under the German flag and two chartered ones under Norwegian registry, but with the funnel marks of their German charterers. With 53 whale catchers and an aggregate tonnage amounting to 96,884 gross tons this made Germany the world's third-largest whaling nation, after Norway and the UK, and before Japan. In something like a gold rush, another company, the "Walfang-Kontor Bremen" was founded, drafting plans for an eighth whaling fleet to join the others by 1940/41.

There were only two German shipmasters with whaling experience, captains Otto Kraul (1892-1972) and Karl Kircheiss. Kraul, having worked for Argentinian whaling companies around South Georgia and off Patagonia and for the Soviet *Aleut* whaling expedition in the North Pacific, acted as whaling manager on *Jan Wellem* in 1936/37 and 1937/38, under R. Schönwald as master. Kircheiss, with much less whaling experience than Kraul, but with more skills in blowing his horn, was made captain of *Wikinger* in 1938/39.

The German fleet adopted Norwegian methods, and used many Norwegians in its crews – especially as harpoon gunners, although German gunners were trained. In 1937-38, its second whaling year, the German fleet secured 11.4% of all Antarctic catches and 10.7% of all Antarctic oil. The German share of world whaling was around 12% in 1938-39 [22].

The German whale oil share eventually helped reduce the quantities imported from Norway by about a quarter. Germany cut its imports from Norway from 230,469 tons in 1935, to 115,580 tons in 1936 and 107,000 tons in 1937-38, thus saving significant amounts of foreign currency.

Optimism concerning German whaling proved short-lived. The fleets had already been fitted out for the 1939-40 Antarctic season, when the outbreak of war in September 1939 terminated all efforts. The floating factories were requisitioned as tankers and military transport vessels, and the whale catchers as minesweepers, submarine chasers and naval patrol boats.

The Man Behind the *Schwabenland* Expedition.

The man in charge of German whaling was Councillor of State Helmut Wohlthat (1893-1982), [23] an economist with a master's degree in political science from New York's Columbia University (1932), who had lived in the USA and Mexico and become an expert in the international fats and oils trade. Wohlthat was intimately familiar with Germany's need to obtain more whale oil [24]. Before becoming Councillor of State for Special Duties within the Four Year Plan, and soon after the Nazis took power, he had initially been put in charge of the newly-founded fat monopoly institute, later renamed the Reich Office for

Catcher
Treff from
Jan Wellem

The whaler
Walter Rau

Milk Products, Oils and Fats, which was responsible for increasing oil seed production and regulating the consumption of oils and fats within the framework of the national emergency Fat Plan. He had then worked for Economic Minister Schacht as head-of-department in the Ministry of Economics, with huge responsibilities aimed at removing the negative trade balance of Nazi Germany, under Minister Schacht's New Plan, the motto for which was 'Foreign Trade without Foreign Currency' *(Aussenhandel ohne Devisen)*. Later that year he was put in charge of the Reich-Institute for the Regulation of Foreign Exchange

Helmut Wohlthat

in which position he practically controlled the import of oils and fats. After the increase in whale oil import prices in 1935, it was his expert advice that changed the official position of the Reich concerning German whaling [18, 25, 26]. He must be regarded as the mastermind of the new German pelagic whaling industry, holding paramount responsibilities for its economic and legal implications.

From the start, Wohlthat and his colleagues strove to secure a long-term basis for the new whaling industry. This was attempted in such diverse fields as (a) operations, logistics and production, (b) international law, (c) scientific research, and (d) by a handbook condensing all these aspects for decision-makers into a convenient format. Part of the systematic effort to secure a long-term basis for Germany's new whaling industry was to establish a National Institute for Whale Research at the Zoological Museum and Institute in Hamburg in autumn 1937.

Given its growing interest in whaling, Germany was concerned at the international level with any efforts to regulate whaling, and with anything that might restrict its right to exploit the whale-rich waters of the Antarctic. To protect its interests, Wohlthat led the German delegation to international whaling conferences in London in 1937, 1938 and 1939. His scientific advisor at those meetings was Dr Nicolaus Peters (1900-1940), Director of the new National Institute of Whale Research. Germany signed the 1937 Whaling Agreement, but did not ratify it so as not to hamper herself by legal restrictions during her learning phase.

As an aside, but highlighting Wohlthat's key role in Nazi economic policy, his participation in the London whaling conference of July 1939 was looked upon as camouflage for secret talks with high-ranking British politicians, economists and industrialists. *Time Magazine* called him "Hitler's star travelling salesman", and suspected that a tentative scheme drafted in these talks to prevent the impending war was intentionally blown by Wohlthat [27].

The operation of the German whaling fleet in the South Atlantic, far from home, raised the question of whether or not its efficiency might be improved by establishing an Antarctic base, much like the Argentine, British and Norwegian whaling stations on South Georgia. This question was thrown into high relief by the coming into effect of the 'Australian Antarctic Territory Acceptance Act 1933' on 24 August 1936, which declared certain Antarctic land areas to be Australian territory. The German Foreign Office quickly raised questions about how this might affect the new German whaling industry in the Antarctic. To protect German economic interests, the ministry thought that the occupation of Antarctic areas by the Reich might be an option. A letter dated 27 November 1936 from the German Foreign Office to its embassy in Oslo specified some areas for a possible occupation by Germany, viz 80° W – 150° W, without Peter I Island, or 20° W – 45° E, without Bouvet Island [28]. It also noted that areas might perhaps be included where the Norwegian flag had been raised without them being formally "annexed" by Norway. Occupying territory on the unclaimed Antarctic mainland east of the land and ocean area claimed by Britain could provide a territorial basis for German whaling, and thereby avoid German ships having to pay Britain for whaling concessions. Implicit in the plan was the requirement for a depot of some kind on land as a base for local operations of Germany's factory ships. This idea was shelved temporarily, but the success of the German whaling fleets in subsequent seasons prompted its re-examination, and, in 1938, Wohlthat resuscitated the idea, targeting the 'unclaimed' Antarctic coast east of the British area for reconnaissance. Wohlthat put his plan for securing German whaling to his superior, Hermann Göring, the Commissioner for the Four Year Plan for economic development. Following consultation with other ministries, Göring approved the concept, and on 9 May 1938 assigned resources for a reconnaissance expedition, including a ship and two seaplanes for aerial survey and photographic mapping. The Third German Antarctic Expedition was born.

Needless to say, the background was not scientific curiosity, but international law, power politics and the economics of Antarctic whaling. Nevertheless, geographical and scientific exploration, in addition to economic exploitation were significant assets in manifesting a nation's claim to sovereignty in the event of nations proceeding to divide Antarctica's land and seas up among themselves. Put simply, the claims of whalers and explorers combined were more difficult to push aside than those of whalers alone. The expedition therefore was motivated by the political will and economic necessity – clearly seen by Wohlthat – not to leave the polar and whale research schemes of other nations, with their hidden legal and geopolitical agendas, to the world powers and established whaling nations [23, 24].

The expedition was not the sole means of supporting potential German claims in the Antarctic. The whaling fleets under the swastika flag were publicised as the 'German colony in the Antarctic' [29]. A documentary film titled *Kolonie Eismeer* (Colony in the Polar Sea) was shot on board the German floating factory ship *Wikinger* in the 1938/39 season at the behest of the Reich Ministry of Food and Agriculture and the Administrative Office of the Leader of the Reich's Farmers. The production costs were allocated to the budget of the

Reich-Institute for Whale Research [30]. The film was shown in early 1940. In line with the popular colonial theme, the German floating factories had official German "post offices" on board, unlike all other whaling fleets of the time. That was because the establishment of a regular postal service could be seen as a significant factor in support of a nation's claim to sovereignty over certain areas. In practise this meant that the ship's purser wielded a cancellation stamp for outgoing mail which carried a post office registration number, the name of the floating factory, and its location - "South Polar Ocean" [31].

With the political directions decided, it would now be necessary to incorporate into the plans for the expedition the ideas for scientific exploration that had been proposed by Kosack in 1935, so as to make more of the expedition than just a whaling venture. The scene was now set for a German contribution to geographic exploration of the Antarctic continent – something that became a prime goal of the coming expedition – and to add a host of scientific activities en route to and from Antarctica and along the Antarctic coast.

References

1. Neumayer, G. von, 1901, Auf zum Südpol! 45 Jahre Wirkung zur Förderung der Erforschung der Südpolar-Region, 1855-1900. Vita Deutsches Verlagshaus, Berlin, 485 pp.

2. Lüdecke, C. 2004a. The first International Polar Year (1882– 83): a big science experiment with small science equipment. History of Meteorology 1, 55–64. http://www.meteohistory.org/2004proceedings1.1/pdfs/06luedecke.pdf

3. Berger, F.; Besser, B P., und R.A. Krause, 2008, Carl Weyprecht (1838-1881) - Seeheld, Polarforscher, Geophysiker: Wissenschaftlicher und privater Briefwechsel des österreichischen Marineoffiziers zur Begründung der internationalen Polarforschung. Verlag der Österreichischen Akademie der Wissenschaften, Wien, 587 pp.

4. Summerhayes, C.P., 2008, International collaboration in Antarctica: the International Polar Years, the International Geophysical Year, and the Scientific Committee on Antarctic Research. Polar Record 44 (231): 321–334.

5. Chun, C., 1900, Aus den Tiefen des Weltmeeres. Gustav Fischer, Jena, 549 pp.

6. Lüdecke, C., 1995. Die deutsche Polarforschung seit der Jahrhundertwende und der Einfluß Erich von Drygalskis, Berichte zur Polarforschung 158, 340 pp, 72 pp. appendix.

7. Kosack, H.-J., 1935, Map of Antarctica 1: 10.000.000. Archive, Geographical Institute, University of Göttingen. Unpublished.

8. Kosack, H.-J., 2 July 1935, Note to Professor Meinardus. Archive, Geographical Institute, University of Göttingen. Unpublished.

9. Burleigh, M., 2001, The Third Reich; a New History. Pan Books, London, 965 pp.

10. Ferguson, N., 2006, The War of the World: History's Age of Hatred. Allen Lane, Penguin. London, 746 pp.

11. Schama, S., 2004, Landscape and Memory. Harper Perennial, London, 652 pp (p.64).

12. Fischer, F., 1967, Germany's Aims in the First World War, WW Norton, London and New York, 252-3, 278 and 313-6.

13. Benz, W., Graml, H., and H. Weiß (eds.), 1997, Enzyklopädie de Nationalsozialismus. Deutscher Taschenbuchverlag,

München, 900 pp.

14. Brandt, K., 1938, The German Fat Plan and its Economic Setting. Stanford Univ. Calif., Food Res. Inst., Sept. 1938. Fats and Oils Studies No. 6, 344 pp.

15. Tooze, A., 2006, The Wages of Destruction: the Making and Breaking of the Nazi Economy. Allen Lane, Penguin, London, 800 pp.

16. Ferguson, N., 2002, The Cash Nexus.: Money and Power in the Modern World 1700-2000. Penguin Books, London, 553 pp.

17. Brandt, K., 1940, Whale Oil: An Economic Analysis. Stanford Univ. Calif., Food Res. Inst., June 1940. Fats and Oils Studies No.7, 264 pp.

18. Scholl, L. U., 1991, "Whale Oil and Fat Supply. German Whaling 1936-1939", International Journal of Maritime History, 3 (2), 1991, 39-62.

19. Henkel & Cie, (ed) 1939, Der wiedererstandene deutsche Walfang dargestellt an der Entwicklungsgeschichte der Ersten Deutschen Walfang-Gesellschaft in Verbindung mit einem Reisebericht über die 2. "Jan Wellem"-Expedition von Wolfgang Frank. Bagel, Düsseldorf, 146 pp. (Description of the restart of German Whaling and a description of the Whaling aboard "Jan Wellem" in the 1937/38 season.)

20. Winterhoff, E., 1974, Walfang in der Antarktis, Stalling AG, Oldenburg, 234 pp. (History of German Whaling)

21. Barthelmess, K., 1993, A Century of German Interests in Modern Whaling, 1860s - 1960s. In: Bjørn L. Basberg, Jan Erik Ringstad & Einar Wexelsen (eds.): Whaling and History - Perspectives on the Evolution of the Industry (= Kommandør Chr. Christensens Hvalfangstmuseum, publikasjon 29). Sandefjord, 121-138.

22. Barthelmess, K., 2005, Competing with Norway for Antarctic whale oil – Britain and Germany. In: Nihon Geirui Kenkyujo (ed.): Learning from the Antarctic Whaling. Report and Proceedings, International Symposium Commemorating the Centennial of Antarctic Whaling. Tokyo: Institue of Cetacean Research, 31–66.

23. Ritscher, A., 1942, Wissenschaftliche und fliegerische Ergebnisse der Deutschen Antarktischen Expedition 1938/39, Hrsg. im Auftrag der Deutschen Forschungsgemeinschaft. Koehler & Amelang, Leipzig. Vol. 1: Text, 304 pp., Pictures and Maps 57 plates and 3 maps.

24. Lüdecke, C., 2004b, (see English resume on page 100: Secret Mission to the Antarctic: The Third German Antarctic Expedition –1938/39 – and the plan to occupy territory to protect the German whaling industry). "In Geheimer Mission zur Antarktis: Die Dritte Deutsche Antarktische Expedition 1938/39 und der Plan einer territorialen Festetzung zur Sicherung des Walfangs". Schiffahrtsarchiv 26 (2003) Deutsches Schifffahrtsmuseum, Bremerhaven, und Convent Verlag GmbH, Hamburg, Vol. 26, 75-100.

25. Scholl, L. U., 1988, "German Whaling in the 1930s". In: Lews R. Fischer, Helge W. Nordvik and Walter E. Minchinton (eds.): Shipping and Trade in the Northern Seas 1600-1939. Yearbook of the Association for the History of the Northern Seas, Bergen, 103-121.

26. Bohmert, F., 1982, Der Walfang der Ersten Deutschen Walfang Gesellschaft. Ein Beitrag zur Geschichte des Unternehmens Henkel. Düsseldorf: Henkel, 1982, 159 pp. Also issued in a shortened, but illustrated version as: Vom Fang der Wale zum Schutz der Wale. Wie Henkel Wale fing und einen Beitrag zu ihrer Rettung leistete (= Schriften des Werksarchivs der Henkel KGaA Düsseldorf, 14). Henkel & Cie, Düsseldorf: 149 pp.

27. Anon, 1939, "Smoke and fire". Time magazine, 31 July 1939 http://aolsvc.timeforkids.kol.aol.com/time/magazine/article/0,9171,761769,00.html

28. Foreign Office, 27 November 1936, Letter of the Foreign Office to its embassy in Oslo. Political Archive of the Foreign Office, Bonn, AA Oslo Fach 201, Pol 3, 8b, Bd, 152, Unpublished.

29. Wegener, K. A., 1938, "Die deutsche Kolonie in der Antarktis". In: Peters, N., 1938, Der neue deutsche Walfang: Ein praktisches Handbuch seiner geschichtlichen, rechtlichen, naturwissenschaftlichen und technischen Grundlagen. Hansa, Hamburg: 1-5.

30. Bundesarchiv Koblenz R15V/288 (correspondence of 03/11/1938). Unpublished.

31. Noltemeyer, W., 1949, "Deutsche Schiffspost im Südlichen Eismeer". Reprinted in: Postgeschichtliche Blätter Hamburg, 29, 1986, 41 – 46.

CHAPTER 2: PLANNING AND MANAGEMENT

Competition with Norway

In 1938, nobody knew much about Dronning Maud Land. The only people to have seen parts of its coast were the Norwegians. During the *Norvegia* Expedition in the southern summer of 1929/30 they had photographed the coast from a seaplane between longitudes 60°E and 20°W [1,2,3]. Rather than land, it turned out to be the seaward edge of a floating ice shelf. Based on that survey, Christensen stated that he claimed this stretch of coast for Norway, but the claim was not formalised at the time through the Norwegian parliament. The Norwegians' interest in this area was the same as that of the Germans. They wanted to expand their commercial whaling into waters east of the British sector, so as to be able to hunt whales without having to pay dues to Britain, which they did when whaling around South Georgia and the South Shetlands Islands in Britain's Falkland Islands sector [4].

At about the same time as the Norwegians had been undertaking their survey, the British and Australians had together been surveying the coast yet further east. Indeed, the Norwegian and the British/Australian survey areas overlapped between 45°E and 60°E. To avoid any jurisdictional disputes the three nations agreed in 1933 that the mutual boundary lay at 45°E. That did not stop Christensen from worrying that eventually the British might also claim the sector that he wanted for Norwegian whaling between 20°W and 45°E. To forestall any such possibility, the Norwegian Foreign Ministry told the London Foreign Office in January 1934 of their interest in claiming that territory. London said it wasn't interested, which may perhaps help to explain why Norway did not formally press its claim by an act of parliament at that time. Having established the boundaries of the territory, Christensen felt comfortable enough in 1938 to give it a name - Dronning (i.e. Queen) Maud Land [3,5]. But what lay inland from the shoreline remained a mystery – a blank on the map.

In 1938, then, this was virgin, frontier territory. Nobody formally 'owned' it yet, though other nations were aware of the Norwegians' interest. This no man's land was a tempting prize for a Germany with an interest in expanding its whaling fleet to gain supplies of much needed oil, and with imperial ambitions. If they surveyed the area and claimed it formally before Norway did, they would be on a par with imperial Britain, which already owned chunks of the icy wastes of the continent. And with a base in the area their whalers also would not have to pay dues to Britain. Claims would be all the stronger if supported by occupation, which the Norwegians had not planned for.

Aside from the hunt for a suitable base for the German whaling fleet, the challenge of geographical discovery, and the possibility of gaining some Antarctic territory perhaps rich in unimagined mineral resources, the expedition was destined to include some time for science, to continue the great traditions of German polar exploration that began with the work of Drygalski in Kaiser Wilhelm II Land (90°E) in 1901-03, and of Filchner in the southern Weddell Sea in 1911-12. While these earlier expeditions provided the leaders of the 3rd German Antarctic Expedition with some guidance in terms of the general conditions to be expected (and indeed Drygalski had visited the leader of the 3rd expedition in his office in 1938 to provide advice) [6] they had taken place in different geographic areas from that targeted by the 3rd expedition, and had not involved aerial photographic surveys, so were strictly speaking not entirely relevant. Besides, Christensen's Norwegian forays into the area had been peripheral to say the least, and offered little information helpful to the evolving German plans.

The Germans were well aware both of the Norwegians' activities and interests and of their use of aircraft for Antarctic exploration, not least because Adolf Hoel (1879-1964), the Director of Norway's Svalbard and Arctic Ocean Research Survey, NSIU, had presented a paper at the Lilienthal Society in Berlin on "The use of airplanes and airships in the exploration of polar regions", which was published in the journal of the Berlin Society of Geography [7,8]. Hoel had travelled to Berlin on the occasion of the 110th anniversary of this society on 14 May 1938 to give a speech on the history and exploration of Svalbard. During the meeting he was honoured with the Ferdinand von Richthofen Gold Medal for his achievements in polar research.

Knowing the interest of the Norwegians in this part of the Antarctic, the organisers of the German expedition decided to keep their plans secret [9]. As Roald Amundsen had done 27 years previously to deceive his rival, Robert Falcon Scott, the expedition was officially listed as directed to the Arctic. Orders for materials specified that they were for an Arctic expedition.

The Plan – A Flying Visit

The Naval High Command recommended three possible routes for the German expedition, and marked them on a map from the British *Discovery* Reports: along the 0° Greenwich Meridian, at 90°W, and at 120 °W. This map, together with the proposal for the scientific research programme, was classified with the stamp "Geheime Kommandosache" (top-secret document) and sent to five of the organisations involved in detailed planning [10]. The shortest route along the Greenwich meridian was most favoured, because it led directly to the German whaling grounds south of Cape Town.

24

The Dornier - Wal flying-boats, *Passat (top)* and *Boreas*

The expedition also had a hidden military dimension. On their return journey they were to visit the tropical Brazilian islands of Trinidade and Martin Vaz, in the western South Atlantic 1000 km east of Vitória, to check on the suitability of the islands as bases for U-boats in the event of war [9].

The overall plan called for a series of expeditions to Antarctica, each building on the success of its predecessor. Since the objective of the first was reconnaissance, the organisers decided to keep costs down by only carrying out an aerial survey using state-of-the-art photogrammetric techniques as the basis for making a topographic map of the region. But the lack of an accompanying land expedition to determine ground control points for the aerial survey map led to some wrong assumptions in its construction. In the long run that would not be a problem provided a follow-up expedition could carry out land-based exploration to establish ground control points while the coastal base was being built.

AERIAL SURVEY

The success of their plan would make the Germans only the fourth party to carry out a systematic survey of inland Antarctica. The first aerial photographic survey flight over Antarctica was made only a decade earlier on 18 February 1929 by Capt. Ashley McKinley (US Army Air Corps) on an expedition to the Ross Ice Shelf led by US Navy Commander Richard Byrd [12]. During their sojourn at their Little America base on the ice shelf, Byrd's group took aerial photographs with 60% overlap and tied to ground control points to facilitate accurate mapping over a large area. Later, as Rear-Admiral Byrd, he continued this work over and around the Ross Ice Shelf from his Little America II base during his second expedition, in 1933-35. Byrd's aircraft flew from landing strips on the ice [13]. In December 1936, the Norwegian Lars Christensen used a different technique, a seaplane that could take off from and land on the ocean, to be recovered from ships offshore, which had been trialled on the *Norvegia* expedition in 1929-30. Working from the *Thorshavn*, his seaplane made an oblique aerial photographic survey of the coasts discovered on the *Norvegia* voyages, using a camera designed to overlap each frame by 60% to provide stereoscopic images suitable for map-making. Working westwards from 85°E to 20°E, they found and photographed a chain of mountains near the coast between 34°E and 40°E. On 6 February 1937, near longitude 26°E, they flew inland and found another long continuous chain of mountains, now known as the Sør Rondane Mountains, some 200 km from the coast [3,5]. They did not fly over the land or the ice shelf between 20°E and 20°W – the area of interest to the Germans.

To substantiate a potential future claim to territory, plans were made for the German airmen to drop onto the ice at 20-30 km intervals 1.5 m long weighted aluminium darts whose tails were engraved with the national symbol – the swastika [11]. In addition they were supposed to drop a weighted German flag at the furthest point south on each flight.

The Germans planned to steam in by ship during a short summer campaign, survey by air, and steam out again – fast, efficient, effective (and, most of all, relatively cheap). For aircraft, they would use the facilities of Lufthansa's South American mail service, with its two 10-ton Dornier-Wal flying boats, *Boreas* and *Passat* [14,15], and their launch vessel – the *Schwabenland*.

Clearly the Germans would have to be lucky with the weather and the pack ice to avoid delays. Whatever they did they would be taking a gigantic gamble, like all polar explorers before them, by setting off into the unknown without maps or rescue teams, and with the crudest of navigational equipment. They were brave men engaged in a perilous enterprise. It must have been comforting to them to know that while many of them were complete novices to Antarctic exploration, their party was seeded with some veterans hardened by experience in the Arctic.

The planes were of an unusual design, monoplane seaplanes with two 'push-pull' propellers located fore and aft on top of the wing, below which the hull was suspended. The planes would be under the command of two Lufthansa pilots Rudolf Mayr (flying the *Passat*) and Richard Heinrich Schirmacher (flying the *Boreas*). Each plane was equipped with sophisticated aerial photographic equipment allowing collection of the overlapping frames required for mapping.

Rudolf Mayr

Richard Heinrich Schirmacher

The planes would be launched from their floating airport, the 8,500-ton catapult ship *Schwabenland*. Built in 1925, this 143 m long ship first served as a freighter sailing to India under the name *Schwarzenfels* [11]. In 1934 it was remodelled as a catapult ship to become the floating airbase for transatlantic air traffic on the Europe to South America run for the Deutsche Lufthansa, under the name *Schwabenland*. Its engines drove it along at around 11 knots and it was large enough to accommodate two 10-ton planes and their launch and recovery equipment. From the bow the ship looked like a freighter with two masts. It had a black hull shading to red below the water line, and a brilliant white superstructure, which carried the bridge and the passenger quarters between the masts. Aft of the superstructure came the grey-painted catapult equipment and the two silver aircraft. Lufthansa's logo decorated the single funnel.

Aerial reconnaissance from planes based on ships was not new, but the concept of undertaking a systematic aerial survey with two planes from a floating base offshore was indeed novel, as was the use of a ship to catapult the planes into the air. Nevertheless, this would not be the first time that German scientists had photographed Antarctica from the air. Emil Philippi did so from a tethered balloon on the Wilhelm II Coast on 29 March 1902 during Drygalski's expedition. Ernest Shackleton beat him to it by a few weeks in McMurdo Sound on 4 February that same year from a tethered balloon on Scott's first expedition.

Schwabenland

FLYING IN ANTARCTICA

Aside from being the fourth comprehensive continental aerial photographic mapping expedition in Antarctica, the German team was among the first seven groups to use aircraft anywhere in Antarctica for any purpose [16]. First had been Hubert Wilkins' team in 1928-29 and again in 1929-30 over the Antarctic Peninsula. His second expedition overlapped with those of the Norwegians operating from the *Norvegia* in 1929-30, and the British-Australian-New Zealand Antarctic Research Expedition (BANZARE) operating from the *Discovery* in the Indian Ocean sector between 45°E and 160°E in 1929-30 and again in 1930-31. Besides Byrd's two expeditions (1929-1930, 1933-35), John Rymill explored the Peninsula by air during the British Grahamland Expedition of 1934-37, and Christensen the Indian Ocean sector in 1936-37. Lincoln Ellsworth flew across Antarctica from Dundee Island at the tip of the Antarctic Peninsula to Byrd's Little America II base on the Ross Ice Shelf in November-December 1935, and planned to survey parts of the coast in the Indian Ocean sector in the 1938-39 season. Alas, the weather and the pack ice were against him, and just a few flights were managed between longitudes 70° E and 80° E near the Amery Ice Shelf, where he discovered the American Highlands on 11 January 1939, just before the Germans reached Antarctica. Nevertheless, Ellsworth achieved his goal, claiming a vast area of the continent for the USA. It was not just the Norwegians, the British and the Germans who were interested in claiming pieces of Antarctica.

Manning the Expedition

Aside from the planes and the ship, the third key to success would be the people. Their selection was a top-down process – hardly surprising, given the imperatives of the German Fat Plan. The scientific team, the flyers and the photographers were appointed by various ministries and non-governmental organizations, and given special leave to join the expedition. Selection sees to have been based largely on prior polar experience, with little or no attention being paid to political affiliations. Indeed, the evidence suggests that very few of those selected were members of the National Socialist Party[17]. The ship's crew appear to have been given little choice; they knew their ship and others did not, so they had to go south.

Enter Alfred Julius Fritz Ritscher (1879-1963), a seasoned polar explorer, ship's captain and aircraft pilot. Ritscher had not been to the Antarctic, but had been captain of the *Herzog Ernst* during the fateful Schröder-Stranz expedition to Svalbard in 1912 [18,19]. He

29

knew all too well how tough polar exploration could be. The *Herzog Ernst* had become frozen in to the ice off the northeastern coast of Spitsbergen when winter arrived suddenly and unexpectedly in September 1912. The party split up, and Ritscher and two others stayed in an empty seal hunter's hut on the coast. Their condition deteriorated. In December, in the full 24-hour darkness of winter, realising they would all die without help, Ritscher took advantage of the next moonlit period and set off with his dog "Bella"

Captain Alfred Ritscher

and very few provisions - three pieces of cooked but frozen reindeer meat the size of a fist, and four kilos of uncooked barley, - on a dangerous march of 210-km - towards the settlement of Advent Bay (today called Longyearbyen), guiding himself by the stars [18]. Day and night the temperature stood between -27 and -39°C. He marched like a machine, stopping occasionally for brief naps during which he was quickly covered by a blanket of snow. To avoid sleeping for long enough to freeze to death he used his alarm clock to wake himself after 10 to 15 minutes, then got up and marched some more. His hopes of finding a hut en route where he could cook his barley for the festive meal of which he dreamt all day every day were dashed. The fates seemed to be against him. Reaching Isfjord on Christmas Eve he found his path blocked by a lead of open water. Luckily the wind shifted and the lead closed enough for him to jump across it from floe to floe, sometimes breaking through the thin ice and getting wet feet. Miraculously, after 9 days and nights without food and with hardly any sleep, he stumbled into the settlement, nearly starved and almost frozen to death. He had survived, though losing half of the little finger of his right hand and half of his right foot and the big toe of his left foot to frostbite in the process. When the moon shone again on 19 January 1913 a rescue party started out, accompanied by "Bella", but had to return due to the fierce cold. At last it was able to leave Advent Bay on 24 January and found Ritscher's small crew and two expedition members, but not the other seven missing men. The following summer the ship was broken free of the ice, and Captain Ritscher had the pleasure of sailing it home.

On 20 July 1938, Rear-Admiral Dr Conrad, of the Naval High Command personally asked Ritscher to take over leadership of the Antarctic expedition because of his unusual talents [20,21]. He was the only German sea captain, apart from whaling captains, to have ice experience at sea (though only in the Arctic). In addition, and unlike the whaling captains, he had also gained extensive ice experience on land, and, even more, he was an airplane pilot, having commanded an aircraft company (Feldflieger) of the German Navy in Flanders during the first World War. He knew what aircraft could do, and – equally important - what they could not do. In the minds of the German Navy, for whom he worked in a civilian capacity, the slim 60 year old lightly bearded merchant captain of about 1.80 m height with his pale blue eyes and blond hair was the only suitable man for the *Schwabenland* job. A subsequent letter on 5 October 1938 from the Office of the Four Year Plan confirmed the appointment, back-dated to 1 September of that year [22].

Alfred Ritscher was born on 23 May 1879 in Bad Lauterberg in the middle of Germany, the son of a medical doctor. Instead of following in the footsteps of his father, he left high school (the Gymnasium at Wittenberg) in 1897. Two more years would have been needed for him to pass the final exam to enter university, but that was not his chosen path. He left school early to begin a career in the merchant navy, where he would eventually earn his captain's ticket. Like all young Germans at that time he was expected to spend some time in military service as well. From 1903-1904 he served as volunteer in the German Navy, and he continued to participate in naval reserve exercises until autumn 1911, when he was gazetted first lieutenant. In his civilian capacity he earned his living as an officer aboard ships of the Hamburg-Süd and Hamburg-Amerika Lines until October 1911. He then moved to the Nautical Department of the Reich Navy Board in Berlin, where he worked from November 1911 to 31 June 1914 as a civilian scientific employee on editing the Maritime Handbooks for various regions. During that time he came to know Schröder-Stranz, and took leave to participate as captain of the vessel *Herzog Ernst* in the Schröder-Stranz expedition between 1 August 1912 and 1 September 1913.

Ritscher got his pilot's licence in 1915, during the First World War. It enabled him to serve as a navy-army-pilot, and later as commander of the army aircraft men (Kommandeur der Landflieger) at the navy station in Wilhelmshaven on the North Sea coast. During the war he was decorated with the Iron Cross and the Knight's Cross. After the war he returned to the Nautical Department in Berlin where he continued editing the Maritime Handbooks until they were terminated for lack of financial support at the end of September 1919.

Ritscher was very interested in art, and painted watercolours in his leisure time. On 30 August 1915 he married the talented and wealthy Jewish artist Susanne Loewenthal [23]. They had two children, a son born in 1916 and a girl born in 1918. To earn a living for his young family after the war he accepted several civilian jobs in Hamburg, one as military-technical leader of the civil defence force and another as a company leader in the security police. In July 1920 he started training in business, and ended up first as an accountant in industry and then as a self-employed businessman, working with a partner to sell technical equipment for modern seagoing vessels. On 1 July 1924 he was able to return to his old job at the Nautical Department, and he moved back to Berlin with his family. When he realised that there was no chance of promotion within the Reich Navy Board, he moved to the newly founded Deutsche Luft Hansa AG (later called Lufthansa) on 15 April 1926. There he led the navigation department and acted as deputy for the department for securing air routes. Because of his work he travelled a great deal, which took him away from his family.

Finally, it was time for the Ritschers to settle down. In February 1927 Ritscher's wife bought a two-storey Art Nouveau villa with a large garden at Schöneiche, a little village east of Berlin and close to Lake Müggelsee. In September 1929 Ritscher was asked to come back to the Naval High Command to help to rebuild naval aviation, especially through the development of modern instruments for air navigation; he started work there more or less right away, on September 11th. After a few years he learned that he might stand a chance of being promoted to become Senior Executive Officer (Regierungsrat) in his former job at the Maritime Handbooks Division. This was a position he had coveted ever since he entered the Nautical Department, and he transferred back there to take it on 1 May 1934.

It was while Ritscher was working for the Naval High Command that Hitler came to power, an event that was to have dire consequences for the Ritscher family. By 30 January 1933 Hitler was Chancellor of Germany, and a torrent of anti-Jewish legislation appeared, not least of which was "The Law of the Restoration of the Civil Service", which was introduced on April 7 that same year, and which made 'Aryanism' a necessary requirement in order to hold a civil service position. Things were beginning to look distinctly uncomfortable not just for Jews, but for those who were married to one. It became painfully obvious to the Ritschers that keeping a job in a governmental position, raising a family, and earning promotion under the new National Socialist regime would become extremely difficult for anyone married to a Jewish partner. Under the circumstances it would appear to be no coincidence that the Ritschers were divorced in September 1933 before Alfred was promoted. But Susanne did not disappear. She had to leave her own house and move to a neighbouring village, but continued to take care of her two children and the household every day until 1937, when the children completed their schooling. With the help of many people, including her ex-husband, her origin and whereabouts were concealed from the authorities, not least due to a faked suicide in 1944. Thanks to good luck, and the help of friends and family, Susanne Ritscher was the only one of her Loewenthal family besides her children to survive the Nazi regime; she died in 1975. The children were brought up as Protestant Christians. They were officially considered to be offspring of a so-called "privileged intermarriage" and thus were not made the object of any persecution, although they suffered some general disadvantages.

Captain Otto Kraul, ice pilot

Alfred Ritscher was not the only old polar hand on the ship. Advice on ice conditions in Antarctic seas would come from a seasoned polar whaler – 47-year old Captain Otto Kraul, who liked to be called Kapt'n Kraul. Kraul had sailed most of the seven seas [24]. The season before (1937/38) he had been whaling manager on the German whaling ship *Jan Wellem*. Evidently he was quite a character – a real 'old salt'. Kraul started his career in whaling as a worker at the whaling station of the Compania Argentina de Pesca in Grytviken during World War I [25]. Then he became seaman on a whale catcher, was promoted pilot, and later in the 1920s sometimes held the well-paid position of whale shooter. In1928 he earned his captain's ticket. Theoretical learning was not his strong point, and in his final examination he failed in physics, meteorology and oceanography, passing the other subjects with the lowest possible grades. Kraul's strengths were practical, and he could tell the most exciting stories about his experiences.

The other senior member of the leadership trio was Alfred Kottas (b.1885), the captain of the *Schwabenland*. There was no question of choosing someone else to captain the ship and look after its 63-crew members, something he had been doing for several years.

A number of other members of the expedition also had some polar experience. Rudolf Mayr had flown a Dornier Wal, the *Perssuak*, during the Danish Lauge Koch expedition to Svalbard and Northeast Greenland in the Arctic in May 1938 [26,27]. Mayr was a very experienced pilot who had performed a number of pioneer flights, as well as 36 flights on the South Atlantic mail route, some of them with *Perssuak*. In his flying for the Danes in Greenland he had been accompanied by aircraft mechanic Franz Preuschoff, who would sail south with Mayr on the *Schwabenland*.

This being a prestigious national expedition, the pilots, aircrew, and catapult crew were chosen by Lufthansa from their most experienced personnel. Besides Mayr (who would later become Lufthansa's first Boeing 707 pilot, in 1958), they picked Richardheinrich Schirmacher as second pilot.

Dr. Ernst Herrmann

The expedition's geographer, Dr. Ernst Herrmann (1895-1970) [17], also had polar experience. He had obtained a PhD in Geology from the university in Berlin before becoming a voluntary teaching assistant at the Mineralogical and Petrographic Institute in Berlin. He earned enough to carry out small privately organised geological and glaciological expeditions, which he did to Sweden, Norway and Iceland (between 1924 and 1934). In the northern summer of 1938 he undertook a private expedition to Svalbard using the new slow-flying Fieseler Storch aircraft to explore the Far North. He used a still camera from the air for what became his travel report, published as a popular book, and made the first coloured aerial movie in the Arctic [28].

Besides his weakness for the polar world, Herrmann had a special interest in volcanoes. In recognition of his expertise, he was appointed a member of the Santorin-Expedition to investigate the eruption of one the volcanoes of the Mediterranean island of Santorini, in 1925-26. He later participated in expeditions to volcanoes in Iceland and Italy (in 1932, 1936, 1937 and 1939).

Herrmann was a tall man of 1.90 m weighing 80 kg, a typical German with blond hair and grey eyes. He described himself as a teacher and polar researcher. During the First World War he had been injured in the forehead, which gained him a medal and an exemption from service both in 1915 and later in 1944. Since 1923 he had been a member of the Freemasons, which explains why he never became a member of the National Socialist Party and why he was never promoted as teacher. In addition to his teaching at a secondary school, he managed to nearly double his income in some years with the publication of books and papers, as well as giving lectures at many places in Germany and for the radio. In 1947 he became docent of geography in the little town of Bederkesa and at the teacher training college in Celle, and later in Osnabrück. His later books included "Die Pole der Erde" (The Poles of the Earth; 1950) and "Die Werkstatt Vulkane" (The Volcano Workshop; 1963).

As well as being the expedition's geologist and geographer, Herrmann was employed along with geophysicist Leo Gburek (1910-41) to measure water depths and make observations on Antarctica and its adjacent islands. Gburek was a tutorial assistant at the Geophysical Institute of the University of Leipzig, and like Herrmann, quite an experienced polar researcher. He had participated in two expeditions to Svalbard, in 1937 and 1938, where he mainly carried out magnetic measurements and made some additional meteorological observations. There he had met Herrmann, and the two of them had become friends.

Another polar man was photographer Max Bundermann (b.1904). As a representative of the professional photographic firm Hansa-Luftbild, he had participated in a scientific expedition of Norway's Svalbard and Arctic Ocean Research Survey (NSIU) to north-east Greenland in 1932, which used Christensen's Lockheed Vega *Qarrisiluni* for aerial surveying [4]. Bundermann took 2109 photographs there during ten flights, covering an area of 30,000 km². The other aerial photographer on the *Schwabenland* was Siegfried Sauter (b. 1916). From June 1934 until April 1935 Sauter attended the HJ (Hitler Jugend) Flying School at Böblingen and became a glider pilot. Subsequently he entered the newly established air force, where he mainly worked in aerial photography. In 1937 he joined Bundermann at Hansa-Luftbild.

To supply Ritscher and his two pilots with reports on weather conditions, a meteorological team of four was appointed, led by Dr. Herbert Regula (1910-80), a meteorologist from the Deutsche Seewarte (German Maritime Observatory) at Hamburg. Along with Regula's team came Heinz Lange (b. 1908), specialist in radiosonde ascents, from the Reich Weather Service; Walter Krüger (b. 1905), a precision engineer, who had participated aboard *Meteor* in the German Atlantic Expedition of 1925-27, and who later maintained radiosondes for the Reich Weather Service, and Wilhelm Gockel (b. 1908), a repairman from the Marine Observatory in Wilhelmshafen. Regula had already gained a lot of seagoing experience, when he served as on-board meteorologist on the catapult ship *Westfalen*, which carried out the same function as *Schwabenland* between Bathhurst in West Africa and Pernambuco in Brazil during the period October 1923 - November 1934. *Westfalen* had been the original choice as the expedition ship, but was unavailable so *Schwabenland* was used instead [9].

Recognising that the ship would spend at least three months at sea – one month steaming down the length of the Atlantic, another month or so patrolling the Antarctic coast while the planes flew over the land, and at least another month to return home - an oceanographer and a marine biologist were appointed to take samples en route. The oceanographer was Karl-Heinz Paulsen (1909-41), a member of the National Socialist Party, who had already carried out Antarctic oceanographic work on the whaling factory ship *Jan Wellem* in 1937/38 for his PhD. The marine biologist was Erich Barkley (b. 1912) - an officer of the naval reserve working at the Institute for Whaling Research in Hamburg, who had seven months experience in Antarctic seas aboard the whaling ship C.L. *Larsen* in 1937/38. The scientists and the pilots were appointed to their duties in October [11].

Making it Happen - the Role of Helmut Wohlthat

Usually in a polar expedition, the leader, like Amundsen, Drygalski, Nansen or Shackleton, provided the driving force and obtained the money, the people, the equipment and the ship. Not so in this case. The enterprise was the brainchild of Councillor of State Helmut Wohlthat. From his experience at the Reich Office for Milk Products, Oils and Fats, and his work for Schacht's New Plan, Wohlthat was intimately familiar with Germany's need to obtain more whale oil. It was the success of the growing German whaling fleet in the 1937/38 season that had prompted him to reactivate the Foreign Ministry's plan to acquire territory in the Antarctic, and which led ultimately to the need for a reconnaissance expedition to scout for a location for a base for the local operations of Germany's factory ships.

Wohlthat worked with representatives of the Naval High Command, the Air Force, the Ministry of Finance, the Ministry of Food and Land Economy, Lufthansa Berlin, the Hamburg shipyard, the *Schwabenland's* owners - North-German-Lloyd, and the Secretary of the expedition, Dr. Herbert Todt, to acquire the ship, assure its provisions, collect the necessary equipment and crew for aerial surveys and scientific activities, man the vessel, and carry out the necessary refits and trials [11,29]. This was not an easy task, shipyards at that time being devoted to the production of military vessels. However, given the importance of the Four Year Plan for economic development, in this case the economic card trumped the military one.

In line with the need to keep the destination of the expedition secret, so as to deflect attention from the political implications of the planned land grab, Wohlthat sought a scientific cover for the expedition. Having failed to obtain it from the Kaiser Wilhelm Gesellschaft (fore-runner of the organisation that today runs the Max Planck Institutes), Wohlthat got the German Research Council to take on the official sponsorship a mere 10 days before the expedition left for the ice, although the money came from the Four Year Plan [9]. The cost would be some 2,440,000 Reichsmarks; Appendix 3 lists the total costs of the expedition, broken down into different categories.

Having found the scientific sponsorship, the ship, the planes, the men and the money, it was time to fit out the vessel and send the expedition on its way.

References

1. Riiser-Larsen, H., 1930, The 'Norwegia' Expedition of 1929-1930. Geographical Review, 555-573.

2. Christensen, L., 1935, Such is the Antarctic. Hodder and Stoughton, London, 265 pp.

3. Christensen, L., 1939, Recent Reconnaissance Flights in the Antarctic. Geographical Journal. 192-203.

4. Barr, S., 2003, Norway – a consistent polar nation? Kolofon, Oslo, 593 pp.

5. RGS, 1939, The Course of Antarctic Exploration Between Longitudes 20°W and 110°E: Notes on the Map Compiled to Accompany the Paper by Mr. Lars Christensen. Geographical Journal 94, 204-208 and map following page 272.

6. Additional information on Ritscher's biography was given by personal communication to CL by his second wife, Ilse Ritscher. Unpublished.

7. Hoel, A., 1938, Die Verwendung von Luftfahrzeugen bei der Erforschung der Polargebiete. Zeitschrift der Gesellschaft für Erdkunde zu Berlin (5/6), 161-175.

8. Ritscher, A. 1940, Die photogrammetrischen Vermessungsflüge der Deutschen Antarktischen Expedition 1938/39. Mitteilungen der Deutschen Gesellschaft für Photogrammetrie 4, 147-150.

9. Lüdecke, C., 2004, (see English resume on page 100: Secret Mission to the Antarctic: The Third German Antarctic Expedition 1938/39, and the plan to occupy territory to protect the German whaling industry). "In Geheimer Mission zur Antarktis: Die Dritte Deutsche Antarktische Expedition 1938/39 und der Plan einer territorialen Festetzung zur Sicherung des Walfangs". Schiffahrtsarchiv 26 (2003), Deutsches Schifffahrtsmuseum, Bremerhaven, und Convent Verlag GmbH, Hamburg, Vol. 26, 75-100.

10. OKM 3 November 1938, in Ritscher's estate Bh1 OKM Unpublished.

11. Ritscher, A., 1942, Wissenschaftliche und fliegerische Ergebnisse der Deutschen Antarktischen Expedition 1938/39,

Hrsg. im Auftrag der Deutschen Forschungsgemeinschaft Vol. 1. Koehler & Amelang, Leipzig.

12. Byrd, R.E., 1930, Little America: aerial exploration in the Antarctic, the flight to the South Pole. Putnam and Sons, New York. 422 pp.

13. Byrd, R.E., 1935, Discovery: the story of the Second Byrd Antarctic Expedition. Putnam and Sons, New York. 405pp.

14. Ritscher estate, private possession, Braunfels. Unpublished.

15 Ritscher, A. 1939, Deutsche Forschung in der Antarktis. Dornier Post (5), 102-105.

16. Bertrand, K.J., 1971, Americans in Antarctica, 1775-1948. Special Publication 39, American Geographical Society, New York. 554 pp.

17. Herrmann's estate, private possession, Bonn (relevant copies held by Lüdecke); containing additional information on Herrmann's biography and the biographies of the Schwabenland crew. Unpublished.

18. Ritscher, A., 1916, Wanderung in Spitzbergen im Winter 1912. Zeitschrift der Gesellschaft für Erdkunde zu Berlin, 16-34.

19. Barr, W., 1984, Lieutnant Herbert Schröder Stranz's expedition to Svalbard, 1912-1913: A study in organizational disintegration. Fram: the Journal of Polar Studies, 1 (1), 1-64.

20. Stocks, T., 1963, In Memorian Alfred Ritscher 1879-1963. Deutsch Hydrographische Zeitschrift 16 (2), 87-92.

21. Conrad, 20.7.1938, letter to Rischer. Ritscher's estate, Bh1, OKM. Unpublished.

22. VJP 5.10.1938, letter to Ritscher. Ritscher's estate, Bh1, VJP. Unpublished.

23. Pietsch, J., 2006, Karriere geht vor: Susanne Ritscher, In: J. Pietsch "Ich besaß einen Garten in Schöneich bei Berlin": Das verwaltete Verschwinden jüdischer Nachbarn und ihre schwierige Rückkehr. Campus Verlag, Frankfurt/Main, 123-135.

24. Kraul, O., 1939, Käpt'n Kraul Erzählt. F.A.Herbig, Berlin, 240 pp.

25. Kraul's estate, in the possession of Klaus Barthelmess. Unpublished.

26. Koch, L., 1940, The seaplane Expedition to Peary Land 1938. In: L. Koch, Survey of North Greenland. Meddelelser om Grønland 130 (1)

27. Tilgenkamp, E., 1957, Schwingen über Nacht und Eis. Verlag Neues Deutschland, Berlin, 351 pp.

28. Herrmann, E., 1942, Mit dem Fieseler-Storch ins Nordpolarmeer. Safari Verlag, Berlin. 276 pp.

29. Herrmann, E., 1941, Deutsche Forscher im Südpolarmeer. Safari Verlag, Berlin, 184 pp.

II
JOURNEYS

CHAPTER 3: THE JOURNEY SOUTH

Preparing the Ship

One of Ritscher's first tasks was to modify the *Schwabenland* to meet the expedition's needs [1,2]. Even with the help of the Reich Ministry of Trade and Industry it was not easy to find a shipyard to adapt the vessel for its new task, because most of them were occupied with contracts from the German State – many of them for military work associated with rearmament. Eventually, the Deutsche Werft (German Shipyard) in Hamburg agreed to undertake the urgent modifications, which took six weeks, between 28 October and 15 December 1938, when *Schwabenland* was in dry dock. The ship had to be fitted internally with additional cabins for the 12 extra people (9 members of the scientific party, two aerial photographers, and one ice pilot), laboratories, and storage space for science. Echo-sounding equipment had to be installed in the hull, space had to be made for launching the meteorological balloons and storing the gas bottles, winches had to be set up for lowering sampling equipment for physical oceanography and biology, and meteorological instruments had to be attached to parts of the superstructure. A dark room and associated store and workspace were needed for the photographers. There was no way that *Schwabenland* could be turned into an icebreaker, but the bow was strengthened to provide protection in case the ship rammed into Antarctic ice floes. Nothing much could be done to strengthen the ship's thin steel hull, but to prepare the ship for the dangers of ice navigation, fitters reinforced her waterline with a steel belt, and replaced her two bronze propellers with more durable cast iron screws; 3,500 tons of sand and rock ballast were added to lower the screws below the level of ice floes, and 18,500 empty casks filled the holds to increase buoyancy in case ice punctured the ship's hull [2]. Captain Kottas would have to be careful not to be caught in closing leads between the floes. The idea was to stay in clear water, where the planes could land, not to push forward through ice-covered seas.

The ship would be home to 82 people from a wide range of organisations. The scientific expedition members were appointed by various ministries or other institutions in the last few weeks before sailing, and began obtaining, adjusting and testing their equipment. When they arrived on the ship they had to navigate their way cautiously around the decks through the chaos of refurbishment, stepping gingerly over power cables, avoiding the protruding edges of steel plates, and ducking under beams, all the while shielding their ears from the noise.

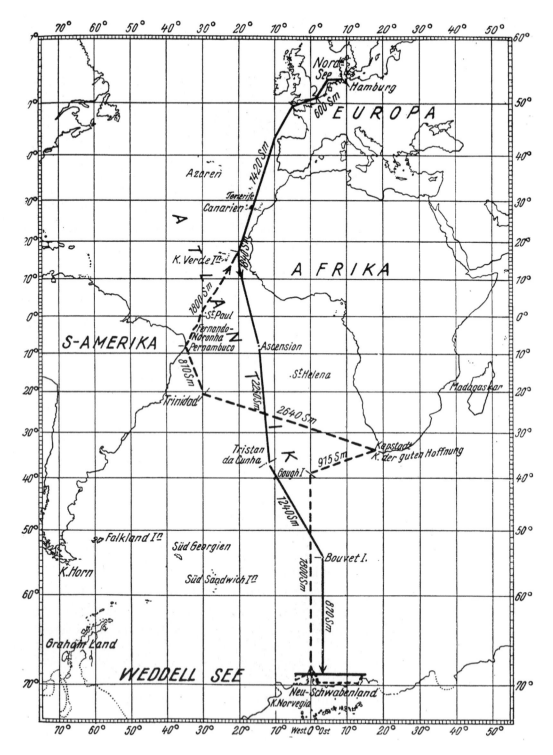

Schwabenland's journey

One day in late November Ritscher called all the expedition's members together, including the ship's captain, officers, and crew as well as the ice pilot Captain Kraul, for a showing of Commander Richard Byrd's movie of his most recent American Antarctic expedition (1933-35). This would give them an idea of the hazards before them, but at the same time hopefully build confidence by demonstrating that their task was feasible. Most of the audience were quite young, but keen to do their very best for the expedition. Ritscher could not resist a feeling of pride to be venturing to the white wilderness of Antarctica with these brave young men as ambassadors of a resurgent Germany.

At the end of the refit the *Schwabenland* sailed on a test cruise on 15 December. Aboard were some 50 prominent representatives of the various ministries that had been brought together under Helmut Wohlthat, with Goering's blessing, to support the expedition, along with directors of the institutes that had appointed the scientific party, representatives of Lufthansa, which had supplied the planes, and fitters and others from the shipyard who were there to make sure that everything on the ship worked as planned. Councillor Wohlthat gathered scientists, aircraft crews and ship's officers together in the saloon to talk with them about the expedition and explain its national importance. Finally he wished them good health, success, luck, and a safe journey home with good results, concluding with a "Heil Hitler!" This was a reminder, should anyone need it, that one was never far away from the politics of the Third Reich; indeed, the ship carried a 'political leader' or 'minder' in the shape of Nazi Party member Karl-Heinz Röbke, the ship's 2nd Officer. He was there to ensure the survival of political correctness even in the far off wastes of the Antarctic – this was after all a state-sponsored expedition, though efforts had been made to conceal that by obtaining at the last minute the nominal sponsorship of the German Research Council.

The Journey Begins

Tests completed to everyone's satisfaction, *Schwabenland* was ready to leave Hamburg docks on Saturday 17 December 1938, with the two glistening silver Dornier flying boats perched on the after deck next to the catapult that would launch them into the unknown polar world. It was a sunny day at -13°C, with a cold easterly breeze from Russia and the smell of the sea in the air. They were off to the other end of the Earth, to use the latest German technology to map the unexplored coast and interior of Antarctica from the air – a daring feat if they could manage it. They would not have long to do it – mid December was already late to be leaving for the short southern summer season typical of the Antarctic. The last official visitors and family members of the participants came to say goodbye. Dr Todt, the expedition's Secretary, brought aboard the last pile of administration and private mail, office equipment and - most important - the expedition's cash box. Miss Ilse Uhlmann, the secretary of the bureau of the Expedition, who became Ritscher's second wife on 29 March 1941, wrote the last telegrams and letters. Then the visitors left.

At 15:30 the expedition members were standing at the rail when the mooring ropes were untied, a tug pulled the 8500-ton ship away from the dock, and they were off on their long journey. The first thing the scientists needed to do was to look for their personal luggage and boxes which had been piled up in the storage rooms without any plan. They also tried to find out from each other and from Kapt'n Kraul as much as they could about what they had to expect in the Southern Ocean and Antarctica. The old salt was full of delightful stories of penguins, icebergs and sea elephants. Besides, the German Research Council had provided 33 volumes on previous expeditions, among them for example that of James Cook, who had been first to cross the south polar circle, in January 1773, and reached almost 70°S on the Greenwich meridian in their target area.

On Sunday 18 December low temperatures and snow in the North Sea made a stay on deck rather unpleasant so the crew asked for their polar clothes. Fortunately the newcomers did not suffer too much with seasickness, although an easterly wind was blowing at Beaufort Force 7 causing sea state 5. In the beginning the heating system did not work well. And the first day out one of the stoves in the galley broke down. Never mind, all would be fixed, according to the Chief Engineer, Karl Uhlig (b.1885), known to all as 'Chief'. A greater problem had been the engine cooling water tube, which broke several times during the voyage, but luckily could always be repaired on-board.

There was still a lot of sorting out to do and it took them quite some time to organise the material delivered aboard during the last days in Hamburg and to store it in the right places. The proper instruments and materials for the various tasks had to be distributed among the different working groups, for instance for echo-sounding or for meteorology.

Schwabenland steamed down the English Channel, passing Dover in pitch dark at 0400 on the morning of 19 December. At 1100 the next day Regula and his colleague Lange carried out the expedition's first scientific task – launching a radiosonde, a 1.5 m diameter hydrogen-filled balloon carrying a tiny 1 kg instrument package for measuring air temperature, pressure and humidity at different heights and radioing the information back to base. The launches were scheduled to take place daily. For the first, a novelty, Regula had an audience of 15 – mostly the scientific crew with nothing much else to do at this early stage. By the fourth launching the novelty had worn off, and the audience had dropped to zero. Regula used a theodolite to measure the direction and speed of the balloon; his assistants, Krüger and Gockel buckled on headphones and followed the radio signals with a stopwatch. From time to time they were helped by the geophysicist, Gburek, when he was not occupied with his own measurements of solar radiation and counting aerial dust particles. The radiosonde data would be used to determine the meteorological condition of the upper atmosphere up to around 20 kilometres, well into the stratosphere, and the strengths and directions of the winds at different heights – essential information for weather forecasts and for briefing the pilots before and during their flights. The temperatures up at 20 km were around -50°C.

As usual the ship's party ate in different messes, but aboard everybody got the same menu. The sailors ate forward in the fo'c'sle; the engineers and diesel mechanics ate aft; the Lufthansa staff ate together. The ship's officers, expedition leader, ice master and scientists ate in the saloon, which became rather overcrowded as a result. To alleviate the overcrowding the two pilots suggested that they should eat in Schirmacher's cabin next door to the saloon, and offered a third seat each day to one of the saloon members to give everyone a turn. After lunch these three joined the others and took dessert in the saloon. For relaxation there were chess, table tennis, cards and light reading from the ship's library of 150 volumes.

On 21 December the ship passed Cape Finisterre at the western tip of Spain, leading the scientists to reflect that a few hundred kilometres to the east German planes were dropping 500 kg bombs, and people were dying in the streets as the Spanish Civil War raged on. Fortunately the *Schwabenland's* civilian aircraft would only be put to peaceful scientific uses.

By now, the oceanographer, Paulsen, had begun to measure various parameters of the sea surface, while the geographer, Herrmann, together with Herbert Bruns (b.1908) - the specialist electrician from the Atlas factory that made the ship's echo-sounding machine - had begun to organise the process of using sound pulses to determine the shape of the seabed. The principle is very simple. A transmitter in the hull emits a high-pitched 'ping' into the water, and the scientists use a stopwatch to measure how long each 'ping' takes to bounce off the seabed and return to a microphone. They then convert that time into a depth, by taking into account the effect of temperature and salinity on the speed of sound in seawater, which averages 1500 m/sec. At that speed, an elapsed time of 7 seconds between 'ping' and echo is equal to a water depth of $7 \times 1500 \div 2 = 5250$ m. During their journey they would discover new underwater features by this means.

Biologist Erich Barkley from the Institute for Whale Research was very busy preparing for his investigations before getting to the working area. The catching nets had to be overhauled and the laboratory for storing his biological samples had to be set up.

At the same time the pilots and their aircrew had to make sure all of the equipment for their aircraft was in good working order, including equipment needed in case of forced landings. They also trained in the use of the new level-sextant for navigational positioning during flight. In this device the level took the place of the horizon when it was foggy.

On 22 December the *Schwabenland* was passing Lisbon. The weather was splendid, and some scientists took the first opportunity to sunbathe. It was time to relax, and beards were sprouting. At 23:00 they passed Cape Vincent in the Algarve of Portugal, almost the southernmost point in Europe.

On 23 December everyone was getting ready for the Christmas festivities: practicing carols; building trestles and benches; and putting up decorations, while the galley staff peeled potatoes, and cooked ham. This would be the first joint party, when crew and officers would mingle after dinner and people from different decks and stations would get to know one another. 24 December started with a record, when despite a Beaufort wind force of 6-7 the meteorologists succeeded in launching a radiosonde that reached a height of over 30 km. This achievement might secure them a prize from the German Meteorological Society for being first to produce correct temperature and humidity measurements from such heights.

The Christmas Eve festivities began off the Canary Islands with a Christmas dinner in each mess at 17:30. An hour later everybody gathered in the community room for a Christmas song and a brief speech by the expedition leader. The evening continued with beer, fruit, nuts, and more songs - accompanied by the ship's band, comprising an accordion, a flute, a violin, and a zither. As a highlight there was a raffle for gifts. Politics intruded with a radio broadcast from Reichsminister Hess. To general relief it had to be cut short owing to bad reception. Ritscher then talked about his long trek through the polar night in December 1912, when he marched across western Spitsbergen to fetch help for the stranded Schröder-Stranz expedition, and Kapt'n Kraul told some of his amusing polar stories.

Cape Blanco loomed ahead on the African shore. Test soundings showed a correlation of their echo-soundings with the information given on the sea chart. More balloons were released to investigate the meteorological conditions of the Northeast Trade Winds. Now hats came out to ward off the sun. In the evenings the scientists enjoyed the wonders of the tropical night, sipped gin and soda, sampled Christmas cake, and listened to Hawaiian songs on the gramophone – they were in calm seas. On 29 December, when the Trade Wind died, the sea surface seemed almost as if covered by oil, and not a single wave disturbed the drinks or the view.

The South Atlantic

New Year's Eve was a special day. It brought the equator at 15°W, celebrated with a traditional crossing-the-line ceremony. In the afternoon, Neptune, Triton and a host of lesser sea spirits came aboard to baptise 26 landlubbers with a dunking. This was followed by a New Year's Eve party in the common room, with music by the ship's band, many jokes and a good supply of drinks. New Year's Day brought the first flying fish. People queued outside the radio shack to send telegrams home. Next day the ship steamed past the volcanic peak of Ascension Island.

Ritscher established an evening lecture series to combat the general idleness with one or two talks a week. First on the podium was the ship's doctor from Norddeutscher Lloyd, Dr. Josef Bludau (b. 1889), with warnings about the dangers of the tropical heat and polar dangers like frostbite. Later, Kraul talked about moving ships through drift and pack ice.

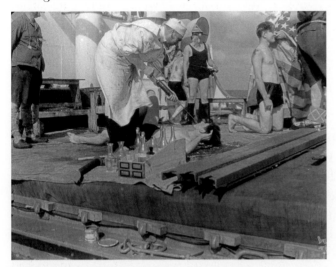
Crossing-the-line-ceremony

Biologist Barkley followed with tales of plankton and whales. The other scientists presented their programmes and explained what help they would need from the crew. Finally, the pilots described the launching and recovery of the aircraft and the need for additional help from the motorboat.

After Ascension, the echo-sounding programme down the centre of the South Atlantic began in earnest, with a sounding taken every half hour where the bottom was flat and at closer intervals where the seabed topography changed rapidly. The topography was rugged and depths changed often, which called for a sizeable echo-sounding team working in 4-hour watches around the clock. On the team were Paulsen, Gburek, Barkely, Bruns and Herrmann, later joined by the two pilots, Mayr and Schirmacher. The soundings averaged around 5 sea miles apart for the 12,000 miles to the Antarctic coast and back.

Living on the ship became routine. Several of those who were not working started with gymnastics at 6:00. Breakfast was served between 7:30 and 8:30. Lunch followed by coffee was scheduled at noon. There was a snack between 15:30 and 16:30, usually followed by work or lectures. Dinner was served at 18:00. Afterwards people passed the time playing chess or skat or reading. The bar was closed at 22:00. At sea on Sundays, Thursdays (the seamen's Sunday), and holidays, meals were richer and a birthday was a special challenge for the pastry cook. Good food and little exercise were making people fat. The doctor borrowed the weighing machine from the kitchen and weighed everyone. Kapt'n Kraul held the record at 119 kg. Most seemed around 10 kilos over their normal weight. Doctor's orders – eat less!

When they crossed 31°S latitude the biologist started his collection of plankton. Herrmann, the geographer, planned his future work and designed a map grid on a Mercator protection at a scale of 1:1,250,000 for tracking the flight routes.

On the evening of 8 January Tristan da Cunha came into view, another distant volcano, this one discovered in 1506 by the Portuguese Admiral whose name it bears, and finally annexed by the British in 1806. The next evening, the first harbinger of the Antarctic arrived in the shape of a radio-telephone conversation with the German floating factory ship *Wikinger*, some 3000 km ahead of *Schwabenland* on the Polar Circle. *Wikinger* provided information about weather and ice conditions. Astonishingly, they had no pack-ice this year at 60°40'S and 26°23'E. Kapt'n Kraul made the most of the opportunity to place an order for a metre of whale sausage and some kilos of whale meat, while he was organising a meeting with *Wikinger* to deliver to them some transmission valves brought from Hamburg.

Captain Ritscher unveiled the final plan for the work programme in Antarctica, and the scientific party discussed the details. He made it his business to ensure that everyone from the chief scientist to the ship's boy felt part of the plan and was committed to its goals. There was much concern about the possibility of one of the planes having to make a forced landing on the ice sheet; about the likely state of the weather, which was known to be stormy on the Antarctic coast; and about the position of the pack ice, which could limit *Schwabenland's* southward penetration. There were plans within plans, for all eventualities. But still there was a risk - even the best-laid plans can go awry. The scientists recalled without being reminded that experienced explorers like Scott and his companions died on the Ross Ice Shelf, and German scientist Alfred Wegener (1880-1930), the inventor of 'continental drift', lost his life on the Greenland ice sheet.

What would happen if one of the planes was forced down 500 km inland from the edge of the ice shelf? "Stay calm", said Ritscher, in a tone that lifted all doubt. "I will get you out." He'd done it before, in Spitsbergen in the Arctic. He could do it again. Ritscher inspired trust as he explained how they would deal with a forced landing on the ice. When the first plane was in the air, the second plane would be made ready on the catapult – which would take an hour - after which it would remain there on standby.

Emergency equipment for the aircraft, in case of forced landing

Every few minutes the first plane would radio back to the ship information about its location (course, speed, time elapsed, and visible landmarks) that could be used to find it in case of a forced landing. The planes would also carry emergency kits with one month's supply of food and a cooker, along with sleeping bags, tents, a portable radio, guns, skis, and a sledge [3].

Mayr and Schumacher busied themselves selecting and weighing supplies for the emergency rations for each aircraft, and packing them in bags, not forgetting the six cigarettes per man per day. The rescue sledges had to be dismantled to fit into the planes.

On the evening of 10 January, uninhabited Gough Island hove into view, another landmark on their journey south, and one surrounded by clouds of albatross and petrels to delight the bird watchers. Just when the steep cliffs of the coast were only about 3 sea miles away, the ship's electricity supply broke down, leaving them drifting towards the cliffs. Luckily the reserve dynamo worked, and they could get going again, much to Captain Kottas' relief.

The weather worsened. They were now in the Roaring Forties, where one depression followed another with monotonous regularity. Air pressure was down to 745 mm Hg (or 990.9 hPa). A strong following wind boosted their speed to 20 knots.

Lectures continued. Regula gave lessons in meteorology, explaining about weather fronts. Gburek talked about the Earth's magnetic field. Experienced master workman Herbert Bolle (b.1908), responsible for the airplanes and the catapult equipment, explained how the planes were launched and recovered. The ship's massive catapult would sling them into the air at 150 km/hour; on their return they would land on the sea and be lifted out by a crane. Herrmann lectured on previous south polar expeditions, especially those of Amundsen and Scott and their tragic race to the South Pole, and Byrd's flight over the South Pole in December 1929.

The Southern Ocean

By 12 January they were well south of Cape Town and entering the wild spaces of the Southern Ocean. The air temperature was down to 6°C; out came the woollens, away went the tropical kit, and on came the heating. Depth-sounding watches continued, 4 hours on, 4 off. On 15 January soundings were being taken minute by minute as the topography steepened, climbed and roughened, fluctuating between 2000 and 1250 m. They were crossing what we now know as the mid-ocean ridge system and its associated fracture zones.

At midday, Bouvet Island came into view. A mere 9.5 km long by 7 km wide, it is another volcano perched, like Tristan and Gough, on the shoulders of the mid-ocean ridge. Although its peak thrusts 900 m above the sea, Bouvet and the massif on which it sits rise up from a sea floor some 5000 m deep, making it like all such islands one of the highest mountains on Earth. At 54° 26'S and 3° 24'E, washed by the Antarctic Circumpolar Current, with an ice cap on top and glaciers reaching down to the sea, it is a bleak, cold, place and rarely accessible from a boat.

BOUVET ISLAND

Bouvet, a dependent territory of Norway, is one of the most remote island in the world. It was discovered on New Year's Day 1739 by Frenchman Lozier Bouvet (1705-81), who found it embedded in impenetrable pack ice. Thinking it to be a promontory of the legendary southern land "Terra Australis Incognita", he named it the Cape of Circumcision, January 1 being the date of the Feast of the Circumcision of Jesus. Later visitors, like Captain James Cook in February 1775, found it was an island and gave it a variety of names. First to land were British whalers, James Lindsay and Thomas Hopper, in 1808, who named it Lindsay Island. Then came the American Benjamin Morrell, on the *Wasp* in 1822, who called it Bouvette's Island, and the British sealer George Norris on the *Sprightly* in 1825, who named it Liverpool Island. Next was the American sealer Joseph Fuller, on the *Francis Allyn*, in 1893, who named it Bouvet or Circumcision Island, and finally Adalbert Krech on the *Valdivia* during the German Deep-Sea Expedition in 1898, who stuck with the name Bouvet, fixed its position accurately, and surveyed the seabed around it for the first time. Surveys of the area continued during the German *Meteor* expedition in 1926, which discovered the 5000 m deep Bouvet Deep nearby. First to land in the 20th century were the Norwegians, on the *Norvegia* expedition of 1929, who hoisted a flag and claimed the island for their king. The rocks collected by the Norwegians turned out to be alkali basalts, rhyolites, obsidian and pumice – not surprising since the geology comprises volcanic tuffs, lava flows and dykes [4].

Passing Bouvet, the *Schwabenland* continued its radio contacts with the *Wikinger*, and arranged to meet her tanker *Anna Knudsen* to collect supplies, including Kapt'n Kraul's metre long whale sausage and whale fillet, and to deposit mail for home. Everyone got busy writing letters. The first icebergs appeared. They were not new to Kraul, Paulsen and Barkley, who had worked down here before as scientists on German whaling ships, but to the polar newcomers – which meant most of the ship's and flight crews - they seemed alarmingly large – colossal tables - and kept the photographers busy. On 17 January 1939, at 63°S, the tanker appeared. Herrmann collected 100 letters and pitched and tossed his way in a small boat across the slack swell to the other ship. To his surprise, whale meat was in short supply. It was a poor season. The steamers hooted as they parted company, one north to Hamburg, the other south to the world of ice.

Kapt'n Kraul had expected them to meet thick pack ice just south of Bouvet, and to have to make a long detour to the east to get around it to the Antarctic coast. Yet all they had seen were a few icebergs; indeed, ice was so rare that on the morning of 18 January, at 68° 10'S, they saw just one solitary berg carrying a number of penguins with a large emperor penguin in the middle. A solitary snow petrel flitted by. Eighty nautical miles further on there was still no sea ice in view, just the occasional whale.

The Antarctic Coast

Coming closer to Antarctica with each turn of the screw, *Schwabenland* reached thin drift ice on the morning of 19 January. Following a conference with Captains Kraul and Kottas, Ritscher changed course from south to south west. As the ship steamed on, the low clouds ahead showed 'ice blink', the effect of reflection from ice below, and towards noon the ice itself appeared. Expecting pack ice, they were astonished to find themselves gazing at shining cliffs at the edge of a substantial ice shelf. As they approached, the glistening front grew higher and could be seen stretching immeasurably far away in the distance to right and left. Ice shelves are parts of the continent's ice sheet that have slid out over the sea and now float there, rising and falling with the tide. They can be anything between a few tens to several hundred metres thick. While their landward edges are solidly attached to the continental ice sheet, their seaward edges are attacked by waves and become unstable. Large pieces break off to form icebergs, some of them tens or even a hundred kilometres long, and usually rectangular in shape. The tabular character of these bergs comes from the flat tops of their parental shelves. Here the cliffs were up to some 30 m high, implying that the ice shelf was some 150 m thick.

The expedition was in luck in that most of the pack ice that mantles the coastal sea in winter had gone. Just as well, since the ship's hull was not strengthened enough for work in ice-strewn seas. During the sunny night of 19 January 1939, they finally reached the edge of the pack ice at 69° 14'S, 4° 30'W only a few miles from the edge of the ice shelf. Away from the pack the sea was clear of ice and they were able to launch their first reconnaissance flight at 4:40 a.m. on the morning of 20 January 1939. It was light at the time – this being the period of midnight sun.

Norway Finds Out

The temperature was a little below zero. The expedition had arrived and it was time for the real work to begin. But, as is often the case when things seem rosy, everything was not quite as ideal as it seemed. While the ship was steaming south, Norway had found out about the German expedition and hurriedly formalised its claim to Dronning Maud Land. Quite by chance, in December 1938 Adolf Hoel, Director of Norway's NSIU, had been visiting various European cities, among them Berlin, in connection with the planning of a proposed polar exhibition in Bergen in 1940 [5]. He had already been alerted to possible

German interests in annexing part of Antarctica, by a visit to NSIU some time before 10 December by Dr. Lehmann, attaché of the German embassy, who had asked him about the principle of making pie-slice shaped claims to Antarctic territory and about territorial occupation in the south, referring to Hoel's recent publication on this subject [6]. Lehmann underlined the private character of his question and that he personally was interested in the study of international law. Hoel willingly gave him valuable references to books and papers. Then Hoel invited Lehmann for a second visit, which must also have been prior to 10 December, during which the Norwegian suddenly remarked "that Germany, if it already wants to occupy, only has the possibility in the region between (about) 40° and 20°E and 80° and 139°W." Hoel stressed that these two regions were in the Norwegian sphere of interest, although Norway had not yet formalised any claim. As the Norwegian did not speak German fluently, Lehmann could not find out whether Hoel knew about the German plans of occupation or whether he only wanted to satisfy Lehmann's interest. The German attaché reported that Hoel was a very well informed person, which allowed him to correlate his knowledge to German needs and – bearing in mind his beneficial contacts in the polar science community - to draw conclusions about possible German interests [7]. Lehmann's report was forwarded to Wohlthat, who sent it to Ritscher with a cover letter dated 14 December in which he only referred to the planned Antarctic expedition of the American pilot Ellsworth, which was the second topic of Lehmann's report. No word about Hoel's possible suspicion!

When Hoel came to Berlin, he tried to contact Dr. Ernst Herrmann, whom he knew from Herrmann's Fieseler Storch expedition to Svalbard the previous year. Told he was away, Hoel telephoned Herrmann's wife who explained that her husband had left on 17 December on a polar expedition [5]. The Hoel story is well known among Norwegian and German researchers [8]. A slightly different (unpublished) version of the story is given by Frode Skarstein of the University of Tromsø (personal communication to CS, 2008), whose sources suggest that Hoel was in Berlin trying to meet with Dr Herrmann on December 10, while Herrmann was still in Germany, and having failed to contact him later contacted Herrmann's wife who told him enough for him to deduce what Herrmann's plans were. Given that it was December, that Hoel's discussions with German officials had indicated which parts of Antarctica were unclaimed, and that the German whaling fleet was active in the South Atlantic, Hoel thought it most likely that the expedition was headed for the as yet unclaimed area south of Cape Town, and raised the alarm at the Norwegian Foreign Ministry on 22 December. As a result, the Norwegian parliament hurriedly laid claim to Dronning Maud Land on 14 January 1939, the day before the *Schwabenland* reached Bouvet. Councillor of State Wohlthat informed Ritscher personally by encoded radio transmission on 17 January about the Norwegian territorial claim. Although the Norwegian Minister of Justice had been authorized to carry out policing measures in this region in support of their claim, Wohlthat told Ritscher "your instructions remain unchanged, stop" [9].

Given that Hoel told the Norwegian Foreign Ministry on December 22 about his suspicions concerning the German plans, perhaps it is no accident that an official announcement of the sailing of the German expedition was made by the German authorities from Hamburg that same day [10], as reported in the New York Times of 23 December [11]. Much the same announcement appeared in the Times of London on 27 December 1938, which reported that that "A German expedition under Captain Ritcher (sic) has left Hamburg on board the steamer Schwabenland for the Antarctic, where.... investigations will be carried out for the German Exploration Society" [12]. This echoed a report in a Berlin paper dated 24 December. The German and New York Times articles noted that the expedition had at its disposal two planes, and that Lufthansa had used *Schwabenland* for catapulting mail planes in the Atlantic [11]. The general drift of the expedition was thus publicly apparent even from this early stage, despite the initial attempts at secrecy. After all, there was no point in Germany keeping its effort secret any longer if the Norwegians already knew about it.

Regardless of the Norwegian claim, the German expedition set about its task of dropping flags as evidence of territorial occupation, something Norway could not claim. The supposed locations of these flags are marked on the topographic survey maps produced after the cruise, and the newly discovered territory was named Neu-Schwabenland, after the ship [13]. As it was for Norway up until January 1939, so it was for Germany afterwards – the German claim to ownership remained informal, never pursued through parliamentary process.

References

1. Herrmann, E., 1941, Deutsche Forscher im Südpolarmeer. Safari Verlag, Berlin, 184 pp.

2. Ritscher, A., 1942, Wissenschaftliche und fliegerische Ergebnisse der Deutschen Antarktischen Expedition 1938/39. Hrsg. im Auftrag der Deutschen Forschungsgemeinschaft Vol. 1. Koehler & Amelang, Leipzig.

3. Ritscher's estate (figure 3.3 relating to emergency equipment) published in Ritscher 1939 Tfl fig. 2.

4. Baker, P.E., 1967, Historical and Geological Notes on Bouvetøya. British Antarctic Survey Bulletin 13, 71-84.

5. Barr, S., 2003, Norway – a consistent polar nation? Kolofon, Oslo, 593 pp.

6. Abs, O., 1957, Professor Adolf Hoel 80 Jahre alt. Polarforschung 27 (1/2), 51-53. Citation is from page 52. This paper confirms that 20 years after the *Schwabenland* expedition German polar researchers thought that the Norwegian claim was triggered by Hoel.

7. Lehmann, 10.12.1938, Note by Dr. Lehmann of 10 December 1938, which Wohlthat send to Ritscher on 14 December 1938. Ritscher's estate AA. Unpublished.

8. Orheim, O., 2008, How Norway got Dronning Maud Land. In Winther, J.-G., Andersen, R.T., Basberg, B.L., Bomann-Larsen, T., Haugland, J.E., Njåstad, B., Orheim, O., and Tveraa, T., (eds), Norway in the Antarctic - from Conquest to Modern Science. Schibsted Forlag, Oslo, 44-59

9. VJP 17.1.1939, Ritscher estate Bh. Unpublished.

10. German Press articles: (i) (probably 22 December 1938), "Deutsche Expedition ins südliche Eismeer"; (ii) (probably 25 December 1938), "Start ins südliche Eismeer - Deutsche Antarktische Expedition 1938/39". Press release 24 December.

11. New York Times, 1938, "Sets out for the Antarctic – German Expedition Carries Two Planes on Motorship". The report is dated December 22 and says the expedition "left today", which was of course 5 days late since the ship sailed on the 17th.

12. Times of London, 1938, German Antarctic Expedition. 27 December issue.

13. Ritscher, A., 1939, Die Deutsche Antarktische Expedition 1938/39. In: Vorbericht über die Deutsche Antarktische Expedition 1938/39, Annalen der Hydrographie und Maritimen Meteorologie VIII. Beiheft, 9-19, map.

CHAPTER 4: OPERATIONS IN THE ANTARCTIC

The Survey Flights

The first flight, on the afternoon of 19 January 1939, was a test flight – a necessary prelude to the long and dangerous reconnaissance flights over the interior - and took place as soon as the ship reached the ice edge [1,2]. Bolle and his crew of mechanics in blue overalls had pored over their two charges for days, checking everything, tightening nuts and bolts, and giving the motors test runs. The pilots had worked to get the aircrafts' loads down to a bare minimum. The fully loaded *Boreas* was now poised on the catapult, while Schirmacher and his aircrew waddled around on the deck in brown flight suits like large teddy bears. They climbed into the plane; Schirmacher triggered a signal light; Bolle pressed a lever; and the *Boreas* was launched.

As planned, the plane communicated with the ship by radio, using Morse code. When they flew over the ice edge near the ship they realised that it was not the edge of the ice shelf proper, but bounded a thin ice strip behind which was a wide bay. Beyond lay the real ice shelf. They radioed the information to *Schwabenland*, which duly steamed south and west to round this promontory and moor inside the bay at 69° 10'S and 4° 25'W. An hour later, at 1722, the *Boreas* returned, the test flight over. Everything had worked perfectly.

Overnight the mechanics overhauled the plane and filled it up with gasoline, while Regula and his team began to map the recent weather systems. The meteorological information for the flight was ready by 0300 on 20 January. Under the southern midnight sun the sky was bright and clear. Everything was ready for the first photographic survey flight, and everyone was excited at the prospect of achieving their mission. With Schirmacher, the pilot, went Loesener as mechanic, Gruber as radio operator, and Sauter as photographer. *Boreas* was airborne again at 0438 GMT for Long Distance Flight 1. Schirmacher flew around the ship with a waggle of wings, then away to the south. Those left behind watched as *Boreas* shrank to the size of a small black dot then disappeared into the distance.

On the bridge, the scientific party went over the plans and worried about the dangers faced by their four comrades. Would the benzine mixture and the instruments stand the extreme cold? Might an engine fail, bringing the plane down 500 km inland? If they needed a spare part, the second plane, the *Passat*, could take it to them. There was no reason why a Dornier–Wal could not take off from an ice surface, even though it was a seaplane. After all, Roald Amundsen and Lincoln Ellsworth managed to take off from the sea ice in the Arctic in 1925 after one of their two Dornier-Wals was disabled there. If *Boreas*

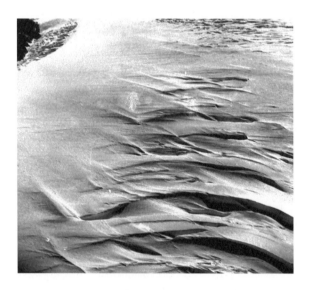

(From top)
Mountains in Neu-Schwabenland;
Drygalski Mountains;
Crevasses in Neu-Schwabenland ;
Conrad Mountain Range

54

crashed or burned, there might be no hope of bringing out survivors, but aside from that Ritscher was confident they could deal with most emergencies and bring survivors home. The planes' emergency supplies were designed to get them to the coast if they were forced down and survived, and the other plane could supply them *en route*. As a first precaution, Ritscher ordered each plane to keep to specified compass courses and to radio the time and direction of each change of course, as well as any landmarks, to enable a rescue plane to follow their track. In case *Boreas* had an accident, Ritscher had *Passat* made ready on the catapult.

Boreas flew south on a compass course of 179° south [3]. The ice seemed smooth, with occasional elevations and no crevasses. At 0630 they flew over a small rocky peak, when, in the distance, to their surprise and delight, they saw rocky east-west trending ridges protruding through the ice – a mountain range! What a discovery! At 0717 they saw a rocky mountain massif perhaps 3-4000 m high in the east. All around, the ice was rising steadily to the south. They were flying at an altitude of 2300 m and about 1200 m above the ground. At 0735 they saw that the mountains stretched far away into the distance to east and west - dark brown, blocky massifs, with occasional needle-like peaks, separated from one another by broad stretches of ice. Behind each ridge another appeared, this was exciting. Here and there were patches of snow-drifts. Locally the ice sheet appeared ridged. Fog filled a valley. The country beneath was still rising to the south. At 0820 they turned back because the ground was still rising, the plane was by then only 100 m above the ground, and they could not gain more height. The mountains seemed to be around 4000 m high, which later turned out to be a considerable over-estimate. Back near the first rocky peak they saw large crevasses in the ice. By 1015 the ice edge was in sight. At 1051 they turned back inland to photograph the eastern part of the newly discovered mountain range. Unfortunately one of the high-tech photo cameras on the starboard side broke down and they had to return to the ship, although the weather was favourable for taking pictures. By 1225 they were over water. About an hour later, at 1335 GMT, they landed on the sea near the ship. Mission accomplished; 'flags and darts dropped as ordered', reported the pilot.

The excitement was infectious. Practically the entire crew crowded onto the after deck to see the aircraft retrieved. Hartmann worked the crane, and plucked the seaplane out of the water. Questions came thick and fast. Film cameras whirred, and shutters snapped, recording the great moment for posterity. Krüger, Bolle and Bundermann, the second photographer would end up spending all night with Sauter, tinkering with the broken camera mechanism to eliminate the problem before the next photo-flight.

Ritscher called everyone together at 1700 in the saloon for a talk on the first flight. The flyers described their discoveries, and reported on how the various bits of equipment had stood the strain of the long cold journey. Later, the crew stayed in the saloon to listen to the news broadcast from Berlin.

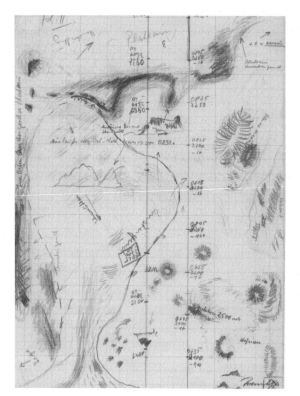

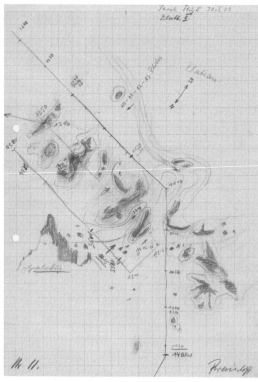

(From top)

On-flight flight track of
Passat - 21 January 1939;

Sketch of the flight track of
Passat - 30 January 1939;

Sketch of "Matterhorn",
21 January 1939

In their efforts to gain height on the flight south, the aircrew had decided to jettison anything not considered essential for safety, which included the heavy metal darts decorated with swastikas. Although this does not appear in the official reports, it has been confirmed in personal communication from Ritscher's second wife Ilse and in letters from Mayr and Sauter to one of the authors (CL) [4,5]. This would explain why the darts were not mentioned in the reports of the subsequent flights. The expedition's maps show that altogether ten flags were dropped at the furthermost turning points of each flight [6].

Long distance flight II took place the next day, Saturday 21 January. This time it was the turn of *Passat*, with Mayr at the controls. As before, Ritscher and Herrmann occupied the chart-room on the bridge, plotting the plane's course as the data came in. During the flights, the most prominent mountains with a characteristic shape were given names like 'Horseshoe', 'Matterhorn', 'Pyramids', 'Block', 'Ball' and 'Skittle', or 'Saddle of Hare' and 'Ring-shaped Pound Cake' ('Napfkuchen') after a tasty German cake. Naming the major features was designed to help the second aircraft orient itself, especially if it had to find the route to bring help in case of emergency.

As before, the plane could only get so far south, before finding it impossible to climb high enough in the thin cold air to get far onto the polar plateau. Suddenly at 0908 they found themselves in a 'white-out', in which the mountains disappeared and the aircrew could not see anything but white all around; they turned away from the mountain range to get into clear air, headed east for 30 km, then switched to the return leg. Each minute of the flight they photographed another 200 square kilometres.

Long distance flight III took place on Sunday 22 January, with Mayr flying *Passat*. All went smoothly and the aerial photography had settled into a routine.

As Regula had warned, the following day the weather was atrocious. The barometer fell, thick clouds blocked the view, and it looked as if the poor conditions would last for a week. A radio message from the whale catcher *Unitas*, 1000 km to the east, reported the same east wind, but stronger - at Force 7. Soon the *Schwabenland* started to roll in the swell that arrived from the east ahead of the storm.

The weather improved on 28 January, and on 29 January the long distance flights restarted, each bringing back photographs of thousands of square kilometres of new land. Schirmacher took Boreas up on long distance Flight IV, which reached 72.30°S before having to turn back because it could climb no further. They covered the eastern part of the mountain mass of what would be named Ritscherland, photographing it from all sides.

Flight V with *Passat*, on 30 January, flew over one set of mountains that was eventually named Drygalskiberge and another eventually named Filchnerberge, to honour the leaders of the two previous German Antarctic Expeditions The appearance of one particular peak was so stunning, and it was so useful as a potential navigational marker that Schirmacher's flight crew gave it the name Gralsburg (Holy Grail mountain), with allusions to Wagner's opera 'Parsifal', about the Holy Grail - something Hitler was keen on. They did not photograph the peak, but Preuschoff sketched it.

Flight VI with *Boreas*, on 31 January, flew over yet more mountains which they named the Wohlthat Massif, a mountain rock mass containing the highest peaks yet seen. On this flight they passed the Gralsburg again, this time photographing it[7]. It sits in the Filchnerberge and is now called Trollslottet Mountain. [8]

This flight combined reconnaissance of a north-south strip with an east-west flight to tie some of the other north-south lines together. The recognisable peaks, which were thought from the previous north-to-south transects to be in particular positions, all seemed to have moved. Evidently the initial maps were all wrong. As revealed later, this is a problem typical of aerial surveys lacking what is called 'ground-truth', some means of ascertaining from the ground precisely where certain landmarks are, so that the aerial survey tracks can later be adjusted to correct for the lateral effects of the wind on the survey planes.

Flight VII, which took place on 3 February, was not as smooth as the others. The scientific party on the ship was worried when Morse messages from *Passat* reported problems with the engine. Eventually the problem disappeared and there were sighs of relief all round, not least because this was the last of the long distance efforts.

While *Passat* was returning, Schirmacher took Ritscher up in *Boreas* for a reconnaissance flight inland from the coast. They suddenly found themselves looking down at a bare rocky area filled with small lakes. This was such a an intriguing discovery that the following day they made a further sortie to photograph the lakes, which they called the Schirmacher Seenplatte – now known as the Schirmacher Oasis. Along the northern edge of the oasis the ice sheet pouring down from the interior ended in a steep ice cliff several tens of metres high. None of the lakes was big enough to land a plane on, which disappointed Ritscher, who noted that the oasis provided favourable conditions for a logistical base for future Antarctic research activity. He was proved right in due course, as the Oasis became home to the scientific stations of Russia (Novolazarevskaya), East Germany (Georg Forster), and India (Maitri) [9].

(From top)
Lakes in the Schirmacher Oasis;
Lakes in the Schirmacher Oasis;
Trollslottet Mountain, formerly 'Gralsburgh', in the northern part of Filchnerberge;
Ice sheet edge - northern edge of Schirmacher Oasis

The Significance of the Geographic Discoveries

In 1939 only around 1.7 million km² of Antarctica's 14-million km² surface had been seen by man. Initially Ritscher thought that during their 57 hours of flying, mostly between longitudes 11°W and 19°E, they had photographed some 350,000 km², and observed around twice as much – some 600,000 km², almost as much as the whole German Reich. A sober appraisal of the results made later in Berlin suggests that the actual area photographed was more like 250,000 km². Whatever the precise result it increased the known area of the continent to around 2.3 million km², or 16% of the total.

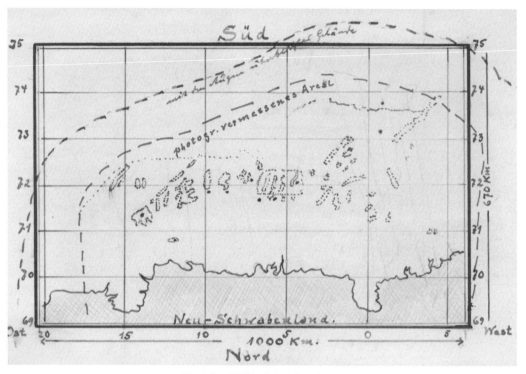

Sketch of Neu-Schwabenland

Under the most favourable conditions, a single flight could theoretically cover an area of some 200,000 km² from an altitude of 3000 m above ground. Patches of fog and cloud prevented such complete coverage, as did the topography. Although some flights penetrated up to 500 km inland, by then they were so low over the polar plateau, flying just 100 m above the ice, that they could only photograph quite small areas. As a result the area covered was much smaller than might otherwise have been the case.

In spite of these local difficulties, they had made some stunning discoveries. They confirmed what Norwegian flights by Riiser-Larsen along the coast west of 5°E had already established

60

in 1930, namely that the coastline was an ice cliff, commonly 10 to 60 m high, bounding the seaward edge of an extensive ice shelf. Because the Germans had flown inland, unlike Riiser-Larsen on the *Norvegia* Expedition, they had discovered that this ice shelf was the seaward edge of an ice sheet that rose slowly and regularly towards the pole, reaching a height of around 1000 m at about 100 km from the coast. There, rocky peaks began to stick out through it; the two closest to the coast they named Kegel and Kugel (Skittle and Ball). They could not tell where the true coast of the continent lay beneath the ice, but it had to be somewhere seaward of those two peaks.

Like the Norwegians in February 1937, who had discovered the Sør-Rondane Mountains at 25°E on a daring inland flight by the seaplane from Lars Christensen's expedition on the *Thorshavn*, the Germans too had discovered mountain massifs some 200 km inland. These were distributed in an 800 km long chain running east-west, more or less parallel to the coast and in a zone about 100 km wide from the Wohlthat Massif in the east to Ritscher Land in the west. In many respects it had the appearance of being the westward extension of the Sør-Rondane Mountains found on Christensen's expedition in 1937.

Within the chain the massifs were clumped into groups having a more or less north-south trend and separated by wide valleys through which glaciers poured down towards the sea from the polar plateau. The rocky peaks rose to between a few hundred and 2000 m above the ice sheet (the higher heights were later reduced based on ground truth data). Beyond them the ice rose steadily poleward for another 20 to 50 km, then more sharply in a 100 m high terrace, south of which spread what they called the Wegener Inland Ice, the local northern part of the white plain of the Polar Plateau that we now know covers all of the Antarctic interior. From the aircraft they could see that this vast high plain, previously seen only by the likes of Amundsen, Scott, Shackleton and Ellsworth, and not in this region, extended a good 200 km further southward, uninterrupted by any rocky protrusions.

They had also discovered the ice-free mountain valleys with frozen lakes in the Wohlthat Massif, and the coastal lowland oasis with ice-free lakes, the Schirmacher Oasis. Frozen lakes were already known from the McMurdo Dry Valleys edging the Ross Sea, but an ice-free oasis was totally unexpected.

If they had had more time, Herrmann, the expedition's geologist/geographer, could have been flown to one of the mountain areas to observe the form of the rocks, and such properties as their colour, surface composition and cleavage, in order to assess their likely character and possible economic potential. But time was a luxury they could not afford. Seeing the sea begin to freeze Ritscher decided they had to leave so as to avoid being caught in the ice, as Filchner had been in the *Deutschland*, when he found himself drifting in the Weddell sea gyre about 27 years before, and as explorers of other nations had been at various times. Herrmann would have to manage with black and white photographs for his geological interpretations.

The Reich's flag planted in the west bight. *(from left)* Mayr, Preuschoff, Ruhnke

Investigating the Ice Shelf and the Ice Floes near the Ship

As the ship was more or less stationary near the ice edge while waiting for the survey planes to return, the scientists aboard had time to investigate conditions on the ice shelf or on the larger of the nearby ice floes. They could get to floes by using one of the ship's boats, but to get to the ice shelf they had to wait until the survey plane was on its way home, at which point the relief plane could be released for local activities. Aside from carrying out scientific investigations, the scientists shot seals and captured penguins.

The first seals, a Weddell and a Crabeater, had been shot on an ice floe near the ship on Saturday 21 January [10]. Before long the seal meat found its way into the cooking pot. Some of the men would love to have had the seal skins for coats for their wives back home, but they would end up in a museum. Barkley, the biologist, was surprised not to find any of the fur seals that used to be the basis for a sealing industry on the offshore islands. He and Kraul put the lack down to over-exploitation of fur seals. But there might not have been any fur seals here anyway. The typical Dronning Maud Land seals are Weddell or Crabeater seals; fur seals, by contrast, are common on sub-Antarctic islands.

The following day Barkley, Gburek, Bruns and Herrmann headed off by boat to a nearby ice floe to do some research and shoot some photos. They erected a theodolite to make some magnetic measurements, only to find that the floe rocked so much because of the swell that delicate observations with a sensitive magnetometer proved to be impossible.

Later that day, when *Passat* was about to land, Schirmacher took *Boreas* up for an aerial pleasure flight of almost four hours to show Ritscher Kegel and Kugel, the first nunataks discovered during the expedition The expedition leader came back full of enthusiasm about the vast landscapes, and enjoyment at having flown the plane in this unique area. Indeed, it would appear from Herrmann's account that Ritscher, the old pilot, actually flew the plane himself for a while during that trip [2].

With the stormy weather starting on Monday 22 January there was no work to do, so the scientists repaired to the common room to sing. Gburek took the role of song-master; Paulsen played the concertina, someone else played the fiddle, another the zither. The weather remained poor. For many, the main diversion was eating. Scurvy was kept at bay with fresh meat and vegetables from the ship's cold rooms, along with fruit conserves supplemented with Vitamin C and multivitamin tablets. Freshly sliced fresh onions were served at table every day, to add to regular dishes and sandwiches.

Following the return of the good weather, while *Boreas* was returning to the ship on January 29, *Passat* took off to investigate possible landing sites at the edge of the ice shelf, in particular two 25 km deep bights in the shelf edge, where the ice edge seemed much lower than the usual 30 m. Mayr was at the controls, with Herrmann in the crew. In the larger of the two bights, at 69° 55'S, 03° 57'W, the ice edge seemed to be only about 40 cm high, and the water was largely free of drift ice, so they decided to 'land'. One of their first tasks was to use an echo-sounder to determine the water depth, which turned out to be 435 m, suggesting that solid land, the coast beneath the ice shelf, was a good distance inland. Mayr used a spirit level sextant to measure the height of the sun to determine the precise location of the landing site. The landing party planted a German flag in the ice 100 m from the shore, claiming 'Neu-Schwabenland' as a new German colony. They were greeted by a number of inquisitive Adelie penguins, along with an Emperor penguin. Mayr and the others loaded three Adelies and the Emperor into the plane's loading room. They were now en route to the Berlin Zoo. Along with them was a shot seal, much of which would end up as fresh meat for dinner. A special pen was built on the deck to house the penguins, and they were provided with a slide to play on. The difficulty would lie in feeding the birds, which preferred the small shrimp-like planktonic krill that supports the Southern Ocean food web to the cook's supply of herring.

Next day, 30 January, it was the turn of Schirmacher and the *Boreas* to catch more Emperor penguins. This time Gburek got to ride along with the crew, to make some magnetic measurements from the ice shelf. The original bight was full of drift ice, so they found another and landed at 70° 17'S 04° 22'E, where they moored against a 1.5 m high ice edge. Once again the German flag was hoisted. The temperature was a balmy –1°C. Another penguin was captured. It was grey and fluffy, not at all like the other birds. After three weeks at sea it was revealed in its true colours as the grey fluff moulted away to expose the plumage of a young Emperor.

Adélie and Emperor penguins on board

While Schirmacher was flying *Boreas* back to the ship on the following day, Mayr took *Passat* up with the biologist Barkley on board. The bights explored earlier being full of ice, they landed instead at 69° 59'S 03° 30'E beside a large ice floe covered with Emperor penguins. Another five were captured to go back to Germany.

Winter was coming in fast and new sea-ice was forming between the older ice floes along the coast. Ritscher had been lucky to find virtually ice-free seas to work in for so long. But the ship was not ice-strengthened and they could not risk the hull being damaged by collision with a substantial floe or a small berg. Regula, the meteorologist, flew with Schirmacher in *Boreas* on 4 February to check the weather [11]. This happened to be the last photo flight, during which they zig-zagged back and forth across the Schirmacher Oasis again.

Original picture of a
landing on an ice floe with
(below) as used in
Die Weite Welt, 1939

Finally, on 5 February, Mayr took *Boreas* up with Lange and Paulsen on the very last flight, to check ice conditions along the coast and to be sure there were abundant channels through which the ship could wend its way north across the belt of drift ice to the open sea. They took the opportunity to land again at the shelf ice edge, this time at 69° 55'S 01° 40'W, where the ice edge was 1.7 m above sea level. They hoisted the German flag again, and collected two more Emperors.

The by now heavily bearded scientists wanted to take one last close look at the ice, so Captain Kottas arranged for two boats to be lowered for an excursion on 6 February. They snaked their way through the drift ice to some large floes and tied up alongside. Cameras were readied and a lot of posing took place for the benefit of the folks back home. Four seals were shot (two recorded as Weddell and the other two not described) [10], and four Adelie penguins captured (eventually reduced to three when one hopped out of the boat on the way back to the ship). On this very last boat trip one man, Rudolf Burghard, a mess steward, fell into the sea and was rescued by Gburek.

Later that day, at 1510 GMT, the *Schwabenland* finally got up steam and set course for home, accompanied by a long succession of hoots on the ship's foghorn.

References

1. Ritscher, A., 1942, Wissenschaftliche und fliegerische Ergebnisse der Deutschen Antarktischen Expedition 1938/39, Hrsg. im Auftrag der Deutschen Forschungsgemeinschaft, Vol. 1. Koehler & Amelang, Leipzig.

2. Herrmann, E., 1941, Deutsche Forscher im Südpolarmeer. Safari Verlag, Berlin, 184 pp.

3. Schirmacher, R., and Mayr, R., 1942, Flüge über der unerforschten Antarktis. In: Ritscher, A., 1942, Wissenschaftliche und fliegerische Ergebnisse der Deutschen Antarktischen Expedition 1938/39, Hrsg. im Auftrag der Deutschen Forschungsgemeinschaft Vol. 1. Koehler & Amelang, Leipzig, 231-265. General description of flights and flight reports.

4. Mayr, 8.10.1989, Mayr's letter to Lüdecke, Privatbesitz Lüdecke, München, 2pp. (Unpublished)

5. Sauter, 25.5.1992, Sauter's letter to Lüdecke, Privatbesitz Lüdecke, München, 1 p. (Unpublished)

6. Ritscher, A., 1939, Die Deutsche Antarktische Expedition 1938/39. Annalen der Hydrographie und Maritimen Meteorologie. VIII, Beiheft, 9-19.

7. Berliner Illustrierte Zeitung, 1939, Number 21, 25th May 1939; p. 867 (with information on the expedition) and pp. 986-987 (with photographs from the expedition, including one of the so-called Gralsburg and a sketch of the flight tracks outlining the main areas of high rocky topography; these are the same areas that appear on the Australian Antarctic map of 1939). Note that a photo Gralsburg also appears on page 51 of Nazis in Antarctica, Life Magazine, July 3, 1939, pp. 51-53, and in Die weite Welt, Nr. 28, 9. Juli 1939, no page numbers given, title page and 4 pages (Ritscher's estate folder Antarktis bis 1941).

8. Brunk, K., 1986, Kartographische Arbeiten und deutsche Namengebung in Neuschwabenland, Antarktis. Bisherige Arbeiten, Rekonstruktion der Flugwege der Deutschen Antarktischen Expedition 1938/39 und Neubearbeitung des deutschen Namensgutes in Neuschwabenland. Frankfurt am Main: Institut für Angewandte Geodäsie. Geodätische Kommission der Bayerischen Akademie der Wissenschaften, Reihe E, Heft Nr. 24, Teil I, II), 42 pp. + 100 pictures.

9. Bormann, P., and Fritzsche D., (eds.), 1995, The Schirmacher Oasis, Queen Maud Land, East Antarctica, and its surroundings. Justus Perthes Verlag, Gotha, Petermanns Geographische Mitteilungen, Erganzungsheft Nr. 289, 448 pp.

10. Schubert, K., 1958, Wale, Robben und Vögel im Bereich der Deutschen Antarktischen Expedition 1938/39. In: Deutsche Antarktische Expedition 1938/39 mit dem Flugzeugstützpunkt der Deutschen Lufthansa A.G. M.S. „Schwabenland", Kapitän A. Kottas. Ausgeführt unter der Leitung von Kapitän A. Ritscher. Wissenschaftliche und fliegerische , Ergebnisse, Vol. 2, Geographisch-Kartographische Anstalt "Mundus", Helmut Striedieck, Hamburg, 257-275. Whales, seals and birds.

11. Regula, H., 1954 (preprint), 1958, Die Wetterverhältnisse während der Expedition und die Ergebnisse der meteorologischen Messungen. Deutsche Antarktische Expedition 1938/39, mit dem Flugzeugstützpunkt der Deutschen Lufthansa A.G. M.S. Schwabenland", Kapitän A. Kottas. Ausgeführt unter der Leitung von Kapitän A. Ritscher. Wissenschaftliche und fliegerische Ergebnisse. Vol. 2, Geographisch-Kartographische Anstalt "Mundus", Helmut Striedieck, Hamburg, vol. 2, 1. Lfg., 16-40.

CHAPTER 5: THE HOMEWARD JOURNEY

Sampling the Ocean en route to Cape Town

The ship had been busy on the Antarctic coast. Over 500 separate manoeuvres had to be made to accommodate aircraft launches and recoveries, to avoid icebergs and large fields of pack ice and to carry out all the scientific work in Antarctic waters while the ship was close to the coast [1].

Now they had to leave all this behind but, as the ship pointed homewards the work continued, following Ritscher's master plan. This was a prime opportunity to supplement the leading edge South Atlantic oceanographic research carried out by Germany's research vessel *Meteor*, which reached south to 63° 51'S in the German Atlantic Expedition of 1925-27. Oceanographic observations and collections of marine biological samples – as well as the usual meteorological observations, radio-sonde ascents and echo-soundings – would be made all the way to the equator [2]. The only other 'serious' oceanographic work in the section between Antarctica and their next stop, Cape Town, had been that of the British on the *Discovery* (1925-29) and on the *Discovery II* (1929-39). Aside from the work of *Discovery*, *Discovery II* and *Meteor*, little research work had been carried out far south of Cape Town, so new scientific discoveries were expected.

Echo-soundings of the seabed were made, and radio-sondes were launched into the air while *Schwabenland* was underway, but sampling for water and marine life required the ship to be stopped at sampling 'stations'. At each station, *Schwabenland* hove-to, and drifted with the wind – the water being far too deep to anchor. Paulsen, the physical oceanographer, attached his measuring instruments and sampling bottles to the thin hydrographic wire - 4 mm in diameter and 7000 m long - and told the winch driver to pay the wire out through a block attached to a meter that recorded how much wire was out. In deep water it could take a couple of hours for the equipment to approach the seabed, with some fine judgment to ensure that the sampling devices didn't actually hit bottom. The wire was held taught by a weight at its lower end. Instruments were strapped onto the wire at intervals so that temperature could be measured and water sampled at standard depths of 0, 20, 30, 50, 75, 100, 150, 200, 250, 300, 400, 500, 600, 700, 800, 900, 1000, 1200, 2000, then every 500 m to as much as 6000 m or wherever the bottom was supposed to be according to the echo-sounder [3]. The work was done in sets, the shallower depths first, the deeper sets later. When the amount of wire out was close to the supposed depth, the winch-man slowed the rate at which the wire passed through the block until he sensed a slackening in tension indicating that the weight had hit bottom. He then stopped paying out, and headed for breakfast, to allow the Kipp thermometers time to equilibrate with the ambient temperature. After breakfast Paulsen attached a running weight – a small heavy metal block – to the wire. The weight slid freely down the wire. When it reached the first sample bottle it closed the lid and tipped the bottle and its thermometer upside-down. This fixed the mercury level in the thermometer so that the temperature at that depth could still be read when the thermometer returned to the surface. At the same time the bottle had trapped water from that same depth, which could then be tested for its salinity and oxygen content. The weight then continued on its way to close the lid of the next instrument in line, then all the others in turn until it reached the weight at the end of the wire. The bottles and thermometers were then hauled in, and Paulsen recorded the temperature and measured the salinity. Then he prepared the next set of bottles for the next series of depths. He used the data to calculate the density of the water, density being the factor controlling how different water masses move relative to each other, and so the key to ocean circulation. Sampling was a tedious business then, and it still is today. In deep water it could take an uneventful five hours to complete a station like this with several sets for different depth groups. Great patience was required.

On most ships the long wait might be quite tolerable, but on the *Schwabenland* the hydrographic winch was a dreadfully noisy beast christened 'Mad Paula' after its owner, Paulsen. 'Mad Paula' coughed, groaned, squeaked and whimpered as the wire went out, then again as the wire came in, the noise penetrating the mid-ships and fore-ship area and causing many awful sailors' curses [4].

Paulsen was not the only one who was busy on station. While he was working on one side of the ship, Barkley, the marine biologist, was using a quiet electrical winch on the other side of the ship to lower his biological nets down to a depth of around 500 m and back up again to collect samples of plankton.

The echo-sounding watch-keepers loved stations because the sounder was turned off and they could sleep instead of marking the record every half an hour, provided they could plug their ears to avoid the squeals of 'Mad Paula'. The 'tween-decks dwellers were happy too, not to be woken every half hour by the howl of the machine that sent out the echo-sounding 'ping'.

As ever, when a large number of people are cooped up in a small space for a long time, tempers frayed. Lange, a non-smoker, shared a cabin with Gburek, who smoked. Lange opened a porthole to let the smoke out, so he could get to sleep. Gburek meanwhile fell asleep and snored, keeping Lange awake. The ship rolled, and a wave poured green water through the open porthole, soaking the two of them and turning their scientific books and papers to mush. Lange cursed Gburek, and begged Captain Kottas for a rubber dinghy so that he could float around in his cabin next time this happened.

Penguins in swimming pool aboard ship

Perhaps not surprisingly, given the tempestuous nature of the Southern Ocean, Captain Ritscher's best-laid plan didn't quite come off. He had been hoping to visit South Georgia, and had obtained permission in a coded telegram from Wohlthat [5]. Kapt'n Kraul had been looking forward to visiting the island and to enjoying the pleasure of downing a stiff whiskey there with old friends from his whaling days [4]. But in the Southern Ocean it is the weather that rules – that and the demand for stations, stations, and yet more stations. Storms blew up. It poured with rain. Schwabenland rolled and pitched. The old sea dogs could handle it, but the penguins found it all rather a trial. As the bad weather slowed the ship down, Ritscher had to proceed with the original plan. They would keep to the Greenwich meridian and head due north for the Cape of Good Hope, stopping to take samples every two hours or so. The only problem was that the ship was heading for the Roaring 40s, where winds from the west howl eastwards, creating some of the largest ocean swells on Earth. Luckily for the expedition it was still summer, so the roar was not quite as bad as it would be in mid winter.

Nevertheless, the crew had a hard time. To take their minds off the discomfort and the tedium a 'Choral Society' and a band were established. One evening Gburek arranged a circus, starring plump, powerful Hartman as a musical clown towing a plush-covered wooden dog. This had everyone in stitches. Gburek wrote and directed a play, a drama called The King of Salern', starring Preuschoff as king, Hartmann as prince, and Lange as a poor shepherdess; it became the highlight of the journey [4].

Back on deck, Barkley and Paulsen, lowered their gear from either side of the ship simultaneously to save time, and managed to get the wires tangled under the keel, occasioning a further delay. Meanwhile the scientists wrote up their findings, produced maps and charts, and tapped out provisional reports on typewriters, ready to be sent home by fast steamship from the next port of call - Cape Town.

En route they saw few other vessels. Herrmann reported a Norwegian whale catcher coming to take a close look at the *Schwabenland* [4]. It reminded him that the German expedition must have been in bad odour with the Norwegians for having penetrated into Antarctic territory that they thought they owned. Ritscher noted that they saw three whale catchers on their return journey, and on 9 February they encountered the American whaling factory ship *Ulysses*, which had a Norwegian crew [2].

Every day Barkley fed the penguins. They had become accustomed to the food, after a period of force feeding in which Mayr held them tight and used gloved hands to open their beaks so that Barkley could stuff their gullets with fish.

On 14 February the barometer fell and the wind rose to 15 m/sec while the ship waited on station. By the following day the deepening low pressure had ushered in a roaring storm. Everything loose flew about dangerously. The scientists felt their way along companionways, clutching at any possible support and bouncing from wall to wall. With each roll, drawers slid out of Ritscher's writing desk, only to slam shut as the ship rolled back. Eventually they fell out completely, and slid from one side of the cabin to the other.

Things calmed down enough by 16 February to allow a station at 54°S. Because the wind made the ship drift so much the wire led out at quite an angle from the side of the ship. When the wire is not straight up and down it is not possible to know precisely at what depths the instruments make their measurements and collect their water samples – so Paulsen had to correct the data, and even then was not quite sure he had the right answers.

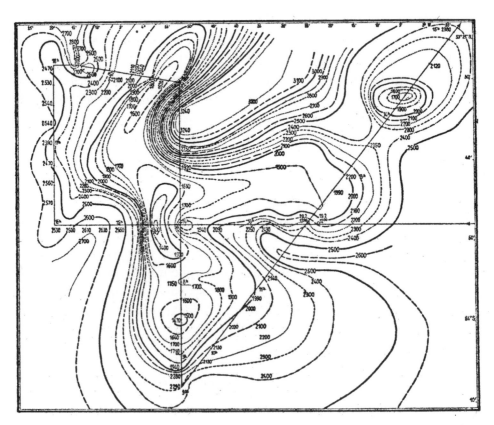

Sounding-map of Bouvet Bank

That day they passed close to Bouvet Island. The early fog lifted, giving them a wonderful view of the island's 200 m thick ice sheet poised above the dark coastal cliffs. Under the ice slept a mid-ocean volcano with an unknown history. Unfortunately, the breakers at the base of the cliff were too high to permit any thought of a landing.

Engineer Bruns and Herrmann used the opportunity to make a 'horizontal' echo-sounding of the north coast [4,6]. This would appear to have been one of the first ever attempts at the technology now known as side-scanning sonar, but as far as we can tell the results were not published.

Nearby, at 53° 30'S and 3° 30'W, the echo-sounder had detected a shallow bank, which they decided to survey. More soundings were collected before they had to heave to and stop work because of thick fog. They drifted ESE, hoping that they would not be overtaken by or run into any icebergs. Herrmann drew a provisional map of the new bank. It would not be the last such map, as all the soundings had first to be corrected for the speed of sound in seawater at this location – a lengthy task in the days before computers.

Cape Town provided a brief but pleasant interlude. The *Schwabenland* arrived on 6 March. While others enjoyed a stroll though the city and a pleasant social evening on board a German fast steamer, Gburek had to work at the geophysical observatory to make some measurements to connect his new Antarctic data with known African conditions.

Before the expedition left on the following day, Reichmarschall Hermann Göring sent a telegram congratulating them on their great success. He was proud of:

...the outstanding employment of the airmen, of the successful work of the scientists, and of the exemplary attitude of the whole crew. You and your expedition have further established the great tradition of German research and accomplished an achievement worthy of the position of Greater Germany in the world. [2].

Wohlthat had hoped that the two aircraft might fly home from Cape Town to bring duplicates of the aerial photos to Germany as quickly as possible [7] but this was not realistic during the one day port stop. Since the last flight on 5 February the planes had been solidly fixed on the ship and could not easily be made available for flying. They remained there until the return to Hamburg [4]. Nevertheless the port stop provided an ideal opportunity to send home some initial reports, among them Ritscher's expedition report and results [8]. His report incorporated an initial list of names of the discovered places and features, including names like 'Hermann-Göring-Land' (later called Neu-Schwabenland) or 'Gralsburg' (later Conradburg). Besides that, he suggested presenting the Emperor penguins either to Göring or to an appropriate zoological garden. It was suggested that the three Adélie penguins be assigned to Hagenbeck's zoological garden in Hamburg. In a letter to his stepbrother Paul Wetz, Ritscher mentioned that he planned to catch fish for the penguins around some of the uninhabited islands of the south Atlantic [9].

The Cape Town press was full of news of the expedition on 6 and 7 March 1939. The Cape Argus from 6 March 1939 carried an article with the title 'Whales being hunted to extinction - Five-year close season suggested by German expert – *Schwabenland's* research in the south'. Herrmann was the expert, describing the scientific work needed to support sustainable whaling and the safety of the whaling fleet. The papers noted the arrival of the first Emperor penguins seen in Cape Town, and mentioned the aircraft, but without any information about their tasks. Evidently Ritscher and his men had kept quiet about their actual objectives. Not until 10 March 1939 did the Cape Times say what the expedition was all about. Under the title 'Germany's Antarctic Claims' it explained that chains of peaks and the polar massif were photographed from the air, noting that the expedition discovered and mapped 350,000 square kilometres of the Antarctic continent. 'Germany will not decide on the course she take to secure her claim to the territory' the article went on, 'until Captain Ritscher has given an account of the expedition and the photographs taken by the expedition have been examined.' As the first reports of the success of the expedition appeared in German press from 10 March onward, it seems likely that the Cape Times was using official German sources, not information gleaned from the visiting scientists.

Cape Town to Recife

At 1700 on 7 March they left the delights of Cape Town for a diagonal run across the South Atlantic towards the port of Recife in the state of Pernambuco on the northeast coast of Brazil. There were interesting echo-sounding data to collect as this line had never been sampled before, because there was no trade route between Cape Town and Pernambuco. The line cuts across and supplemented the 14 east-west lines sampled by the *Meteor* expedition a decade before.

Every two hours Regula measured wind speed over the ocean's surface while the ship lay quiet. Meanwhile, Herrmann filmed waves stereoscopically from the ship's side through two parallel film cameras, to provide Regula with 3-D pictures of wave heights for comparison with the wind data.

On 18 March the Brazilian island of Trinidade came into view. It was another of the Atlantic's volcanos, around 600 m high, and very steep sided. Pitch-black lava plugs rose like needles out of the sea; around them were brown-red volcanic rocks covered by sparse vegetation [4, 10]. *Schwabenland* anchored at Cochoeiro Bay in the lee of this wild island, and was soon joined by a Norwegian whale factory ship and its small whale catchers. While they lay at anchor sheltered from the strong Trade Winds, the sailors, led by Boatswain Stein, painted the outside of the hull to adapt it for the tropics [2,4].

According to the German Sea Handbook the island was occupied only by herds of wild goats, survivors of World War I, when a dozen people were interned here with some goats

(From top)
Trinidade as seen from the
south west;
Pico on the west coast of
Fernando Noronha;
The steep mountains
of Cochoeiro Bay on
Trinidade

for food. Breakers as high as houses beat against the steep black rocks. The scientists enjoyed their time off and sunned themselves on the deck. Troe, the second cook, set himself up as hairdresser, grooming those who wanted to look their best on the run ashore in the Brazilian port of Pernambuco; he was a happy man - one haircut cost 2 flasks of beer.

Reading Herrmann's description of this relaxing day, nobody would suspect that in some ways the visit to Trinidade was the most exciting event of the whole expedition for some of the scientists [4]. The excitement came about because the expedition had to fulfil a top secret military task. Ritscher was required to answer the following questions from the Navy about the Brazilian islands of Trinidade and Martin Vaz [11]:

> *Are there anchorages to give protection for fuel depots, for equipment for auxiliary cruisers, and for other similar military requirements? Are the islands permanently or temporarily inhabited? Are there any installations for telecommunication? Is it possible to supply ships with fresh water? Do the Islands provide animals and plants to supplement U-boat supplies? Do any vessels call at the islands from time to time?* [11]

To answer the questions, Ritscher decided to go ashore with some of the scientists to gather information. The 1st officer, Amelang, took eight people close to the shore in a launch to look for a beach to land on [10]. Spotting what seemed like a good place, Ritscher, Lange, and Herrmann transferred to a rowing boat manned by two seamen and headed for the shore. As the seabed shallowed, the waves steepened and the big Atlantic rollers began to toss the boat around; it was not as safe a spot as it looked from further out. Damp from the spray they turned back. Returning to Amelang's launch they searched for another landing site, finding one in a bay further to the east, where the land ascended gently from the shore. The friendly appearance was deceptive. As they rowed in and the seabed shoaled, the breakers again became higher and higher. Thirty metres from the shore an enormous breaker caught the boat astern and turned it upside down. The men scrambled ashore, where the sun dried their wet clothes. They managed to retrieve the boat and pull it ashore, but when the tide came in the boat was dragged into the breakers and smashed by the waves.

The shipwrecked mariners had neither provisions nor water. Amelang realised that it would be foolhardy to try another landing at this unfriendly spot, and found a better landing site in a bay further to the west. Between this new bay - Principe Bay - and the 'shipwreck' cove the rocks were high and very steep, but there was no alternative. To reach the first party a second group would have to land there and clamber up over the rocks and down the other side, with the aim of bringing their comrades back by the same route. Happily, there were no signs of sharks, only some rainbow coloured fish and some giant sea turtles. Lacking a second rowing boat, Barkley, Regula, and Krüger decided to swim the 50 m to shore. The surf was not too bad, and they made it with just a few grazes from the sharp rocks in the shallows.

Barkley started to climb the cliff to get to the neighbouring bay, but cut his hands and feet on the rugged volcanic rocks. To make progress they needed shoes to protect their feet, and shirts to keep off the fierce tropical sun. The launch crew used a rocket pistol to shoot a rope ashore, and used the rope to send the photographer Sauter to the beach with a camera and a rucksack full of clothes. A grand plan, except that he and the camera and the clothes arrive completely soaked, killing any chance of photographs of the interior.

The climb up the cliff to get to the shipwrecked group was too steep for Krüger and Sauter, but Regula and Barkley made it. Meanwhile Ameland had taken the launch back to the ship and returned with some inflatable rubber boats. Early in the evening Mayr landed in a rubber boat, collected Sauter and Krüger, and brought provisions and drinks for the others. Back on the launch they kept a watch on the bay, and before it got dark they could see two people climbing back down. The original three apparently preferred to stay where they were rather than risk a steep and unfamiliar climb in the dark. Next day at 0500 everyone was rescued with the aid of three rubber boats. The shore party even managed to bring new provisions aboard: Barkley had killed a giant turtle weighing 150 pounds, from which a wonderful goulash was prepared for all aboard the ship.

Ritscher detailed these various exploits and the answers to the Navy's questions in his report to the Naval High Command, which he would deliver on 2 May 1939, shortly after his return to Germany [12]. He noted that landing on Trinidade would be fraught with risk due to the steep cliffs and high swell. The best landing site was a place called 'Boat Harbour', mentioned in the Sea Handbook, which could be reached through a 5 m wide channel between the cliffs and a sandy shore. Conditions might be better during summer when the swell would be lower. Evidently people could mange to live there, or so it would appear from the wooden huts seen on the island. The report confirmed the description of the Sea Handbook: steep cliffs; mountains up to 600 m high; small, but very steep gorges. It seemed to Ritscher that there was probably much rain during the southern winter. In the southern summer and even in March, the southern hemisphere autumn, the southwest and the south coast would have no water at all. Food was abundant, he reported, the domestic animals like goats and black and white pigs having increased since being left behind by the occupying forces of World War I. There were many birds – a source of meat and eggs - and, between January and March, many giant turtles, which crawled ashore to lay eggs and could be easily caught. The only flat land on the island, he noted, lay on the northeastern side, some 30 m above the beach. It was covered by a layer of clay on which a herb with many leaves came up in March and which grew up to 0.5 m in height. There were broken down huts at the southern end of this beach, which could sustain a population of around 20 families if the nearby rivulet was maintained and winter rain was collected. The island was not far from sea-lanes, and Norwegian factory ships stopped there quite often to provide their catch boats with fuel. Due to the heavy permanent swell, ships needed to be equipped with good fenders in case of collision with each other or the rocks.

Both Ritscher and Herrmann would have liked to mention in their published reports of the expedition the exciting story of their landing on Trinidade. First they had to ask the Naval High Command for permission [13]. The answer was no. They were allowed to mention the rest stop at Trinidade, but not the landing, nor their investigation of the interior [14].

Back on the ship they realised they were running out of time to undertake what were evidently difficult landings and surveys – tasks for which they were not well equipped. As a result Ritscher decided they must abandon any further investigation of the other parts of the island, and a planned trip to the island of Martin Vaz. On 19 March they left for Pernambuco, which they reached on 22 March [2,4].

Like Cape Town, Pernambuco provided a pleasant interlude. Some of the crew went downtown while others visited *Schwabenland's* sister ship, the floating airbase *Friesenland*, which was waiting for the next transatlantic aircraft from the north. The penguins were happy, because they were treated to fresh fish, the supply of which should last them for the rest of the journey. Three penguins - two Adelies and an Emperor - had died in the tropics, despite Barkley's efforts to keep them alive.

Pernambuco to Hamburg

On the morning of 23 March, *Schwabenland* sailed again, this time doubling as a mail ship and heading directly for Hamburg. Its own mail went by air to Berlin via Lisbon in a Dornier 17 flying from the *Friesenland*.

The next stop was at the Brazilian island of Fernando de Noronha, another Atlantic volcano, 345 km off the coast of Brazil, whose principal skyward pointing peak is known as the 'Finger of God'. The tall, thin peak is a lava plug, the remnant of the central lava-filled tube of the volcano. The surrounding volcanic cone, made of easily weathered layers of volcanic ash, has long since been eroded away. Unlike Trinidade, Fernando de Noronha (now a World Heritage Site) was inhabited, and decorative little houses clustered together around a paradisiacal natural harbour (the island became a prison in 1942). The locals recognised the *Schwabenland*, which had been there before on its South American mail runs, and rowed out to visit.

Continuing on their way they crossed the equator for the second time at 1600 on 25 March. The scientific programme was now over and the scientists were writing up their final reports. By 29 March it was getting distinctly cooler, and the penguins began to come out from beneath the awning that had protected them from the tropical sun. The Cape Verde islands came in sight; more volcanos.

Poland now occupied much of the radio news, with propaganda being made about Nazi Germany's wish to establish a new border with Poland to connect the German territory of East Prussia with the rest of the Reich, rather than remaining separated from it by the 'Polish Corridor' (the Poles had acquired the corridor from Germany in the Treaty of Versailles at the end of the First World War, and Hitler sought to reverse this and at the same time to make German the so-called Free City of Danzig, which was under control and protection of the League of Nations). It was on March 30, as they sailed north, that Britain and France backed Poland, something that would lead eventually to war. Shipboard conversations turned constantly to the question, like a tongue exploring a new cavity in an old tooth.

But politics was not the only subject of interest. On 1 April they held their last evening songfest: seaman Hock dressed as an Indian and read palms; Ruhnke mined his seemingly inexhaustible fund of jokes. It was time to relax. From the deck outside, the Great Bear was once again visible in the northern sky. Even though they were still only at 26°N, this was a sign that they were almost home. Next morning they passed the Canary Islands, with the peak of Tenerife, yet another volcano, dark against a rose-red sky. *Schwabenland* ploughed on through the swells towards Cape Finisterre and the Bay of Biscay. Passing Spain on this occasion their minds were no longer preoccupied with the German role in the Spanish Civil War, which had ended with the surrender of the Republican forces on April 1.

At Easter, on 9 April, *Schwabenland* was in the English Channel under sunny skies. Boxes and crates were being packed. One by one the crew called home on the radio-telephone in the radio shack. On the 5th the ship lay by the lightship Elbe 3, waiting for a pilot. The weather was beautiful – a fine day for a homecoming. Captain Ritscher pinned a memo to the notice-board.

Comrades! The DAE 1938/39 is at an end. A true team effort, which has built up through four months of joint experience, is now dissolved. But so long as you live, you know that you proved yourselves through good days and bad. The results of the expedition show that you succeeded by standing by one another and all pulling together. As leader of this loyal team I take great pleasure in thanking you all – the flyers, their mechanics, the scientists and the deck and machine crews – for your willing cooperation and I hope that all of you will look back with pride at our now completed journey. I give you my best wishes for your future occupations and your welfare.[4]

By 11 April the ship was back in Cuxhaven at the mouth of the Elbe. Ritscher had already asked to be met with fresh fish for the seven Emperor penguins. The sailors and scientist were in good health [15], having been looked after closely by Josef Bludau, the ship's doctor, and fed well by the ship's cook.

The following day guests arrived on the early train from Hamburg further down the river. Many of them were dignitaries who had been on the sea trials in December. Among them was Councillor of State Wohlthat, the expedition's sponsor, representing General Field-Marshall Göring; Professor Mentzel, President of the German Research Foundation, representing Minister Rust, of Education and the Arts; Rear-Admiral Dr Conrad, representing the German Naval High Command; and Admiral Dr. Spiess representing the German Naval Observatory - the Deutsche Seewarte.

The guests joined the crew on the final leg of the journey down the Elbe from Cuxhaven to Hamburg. A festive air reigned. Ritscher delivered his report of the expedition, and provided some of the early results. The visitors toured the ship, which arrived in Hamburg in the evening. The intrepid explorers were feted with a parade by Hitler's private army the SA - the *Sturm Abteilung* (literally Storm Section), otherwise known as the storm-troopers or the brown-shirts, complete with musical band. Next was a reception in the Town Hall, followed by a festive dinner at the Four Seasons Hotel. Next morning, 12 April, a telegram of congratulation arrived from the Führer himself –

I thank the participants of the German Antarctic Expedition 1938/39 for the report of their return home. I combine with this my hearty congratulations on the successful implementation of the expedition's assigned task. Adolf Hitler. [2]

As with any polar expedition, however, arrival home and telegrams from on high were not the end - at least not for the scientific party. Though their task of collecting samples and data had been completed successfully, to the point that initial reports of the expedition could soon be published [1,2], there was much more work to be done in refining the maps and analysing and reporting comprehensively on the samples and data that had been collected. The war that would break out 5 months later would seriously interrupt those proceedings, so much so that many of the results would not be published in final form for almost 20 years, as a major German contribution to the International Geophysical Year (IGY) of 1957/58.

Still, it would be a while until war started. In the meantime one of Ritscher's first acts on returning home was to hand over seven Emperor penguins and one Adelie penguin to a representative of the Berlin Zoo [16]. The Emperors attracted a lot of attention, apparently being the first live specimens seen in Europe. During the 1937-1938 whaling season *Jan Wellem* was reported to have captured four Emperor penguins in South Georgia to bring them home for a zoo, but they died aboard ship*. Keeping penguins alive was evidently a tricky business, and the Emperors only survived for a short time in Berlin.

*Given what we now know about the distributions of Emperor penguins it seems likely that the specimens from South Georgia were King penguins.

References

1. Ritscher, A., 1939, Die Deutschen Antarktischen Expedition 1938/39. In: Vorbericht über die Deutsche Antarktische Expedition 1938/39. Annalen der Hydrographie und Maritimen Meteorologie. VIII, Beiheft, 1-19.

2. Ritscher, A., 1942, Wissenschaftliche und fliegerische Ergebnisse der Deutschen Antarktischen Expedition 1938/39, Hrsg. im Auftrag der Deutschen Forschungsgemeinschaft Vol 1. Koehler & Amelang, Leipzig.

3. Paulsen, K.H., 1939, Die ozeanographischen Arbeiten. In: Vorbericht über die Deutsche Antarktische Expedition 1938/39. Annalen der Hydrographie und Maritimen Meteorologie. VIII, Beiheft, 27-32.

4. Herrmann, E., 1941, Deutsche Forscher im Südpolarmeer. Berlin: Safari Verlag, 184 pp.

5. Wohlthat, 8 February 1939, Telegram to Ritscher. Bh1 VJP. Ritscher's estate.

6. Hallstein, 1952, Bekanntmachung über die Bestätigung der bei der Entdeckung von "Neu-Schwabenland" im Atlantischen Sektor der Antarktis durch die Deutsche Antarktische Expedition 1938/39 erfolgten Benennungen geographischer Begriffe. Bundesanzeiger 4 (149), 5 August 1952, 1-2.

7. Wohlthat 13 February 1939, Telegram. Bh1 VJP. Ritscher's estate. Unpublished

8. Ritscher, 26 February 1939, Letter to Wohlthat. Bb1 OKM. Ritscher's estate. Unpublished

9. Ritscher, 6 March 1939, Letter to Paul Wetz. Antarktis bis 1941. Ritscher's estate. Unpublished

10. Krüger, 1 May 1939, Unsere Landung auf Trinidad. Bb1 Trinidad. Ritscher's estate. Unpublished

11. OKM, 21 November 1938, Letter to Ritscher. Bh1 OKM. Ritscher's estate. Unpublished

12. Ritscher, 2 May 1939, Letter to OKM. Bb1 Trinidad. Ritscher's estate. Unpublished

13. Todt, 15 May 1939, Letter to OKM. Bh1 OKM. Ritscher's estate. Unpublished

14. OKM, 9 June 1939, Letter to Office of DAE. Bh1 OKM. Ritscher's estate. Unpublished

15. Ritscher's estate file Bb1 (Medizin). Unpublished

16. Rüdiger, H., 1939, Die Deutsche Antarktische Expedition 1938/39. Petermanns Geographische Mitteilungen, 85, 197-198.

III
CONSEQUENCES – 1939 TO PRESENT DAY

CHAPTER 6: DEVELOPMENTS 1939-1945

The First Accounts Appear

News sent home from Cape Town on the return journey on 6 March 1939 was released to the press as an official communiqué, summarised in the international press on 10 March by Britain's Daily Telegraph, which first noted the success of Ritscher's team in mapping part of the continent, then went on to say that the news 'aroused some speculation as to whether Germany intends to claim sovereignty over this territory. It is asserted that while sovereignty is claimed by Norway, this part of Antarctica has never been trodden or flown over by Norwegian explorers' [1].

Much the same report appeared in the New York Times, which also noted that the same day, 10 March, Norway had been quick to remind readers that the area had been mapped and photographed by Lars Christensen and put under Norwegian sovereignty by the Norwegian government on 14 January 1939 [2]. 'A conflict thus appears likely to arise between Germany and Norway over this subject' said Britain's Daily Mail of 10 March [3]. On 14 March, the London Times made much the same report but went on to note that the official communiqué said that 'After Captain Ritscher's detailed report has been studied, decisions can be taken as to the steps necessary to secure the results of the expedition for Germany' [4].

There was another flurry of reports on 12-13 April as the ship reached Germany. The New York Times of 12 April summarised what the expedition had accomplished [5] and the issue of 13 April quoted the German press as reporting on 12 April 'It is a matter of course for the Germany of today that the permanent result of this expedition be safeguarded for the German people in every respect, scientifically, economically and politically' and that '...no other country can have such a justified claim as the explorers who returned today and the Great German Empire which sent them out.' [6,7]. The paper reported the anxiety in Norway about the German claim. Clearly the world was aware of the geopolitical ramifications of the expedition, and that in turn had an effect on US policy on Antarctica. No doubt the reports of the expedition had also piqued curiosity in the minds of scientists with an Antarctic bent, but they were to be disappointed by the slowness with which the results emerged, owing to the outbreak of war.

The expedition had raised public interest in the Antarctic and in whaling. Numerous articles appeared in German newspapers, besides the books and technical reports that the expedition would produce.

Next Steps

Wohlthat called Ritscher and official representatives from various ministries, the German Research Foundation, the Navy, and Deutsche Lufthansa, to a departmental meeting on 27 April, 1939 to discuss what should happen next. As can be seen from the minutes of the meeting [8], one key item of business was what to do about substantiating a possible German claim to the territory they had flown over. They agreed on three courses of action. Firstly, there should be a second expedition. Secondly, any claims based on the first expedition would have to be delayed until they could be supported by scientific papers and articles in journals and magazines. And thirdly, a political opinion on the status of the possible German claim should be drafted ready for publication after the return of the second expedition. The meeting also considered what should be done about formalising the names to be given to the newly discovered mountains. They decided to follow international recommendations, which meant not using the names of politicians or names with special significance in political circles. For that reason the name Hermann Göring-Land, which had initially been proposed for what became Neu-Schwabenland [9], was subsequently dropped, as was the name Gralsburg for one of the peaks in the Filchnerberge. Ritscher finalised his proposed list of names before 6 May, the date by which he had to submit the list to Göring for approval [10], which came through on 5 July [11].

In the meantime, there was growing interest in the expedition from outside Germany. For example, Ernest Walker, commander of a planned private British Antarctic Expedition aboard the *Westward*, which was cancelled after the war began [12], wrote to Ritscher on 14 April 1939 asking for information on the geographical limits of the aerial surveys and the position of the coast line, so as to keep his maps and records up to date [13]. Ritscher asked Wohlthat if he should respond, and if so how much he should tell the Briton. [14] There is no copy of a reply,

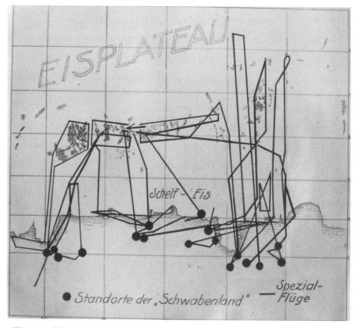

First published map (the so-called "Preuschoff map") with flight tracks and discoveries in Neu-Schwabenland

84

so presumably none was sent because at that time the results were still considered secret.

Nevertheless, on 25 May the information in question was published in a popular German magazine in the form of a rough map outlining the mountain ranges discovered, the position of the shore line, and the tracks of the flight routes.[15] Wohlthat's bureau promptly asked Ritscher's secretary, Herbert Todt, how this publication had come about and who had provided the material [16]. Todt answered that it had seemed desirable to give an impression of the achievements of the expedition to a broad public. Thus they had submitted a preliminary sketch made by the flight mechanic, Franz Preuschoff, of the analysis of the aerial photos - the so-called 'Preuschoffkarte' (Preuschoff's map). This sketch represented a first step towards producing an eventual map. The person in charge at Hansa Luftbild, where the maps were being made, commented that the geographical position and the forms of the landscape shown in the sketch were in most cases not positioned correctly. The 25 May 1939 issue of the Berliner Illustrierte Zeitung (BIZ) also carried a photo of the peak provisionally named Gralsburg, a name that was subsequently dropped from the approved list of names. Pictures of Gralsburg, though without the name, also appeared in magazines in July [17,18].

Preuschoff's crude map in the BIZ made its way to Canberra to be incorporated into the 1939 Australian map of Antarctica [19,20]. The Americans evidently had access to a more detailed and up-to-date publication of Ritscher's map of Neu-Schwabenland than the one in the BIZ of 1939, since a detailed portrayal of the new discoveries, along with names of selected features, was incorporated into the USA's 1943 Hydrographic Chart of Antarctica and the Southern Ocean [21]. Probably the Americans used the large map in Ritscher's 1939 report [22], since the first volume of the expedition's results were not published until 1942 [23], months after war had been declared between Germany and the USA on December 11, 1941.

Ritscher and his colleagues were now busy trying to finalise their reports on what they had discovered. In the early summer of 1939 there was a constant interaction between the expedition's experts and the map-making cartographic team – none of whom had been down to the ice. Aside from advising the cartographers, Ritscher and his colleagues were writing up their results for publication. First to appear in print was Ritscher's report about the expedition and some preliminary results – published as a supplementary issue of the Annalen der Hydrographie und Maritimen Meteorologie of the German Maritime Observatory [22]. It seems most likely to us that publication took place between 1 and 7 September 1939 - just after the outbreak of war. Firstly, the galley proofs in Ritscher's private papers are dated 29 July 1939. Secondly, the print run of 2,100 copies of the large-scale map of Neu-Schwabenland that accompanied the report was not ordered by the publisher until 9 August 1939 [24]. Thirdly, Ritscher wrote to a colleague on September 7 to say that the supplement had been published [25]. And fourthly, the document was not widely available outside Germany, suggesting it had not been distributed before the war started. Indeed, the earliest accession date found for these documents in British libraries was 1946. The copy in the Norwegian Polar Institute is not listed in the accessions received between 1939 and November 1941, a further indication of the lack of international distribution at the time [26]. The copy owned by the ship's doctor, Josef Bludau, bears an inscription dated 1 May 1940 on its title page, suggesting that distribution did not happen swiftly after publication. This copy now sits in the Rauner Special Collection of Dartmouth College Library in the USA (S. Hartwell, personal communication to CS, 2008). Written on the title page is this poignant note: 'Hans Weigert, 30 Dec. '47, Exchange for coffee'. Weigert was a lecturer at Georgetown University in the USA, and it would appear that after meeting Bludau in 1947 and obtaining the book by exchange he passed his copy to Vilhjalmur Stefansson, whose book collection went to Dartmouth College in 1951. The exchange for coffee is a reminder of the hardships of post-war Germany.

Several other reports appeared in 1939, including the first accounts of German whaling expeditions [27,28], and Käpt'n Kraul's account of his life in whaling, with a chapter on the Schwabenland expedition [29]. Meanwhile, Herrmann was working on his popular account of the expedition, which would be published in June 1941 [30,31]. All of the expedition's scientists were finalising their contributions to Volume I of the official report of the expedition, which would be with the printers by 3 June 1941 [23,32].

Although Wohlthat had asked for the large-scale map of Neu-Schwabenland to be ready for him to take to the International Whaling Conference in London (17-20 July, 1939), it was not available until August – as mentioned above. That would explain why there is no record in the proceedings of that conference that Wohlthat handed out copies of the map there [33]. 2000 copies of the three high resolution maps of Wohlthat Massif (at a scale of 1:500,000), and of the western edge of the Humboldt-Gebirge, and the central part of the Wohlthat Massif (at a scale of 1:50,000), were ordered on 24 July 1941 [34]. It took another year until the publication of the first volume of the results, including the maps [35]. A revision of the maps of the western edge of the Humboldt-Gebirge and the central part of the Wohlthat Massif at a scale of 1:100,000 was published in 1985 [36].

To crown the success of the expedition, Deutsche Lufthansa ordered 100 commemorative coins to be made in polished steel [37], which Wohlthat planned to present to the expedition's members on 25 October, when Ritscher was scheduled to give a formal public lecture on the expedition to official guests [38]. Unfortunately the production of the coins was delayed, because of difficulties in the delivery of the forged steel needed for preparing a special ring for the mould for the coins [39]. As a result, the German Science Foundation (Deutsche Forschungsgemeinschaft - DFG) revised the date for the lecture to Saturday, 27 October 1939 at the New Physics Auditorium of the Technical University in Berlin-Charlottenburg [40].

The commemorative coin of the 3rd German Antarctic Expedition 1938/39

Guests were invited to attend in formal dress. That evening, Prof. Rudolf Mentzel (1900-1987), who as President of the DFG represented the official sponsor of the expedition, distributed 30 commemorative coins to the members of the expedition who had been able to attend the lecture [41]. The design from one side of this coin later appeared like a logo of the expedition on the cover of Herrmann's travel account.

Proposed tracks for the 3rd German Antarctic Expedition, from a top secret document of 3 November 1938

Planning the Follow-up Expedition

Besides his many other tasks, Ritscher was also busy planning the next Antarctic expedition; indeed, he had started doing so on the return journey, and was able to hand his plan to Wohlthat as the ship docked in Hamburg. Instead of returning to Neu-Schwabenland, he would go elsewhere. Two things drove his new plan. Firstly, there was no point antagonizing the Norwegians, now that they had claimed Neu-Schwabenland as Dronning Maud Land, especially since their claim had been recognised by Australia, Great Britain, France and New Zealand. And secondly, there was increasing evidence to suggest that there were not all that many whales in that sector of the Antarctic. Instead, Ritscher planned to investigate whaling prospects and the possibilities for a land base in the Pacific sector between 80°W to 130°W, building on a provisional plan already proposed in September 1938 [42]. No nation had yet made any claim to

87

the coast of West Antarctica in the Bellingshausen Sea area. Indeed, it had hardly been explored at all by anyone. The London Whaling Conference of 1939 had recommended this area as sanctuary for whales, which meant that it might be a promising region for German whaling in the 1940/41 season if the Germans refused to endorse the sanctuary recommendation [43].

Wohlthat approved the plan in principle the day after *Schwabenland's* return [44], subject of course to an eventual agreement to it by a meeting of the interested departments and agencies. The task of the Pacific expedition would be the same as before – reconnaissance aerial survey. This time there was an additional focus on determining the possibilities for a follow-up expedition to land with dog sleds to fix ground control points, so as to avoid the cartographic problems raised on the 1938/39 expedition. Whether or not territorial claims would be made would depend on the outcome of the expedition. En route, the Pacific expedition would return to the islands of Trinidade and Martin Vaz to continue surveying them for military purposes.

Ritscher suggested that the Pacific expedition should leave Hamburg on 15 November at the latest so that they could start work in Antarctica by 20 December 1939 and make full use of the southern summer season of 1939/40. To save foreign currency they would sail around Cape Horn rather than through the Panama Canal. Meteorological and oceanographic measurements would be made throughout the journey, while biological sampling would be confined to Antarctic waters. Ritscher wanted to use the more powerful Dornier 24 aircraft for the aerial photogrammetric survey. On 19 June Wohlthat gave the order to prepare the expedition, which if it left on time should be able to operate in Antarctica for six weeks – significantly longer than during the 1938/39 expedition. On Kraul's recommendation the date was brought forward to 20 October 1939 to enable more research on whales to be included. As well as *Schwabenland* the expedition would include two vessels for whale research; these were the 500-ton trawler *Kehdingen* and the 400-ton whale catcher *Wal I*, which would depart on 15 and 11 October respectively, because they were slower than the *Schwabenland*. All three vessels would rendezvous at Deception Island in the South Shetland Islands. Kapt'n Kraul would be in charge of using the two small vessels to investigate whaling possibilities in the Pacific sector. On the way back the expedition would land on South Georgia to carry out further scientific research. That port stop would enable them to follow upon the German research carried out at Moltke Harbour on South Georgia during the first International Polar Year of 1882-1883.

The plan called for two main parallel actions. More or less as before, the two Do 24 aircraft would survey new Antarctic regions within a range of 1000 km from the catapult ship *Schwabenland*. Meanwhile, provided the sea ice broke up, the *Kehdingen* and *Wal I* would attempt a landing at the shelf ice edge, with the goal of setting up a small hut that could operate as a land-based radio transmission station [45,46]. The idea was to land a slowly flying Fieseler Storch that would be used to survey the immediate neighbourhood of the radio station up to a distance of 100 – 150 km, along with a three-engine Junkers Ju 52 with a 9.2 tons take-off weight and a crew of two pilots, which had a longer range and higher maximum flight level than the Do 24. Those characteristics would enable the Ju 52 to follow up on observations made by the less flexible Dorniers. The Junkers and the Fiesler Storch would operate from an ice runway - an approach very similar to that used by Admiral Richard Byrd on his previous expeditions to Antarctica. In support of the aircraft there would be a small land depot for refuelling and to house the pilots between surveys. The hut would also form a base for geophysical research, but no extended land expeditions were envisaged – for example they did not propose to take dog teams for the sleds, though that had been initially considered a possibility; the idea was only to carry out research at and close to the station. All these plans came to naught when Germany initiated what would become World War II by attacking Poland on 1 September 1939. Under the circumstances there was no way that *Schwabenland* could sail south for the 1939/40 southern summer season in the Antarctic. All preparations were stopped officially at a meeting with Wohlthat on 5 September 1939 [47], and the remodelling of *Schwabenland, Kehdingen,* and *Wal I* for expedition purposes was stopped on the following day [48]. But that did not stop further plans being made.

Wohlthat was still keen to see a follow-up expedition take place – after all, it might be a short war, and Germany might win it! Despite the outbreak of war and the abandoning of Ritscher's Pacific plan, he encouraged Ritscher to continue to prepare plans for a German Antarctic Expedition for the 1940/41 southern summer season. Fretting over his disappointment with the results of the aerial survey, and deflected from the Pacific by the advent of new American plans, Ritscher began to think about returning to Neu-Schwabenland with dog sleds to provide the missing ground control points. Having an accurate survey map with good ground control would enable Germany to reinforce its territorial claims – not least because all that the Norwegians had seen was the edge of the floating ice shelf – a weaker basis for a claim than a full-scale land survey. Ritscher thought he could provide what was required by surveying the ground during a three to four week period, working from temporary tented camps at the Schirmacher Oasis and in the Wohlthat Massif. He would get his men and dog teams in and out by plane. As an alternative he proposed flying in with two Dornier 24s to make an aerial photogrammetric survey of Kaiser Wilhelm II Land, which had been discovered by the German South Polar Expedition on the Gauss at 90°E in February 1902. Ritscher proposed using the slow flying Fieseler Storch to land people in the interior to provide ground control. This would have infringed the rights of Australia, which held a 1936 claim to the area between 45°E and 160°E extending to the South Pole. Perhaps because of that, Wohlthat chose the Neu-Schwabenland proposal, and Ritscher started detailed planning. Another later reason for focusing once again on Neu-Schwabenland was that on 9 April 1940 Germany had occupied Norway to deny Scandinavia to Great Britain and to ensure control of the ice free port of Narvik, through which Sweden exported iron ore to Germany. Control of Norway was an interesting geopolitical development in view of the competing claims of Norway and Germany to the same piece of Antarctica.

Once again the planning was all for nothing. At the end of 1940 the war was still grinding on, and *Schwabenland* was still chartered by the Navy. All Antarctic planning was finally abandoned on 1 November 1941, when the expedition's office was closed.

An American Response

Ritscher and Wohlthat did not know as they concocted their Pacific plan that Germany's interests in Antarctica had begun to worry the USA [49]. By early 1939 President Franklin D. Roosevelt had come to believe that a German presence near the Antarctic Peninsula posed a potential threat to the solidarity and defence of the Western Hemisphere should a second world war occur. Quite fortuitously, at about the same time, Rear-Admiral Richard Byrd was contemplating a third private American Antarctic expedition to West Antarctica, facing the Pacific Ocean. Their two interests came together in January 1939, and the following month Byrd met the President to discuss preliminary plans [49]. Roosevelt was interested in aerial and ground exploration to support a possible US claim to all of West Antarctica adjacent to the Pacific Ocean, extending from the Bay of Whales in the Ross Sea to the edge of the UK's claim in the Antarctic Peninsula. Although Byrd's expedition was to have been private, like his previous two, on 13 March he revealed to the press that: "I expect to take possession of lands about a million square miles in extent for my country...." [50].

Things changed rapidly after that, Roosevelt having decided to establish the US Antarctic Service to maintain permanent or temporary stations on the Antarctic continent to fulfil the requirements of discovery and settlement that were essential in support of possible eventual territorial claims [49]. As early as 18 April 1939 the British Daily Mail was reporting that 'The United States government may send an expedition to the South Pole regions to safeguard American interests' [51]. On 21 June Byrd was pointing out in private correspondence that several nations had now claimed territory in the Antarctic, that Germany was rumoured to be planning claims to the Pacific coast of the Antarctic (an allusion to Ritscher's new plan), and that he 'would like to try once again to add more of this territory by aerial reconnaissance and mapping to the territory of the United States before it is too late' [49]. The New York Times of 24 June [52] reported that Byrd would proceed with his project of a third voyage to Antarctica to claim territory for the USA even if Congress should reject plans for a government-sponsored expedition; the same article went on to note that the State Department had informed Congress of Germany's intention to send an expedition to the Pacific coast to claim land there.

90

The USA and Germany were not the only states with interests in Antarctica. At the same time Argentina made plain its intention to vigorously oppose US aspirations to Antarctic territory, and to dispute Britain's existing claims [53]. Argentina based its claims in part on occupation, having maintained a meteorological and magnetic observatory on Laurie Island since 1904. The renewal of Argentine interest was another of the outcomes of the German expedition and its claims.

By 8 July it was announced that Admiral Byrd would lead the US government expedition [54]. On 31 July the link between the US and German activities was made plain in the British press, which reported that the goal of the expedition was 'to substantiate the USA's claim to territory there within the Monroe Doctrine sphere of influence west of the 180th meridian. Germany's announcement of her intention to send a party to the same region this summer is the direct cause of the decision' [55]. The Monroe Doctrine takes the view that the extension by a European power of its sovereignty into the Western Hemisphere constitutes a threat to the United States and justifies war on grounds of self-defence.

It was most unusual for the USA to become officially so active in Antarctica. Byrd may have been a US Navy man, but his two previous US expeditions to the Antarctic had been privately sponsored, and undertaken when he was on leave from the Navy. The expedition of 1939/41 would be the first time since the Wilkes Expedition 100 years before that the US government had become heavily involved in Antarctica [56,57,58]. This expedition would involve 125 men, two ships, and several small aircraft. It sailed in the late northern autumn of 1939 with the object of setting up a base on the Ross Ice Shelf, and a base on the west coast of the Antarctic Peninsula. Docking in the Bay of Whales on 12 January, 1940, they set up West Base, naming it Little America III; the ships then sailed to the Stonnington Island in Marguerite Bay on the west coast of the Peninsula to set up East Base in March 1940. Both bases carried out an extensive programme of land and aerial survey and scientific research until they were closed on 1 February 1941 (West Base), and 22 March 1941 (East Base). It had been intended to keep them open for 5-6 years, but seeing that fears of German occupation of Antarctica had proved groundless, the decision was made to bring the men home. Byrd had been told not to make any claim public without the express permission of the Secretary of State and, in the end, the USA chose never to make claims based on its work, thus negating a major reason for the expedition. Rather like the *Schwabenland* expedition, only a few accounts of the third Byrd expedition emerged, possibly because of the demands of the war.

Roosevelt's proposals soon came to the attention of the German Foreign Office, which passed the news to Wohlthat. It was probably the announcement of the Americans' objective to prepare the basis for territorial claims in the Pacific sector between 80°W and 148°W that made Wohlthat think twice about planning a German expedition to the Pacific sector.

The Effects of War

Ritscher had other worries too. With the outbreak of war, several of the expedition scientists had joined the armed forces. That meant they were no longer available to work up their results beyond the provisional level reported in the Annalen and Volume I of the expedition's reports [22,23]. Indeed, almost all analysis of the expedition's materials was abandoned until after 1945. Under normal circumstances one would have expected the expedition scientists to present their work at scientific conferences and in scientific journals both nationally and internationally. The war put a stop to all that. As a result, the international influence of the expedition was much less than might have been expected.

And as wars tend to do, this one had its own tragic effects. Four members of the small scientific party – a very large percentage for what was such a small group of men - were killed in action: oceanographer Karl-Heinz Paulsen; geophysicist Leo Gburek; biologist Erich Barkley; and meteorologist Heinz Lange. To make matters worse, Otto von Gruber, who was in charge of the post-expedition photogrammetric analysis, died in 1942 at the age of 57, apparently of natural causes. As if that was not enough, some of the expedition's materials were lost during the war, such as the geophysical data, which were destroyed by fire at the Geophysical Institute in Leipzig during a bombing raid, and Barkley's plankton samples. Most of the negatives of the 18 x 18 cm aerial photographic pictures were also destroyed in bombing raids. Fortunately, some meteorological data and the oceanographic material including the echo-sounding data, survived the war, as did many prints of the aerial photographs and the information used to make the maps.

The expedition ship too was a casualty of war. *Schwabenland* was commissioned by the military and used as an air base on the Norwegian coast [59]. In April 1944 it was hit by a torpedo and ran aground on the beach. It was eventually floated off and towed to Egersund, then later to Oslo, where it was used for accommodation (Wohnschiff) [60]. It then appears to have been returned to Kiel, where it was partly dismantled in 1946. The hull was then filled with gas ammunition, taken to sea by Captain Kottas, and sunk in the Skagerak on 31 December 1946.

References

1. Daily Telegraph, 1939, Germany may claim polar territory. 10 March issue.

2. New York Times, 1939a, Reich party reports Antarctic discovery. 11 March issue.

3. Daily Mail, 1939a, Germans find a new "Colony". 10 March issue.

4. London Times, 1939, German Antarctic claims. 14 March issue.

5. New York Times 1939b, Vast Antarctic Area Claimed by Germany; Expedition Returns from Mapping Region on Long Flights. April 12 issue.

6. New York Times, 1939c, Antarctic Colony claimed by Reich. 13 April issue.

7. New York Times, 1939d, Reich to Defend Antarctic Colony; Norway's Claim Defied. 13 April issue.

8. Vermerk, 6 June 1939, Memorandum of a department meeting at the VJP of 27.4.1939, Ritscher,s estate folder Bh1, VJP. Unpublished.

9. Herrmann, E., 1939, manuscript, Ritscher's estate folder Bb1, Geographie. When Herrmann prepared his paper on the geography of the expedition for the preliminary results in the Beiheft (1939) he entitled it: *Die geographischen Verhältnisse des Hermann Göring-Landes*. Herrmann signed this manuscript on board *Schwabenland* on 4 March 1939. It was published under the title *Vorläufiger Bericht über die geographischen Arbeiten auf der Deutschen Antarktischen Expedition 1938/39*. Unpublished.

10. Ritscher's letter to Konteradmiral Conrad, 3 May 1939, Ritscher's estate folder Bh1, OKM. Unpublished.

11. Hahn, 5 July 1939, Hahn's letter to Ritscher of 5 July 1939, Ritscher's estate folder Bh1, VJP. Unpublished.

12. Headland, R.K., 2009, *A Chronology of Antarctic Exploration*. Quaritch, London, 722 pp. Item 2229, 303.

13. Walker, 14 April 1939, letter to Ritscher. Ritscher's estate, B.P.1. Unpublished.

14. Ritscher, 25 April 1939, Ritscher's letter to Wohlthat. Ritscher's estate, B.P.1. Unpublished.

15. Berliner Illustrierte Zeitung, 1939, 600000 qkm am Südpol von Deutschen entdeckt und erkundet 25 May issue no. 21, 386.

16. Hahn, 27 May 1939, letter to Todt, Ritscher's estate, B.P.1. Unpublished.

17. Life, 3 July 1939, Nazis in Antarctica, 51-53. Photo of Gralsburg on p. 51, captioned: *Mountain ranges of black basalt, drowned in 2,000 ft of snow and ice, stood across the German path. An isolated continent surrounded by oceanic deeps, Antarctica has an average height of about 6,000 ft. the highest in the world.* (Ritscher's estate folder Antarktis bis 1941).

18. Die weite Welt, 9 July 1939, Nr. 28, no page numbers given. Photo of Gralsburg (no page number given) captioned: *In wenigen hundert Metern Höhe brauste eins der Expeditionsflugzeuge über diese bizarren Felsgebilde hinweg, die durch Kälteverwitterung entstanden sind und diesen teil der Antarktis ihr Gepräge geben.* (Ritscher's estate folder Antarktis bis 1941).

19. Bayliss, E.P., 1939, Antarctica. 1:10,000,000 map. Property and Survey Branch, Department of the Interior, Canberra.

20. Bayliss, E. P. and Cumpston, J.S., 1939, Handbook and index to accompany a map of Antarctica. Commonwealth Government Printer, Canberra. *The German source is mentioned on page 71.*

21. USHO, 1943, *Antarctica; compiled from all available sources to 1943. Map 1: 11.250.000*. H.O. Chart No. 2562,

US Hydrographic Office Washington DC.

22. Ritscher, A., 1939, Die Deutsche Antarktische Expedition 1938/39. Annalen der Hydrographie und Maritimen Meteorologie. VIII, Beiheft, 9-19.

23. Ritscher, A., 1942, Wissenschaftliche und fliegerische Ergebnisse der Deutschen Antarktischen Expedition 1938/39, Hrsg. im Auftrag der Deutschen Forschungsgemeinschaft, Vol 1 Koehler & Amelang, Leipzig.

24. Frisch, 8 September 1939, Rechnung für 2.100 Übersichtskarten. Ritscher's estate, B.P.1. Unpublished Invoice for 2.100 survey maps of Antarctica. Unpublished.

25. Ritscher, 7 September 1939, Ritscher's letter to Prof. Kayser. Ritscher's estate, folder BP1 Buch/Presse starting 1 April 1939. Unpublished.

26. F. I. Presteng, personal communication to Colin Summerhayes, 2008.

27. Frank, W., 1939, Mit Jan Wellem auf Walfang im südlichen Eismeer. Der Wiedererstandene deutsche Walfang dargestellt an der Entwicklungsgeschichte der ersten Deutschen Walfang-Gesellschaft in Verbindung mit einem Reisebericht über die 2. "Jan Wellem" Expedition von Dr. Wolfgang Frank. Henkel & Cie, Düsseldorf, 146 pp.

28. Spengemann, H., 1939, Auf Walfang in der Antarktis. Concordia, Brühl-Baden, 103 pp.

29. Kraul, O., 1939, Käpt'n Kraul erzählt. 20 Jahre Walfänger unter argentinischer, russischer und deutscher Flagge in der Arktis und Antarktis. Herbig, Berlin, 239 pp.

30. Safari-Verlag, 8 December 1939, letter to Ritscher. Ritscher's estate, B.P.1. Unpublished.

31. Herrmann, E., 1941, Deutsche Forscher im Südpolarmeer. Safari Verlag, Berlin, 184 pp.

32. Ritscher, 3 June 1941, Ritscher's letter to Schreiner. Ritscher's estate, B.P.1. Unpublished

33. International Whaling Conference, 1939, Report of the International Whaling Conference, London, 17-20 July. UK Ministry of Agriculture and Fisheries.

34. Ritscher, 25 October 1941, Ritscher's letter to Justus Perthes, Ritscher's estate, B.P.1. Unpublished.

35. Auswärtiges Amt, 23 October 1942, Thank you letter to Ritscher. Ritscher's estate, A-K2, A. Unpublished

36. Brunner, K., and Hell, G., 1985, Photogrammetrische und kartographische Ergebnisse der Deutschen Antarktischen Expedition 1938/39. Karlsruher Geowissenschaftliche Schriften, Reihe B, Geodätische, Photogrammetrische und Kartographische Berichte Bd. 1, 41-55, 2 maps.

37. Hartmann, 2007, Auszug aus der Ahnenforschung von Alfred Ritscher, geschrieben in den 50er Jahren des 20. Jahrhunderts (überarbeitet und ergänzt von seiner Tochter Gertraude Gisela Hartmann, geb. Ritscher). Unpublished typescript, Braunfels, 20 pp.

38. Deutsche Lufthansa, 16 October 1939, Letter to Firma Gebr. Godet & Co. Ritscher's estate, Bh1 Deutsche Lufthansa. Unpublished.

39. Godet, 12 October 1939, Letter of Firma Gebr. Godet & Co. Ritscher's estate, Bh1 Deutsche Lufthansa. Unpublished.

40. DFG, 10 October 1939, Invitation of Deutsche Forschungsgemeinschaft, Ritscher's estate, Ma1, PQ. Unpublished.

41. Ritscher, 6 November 1939, Letter to Wohlthat. Ritscher's estate, Bh1 OKM. Unpublished.

42. Proposed tracks, 3 November 1938, Ritscher's estate, Bh1 OKM. Unpublished.

43. Wohlthat 11 August 1939, Letter to Ritscher, Entwurf des Auftragsschreibens and die DFG. Ritscher's estate, Bh1

VJP. Unpublished.

44. Lüdecke, C., 2003, In geheimer Mission zur Antarktis - Die dritte Deutsche Antarktisexpedition 1938/39 und der Plan einer territorialen Festsetzung zur Sicherung des Walfangs. Deutsches Schiffahrtsarchiv 26, 75-100.

45. Entwurf, 18 August 1939, Entwurf, Arbeitsplan der Deutschen Antarktischen Expedition 39/40. Ritscher's estate, VAE1 without title. Unpublished.

46. Deutsche Lufthansa 28 August 1939, Notiz: FT-Ausrüstung der zweiten Antarktis-Expedition. Ritscher's estate, Bh1 Deutsche Lufthansa. Unpublished.

47. Niederschrift 5 September 1939, Niederschrift über die Besprechung am 5.91939. Ritscher's estate, Bh1, Vierjahrtesplan. Unpublished.

48. Deutsche Lufthansa 6 October 1939, Letter to Ritscher. Ritscher's estate, Sch1 D. Unpublished.

49. Rose, L.A., 2008, Explorer: the life of Richard E Byrd. University of Missouri Press, Columbia. 540 pp.

50. Christian Science Monitor, 1939, Byrd plans to claim vast acreage for America. 13 March issue.

51. Daily Mail, 1939b, Nations race for Antarctic wealth. 18 April issue.

52. New York Times, 1939e, Byrd Persists in Plan for Antarctic Trip. 24 June issue.

53. New York Times, 1939f, Argentina Claims Antarctic Land in Conflict with U.S. and Britain, 25 July issue.

54. New York Herald, 1939, President Says Byrd will lead Antarctic trip. 8 July issue.

55. Evening Standard, 1939, Roosevelt sends Admiral Byrd on a new Antarctic Expedition. 31 July issue, 14.

56. Dewing, C.E., and Kelsey, L.E., 1955, Preliminary Inventory of the Records of the United States Antarctic Service. National Archives and Records Service, Washington DC, 59 pp.

57. Sullivan, W., 1957, Quest for a Continent. McGraw-Hill, New York, 372 pp.

58. Rose, L.A., 1980, Assault on Eternity: Richard E. Byrd and the Exploration of Antarctica 1946-47. Naval Inst. Press, Annapolis, 292 pp.

59. Nowak, 26 January 1983, Letter to Ilse Ritscher. Ritscher's estate, Antarktis bis 1964. Unpublished.

60. Schön, H., 2004, Mythos Neu-Schwabenland für Hitler am Südpol; die deutsche Antarktis expedition 1938/39. Bonus-Verlag, Selent. 176 pp.

The route of *Jan Wellem* during the first German whaling season 1936/37

Coastal cliffs off
Bouvet Island

Passat on the ice edge,
29 January 1939

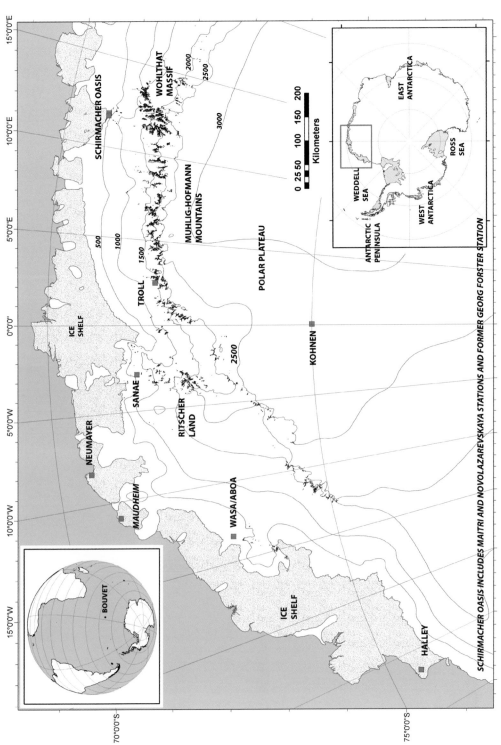

Dronning Maud Land (named Neu-Schwabenland by the Germans) between the eastern edge of the British Falkland Islands
Dependencies and the western edge of the Australian Antarctic Territory

The Hoegfonna peak, part of the Borg Massivet, showing the camp of the Norwegian-British-Swedish expedition of 1949-52

A melting lake in the Schirmacher Oasis, next to the Indian station, Maitri, December 2004

Der neue deutsche Walfang

Ein praktisches Handbuch

seiner geschichtlichen, rechtlichen, naturwissenschaftlichen und technischen Grundlagen

HERAUSGEGEBEN IM AUFTRAGE DES REICHSMINISTERIUMS FÜR ERNÄHRUNG UND LANDWIRTSCHAFT UND DES REICHSWIRTSCHAFTSMINISTERIUMS VON Dr. NICOLAUS PETERS, LEITER DER REICHSSTELLE FÜR WALFORSCHUNG IM HAMBURGISCHEN ZOOLOGISCHEN MUSEUM UND INSTITUT

The German Whaling Handbook of 1938

An Antonov
transport plane
on the frozen
surface of the
Untersee in the
Wohlthat Massif,
December 2004

(below)
Neumayer III
station, February
2009

(left) German postal cancellation stamp from the South Polar ocean

(above) 1983 5-peso Paraguayan postage stamp celebrating *Schwabenland* and its Dornier-Wal aircraft

Schirmacher Oasis plaque showing the location of the former Georg Forster Station of East Germany (l to r), Colin Summerhayes, Henry Valentine of the South African programme, Hartwig Gernandt, the former station chief, Peter Clarkson (SCAR Executive Secretary) and a representative of the Russian Novolazarevskaya station

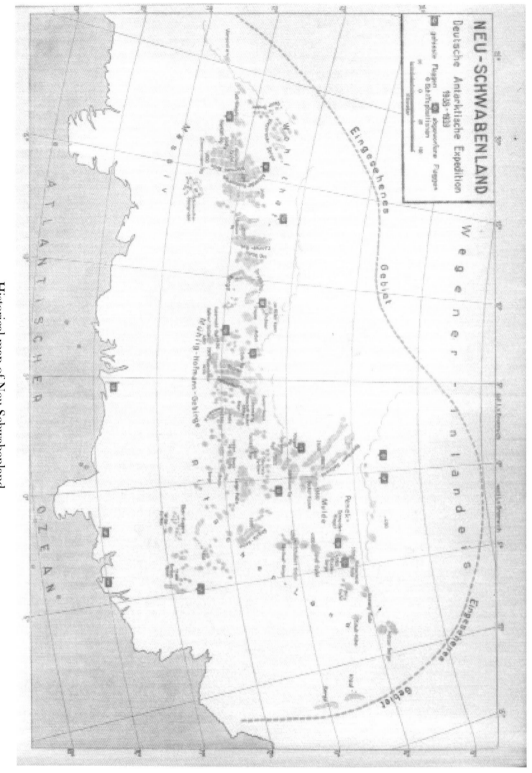

Historical map of Neu Schwabenland

CHAPTER 7: POST-WAR DEVELOPMENTS

Subsequent German Exploration and Science in Dronning Maud Land

After the war, Dronning Maud Land became, and remains, a favourite stamping ground for the post-war German Antarctic research community. By then Germany was divided and there was no interest in setting up a German Antarctic base for Southern Ocean whaling any longer. But there were still Germans with a fascination for Antarctica, among them a German medical doctor Karl Maria Herrligkoffer (1916-91) in Munich, already well-known for the expedition that made the first ascent of the 8125 m peak Nanga Parbat in the Himalayas in 1953. Herrligkoffer planned a German South Pole Expedition to take place during the International Geophysical Year (IGY) [1]. His proposal was intended to continue the long tradition of German Antarctic research and, in particular, to build on Ritscher's pioneering work. He also drew attention to strategic gaps in a possible future war, by citing Antarctica as a potential base for inter-continental ballistic missiles and by drawing attention to the likelihood that both the USA and the USSR might claim Antarctic territory after the IGY in order to gain access to resources of raw material including the uranium found by Byrd during his 1939-41 expedition [2]. Other nations like Germany, he felt, ought to participate in the IGY in order to earn a slice of the post-IGY cake.

Herrligkoffer planned to continue Ritscher's research in Neu-Schwabenland, which had been interrupted by the war. Why did he choose this area, where the Norwegian-British-Swedish-Expedition (NBSX) (1949-52) had worked – something that he did not mention in his outline? The main reason seems to have been that he was primarily a mountaineer, and Neu-Schwabenland was full of hundreds of unclimbed peaks, each representing the chance to establish a first route and a first ascent – it was a mountaineer's Eldorado, especially for someone like Herrligkoffer. He visited Ritscher to request some background material for his expedition, but Ritscher advised him against going, fearing that Herrligkoffer lacked polar experience (G. Hartmann, personal communication to CL 17.3.2008). Instead, Herrligkoffer turned for support to the unlikely figure of Herbert Bruns, electrician of the *Schwabenland* expedition. In his brochure supporting Herrligkoffer's expedition, Bruns called for a 'German South Pole Expedition 1956/58' to promote national claims [3]. Building on what had been discovered by the *Schwabenland* expedition, he outlined a scientific programme and listed the equipment needed, including an icebreaker, which would have to be built, and caterpillar tractors for work on land in snow and ice. Unfortunately for Herrligkoffer and Bruns, there was no money at all for something like research in Antarctica, when Germany was still trying to recover from war and had to rebuild its destroyed cities [1]. Besides the time was not considered right

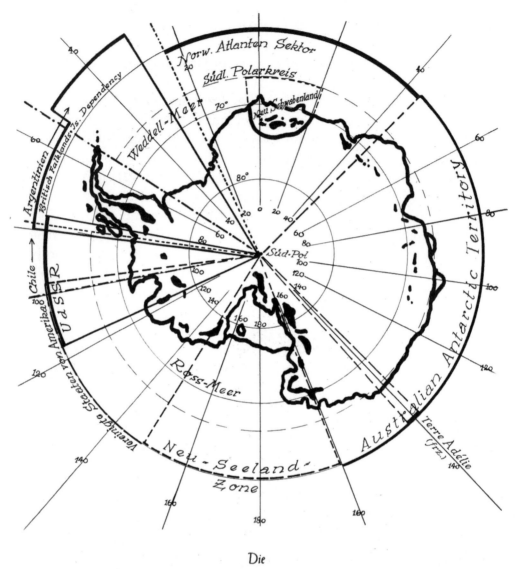

Die

„Deutsche Südpol-Expedition 1956/58"

Ein akutes Problem der Gegenwart

Map of territorial claims, and indication of Neu-Schwabenland, from the title page
of Bruns' booklet promoting Herrligkoffer's expedition

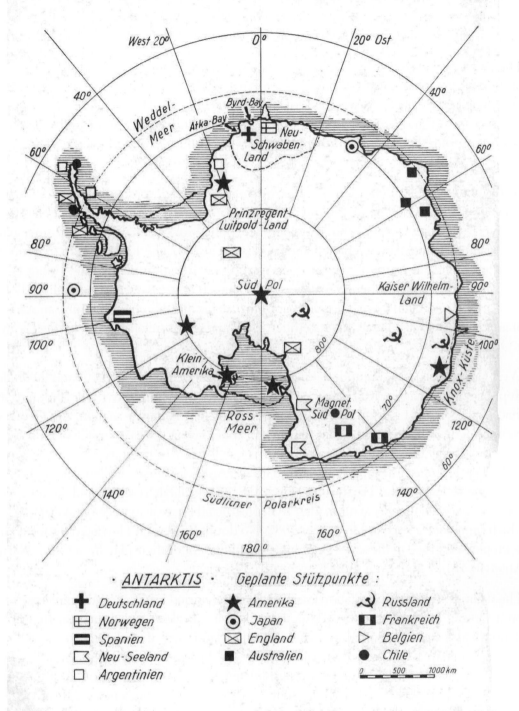

Planned stations of the proposed third International Polar Year (later to become the International Geophysical Year of 1957-58) including Herrligkoffer's proposed station in Neu-Schwabenland

politically for West Germany to be seen to be making claims for Antarctic territory. Then again, the scientific community was not convinced that Herrligkoffer was the right person to lead a scientific polar expedition. The plan came to naught.

The first Germans to visit Antarctic after the war were the East Germans, in 1959, as part of the Soviet expeditions that established themselves in the Schirmacher Oasis in eastern Dronning Maud Land [4]. Research carried out by the German Democratic Republic (GDR) was focused in and around the Schirmacher Oasis and grew considerably in 1976 in association with the activities of the Soviet (now Russian) Novolazarevskaya Station in the Oasis [5].

By October 1980, East German Antarctic research was well developed enough for the GDR to be admitted as a full member of the Scientific Committee on Antarctic Research (SCAR), an interdisciplinary body of the International Council for Science (ICSU - former name: International Council of Scientific Unions). Finally, in 1987, the East German presence was sufficiently large to warrant creation of its own research station, named the Georg Forster Station, in the Schirmacher Oasis. Forster (1754-94) was a German naturalist who had participated in captain Cook's second voyage to the Pacific. The GDR became an Acceding State to the Antarctic Treaty in November 1974, and a Consultative Party to the Treaty on 5 October 1987.

West Germans had begun undertaking research in Antarctica in the 1970s and the Federal Republic of Germany (FRG) became a full member of SCAR in May 1978 [6]. Not long after that, in the 1980/81 season, they constructed their first Antarctic station, the Georg von Neumayer Station, on the Ekström Ice Shelf in Atka Bay on the eastern side of the Weddell Sea close to the location that Herrligkoffer chose for his overwintering station during the IGY. The FRG became an Acceding State to the Antarctic Treaty in February 1979, and a Consultative Party to the Treaty on 3 March 1981. To facilitate research and the resupply of the Georg von Neumayer station, the FRG constructed the research ice-breaker *Polarstern*, which came into service in December 1982. No doubt Bruns and Herrligkoffer would have been pleased to see in these developments the fulfilment of their plan for a fourth German Antarctic Expedition, even though twenty five years late.

The Georg von Neumayer Station gradually became buried by snow, and in any case rested on a moving ice shelf that was taking the station inexorably toward the sea. In 1992 the station had to be abandoned and rebuilt further landward, though still on the ice shelf, as the Neumayer II Station. That same year the Georg Forster Station was closed, as German activities in Antarctic were consolidated following reunification, and the station was removed in 1996. The latest stage in the ongoing German presence in Dronning Maud Land is the abandonment of Neumayer II, for much the same reasons as the abandonment of its predecessor, and the construction of the modern Neumayer III station six kilometres further landward during the austral summers of 2007/8 and 2008/9.

These German developments have been key strands in the steady post-war growth of scientific interest in Dronning Maud Land. Following the establishment of the Norway Base and the Belgian Roi Badouin Base there during the IGY, a number of other national bases were established in this area. The Soviet Union (now Russia) set up its Lazarevskaya base in the Schirmacher Oasis in 1961, replaced later by Novolazarevskaya Station. South Africa took over the Norway base in 1962, naming it SANAE-I, and now has its SANAE-IV base on the nunatak Vesleskarvet. India established its Dakshin Gangotri station on a coastal ice shelf in 1983/84, abandoned it in 1990/91 after it became buried in ice, and moved to its Maitri Station, established in the Schirmacher Oasis in March 1989. Japan established its Syowa Station in 1957 on the east coast of Dronning Maud Land at 39° 35'E; its Dome Fuji Station was established in 1995, 1000 km south of Syowa, at the highest point of Dronning Maud Land, at 3810 m on the Polar Plateau. In 1988, Finland established its Aboa Summer Station in the Vestfjella Mountains, about 130km inland from the coast of the Weddell Sea in western Dronning Maud Land, and Sweden established its Wasa Summer Station alongside Aboa in 1989. Up on the Polar Plateau in western Dronning Maud Land in 2001 Germany began operating the Kohnen Station for drilling ice cores for the European Project for Ice Coring in Antarctica (EPICA). Norway, which abandoned its original base in 1962, established its Troll Station at Gjelsvikfjella in the western mountains of Dronning Maud Land in 1990. The base was expanded to take wintering parties in 2004/05, and a year-round 3 km blue ice runway for 4-engine aircraft was opened in February 2005. Belgium abandoned its Roi Badoin base right after the IGY, but established Princess Elisabeth Station in eastern Dronning Maud Land in 2007/08. Ritscher would have been amazed to see all these bases, and to observe that they were all connected by the Dronning Maud Land Air Network (DROMLAN) comprising long ice runways at Novolazarevskaya and Troll that between them can take 4-engine transport planes from Cape Town year round, and from which small planes like the German Dorniers (Do 228-101) and the new Basler (BT-67) ferry researchers and construction workers between the bases and out to summer field camps.

As an indication of the standing of German science in Antarctic, Professor Jörn Thiede, Director of the AWI from 1997-2007, served as President of SCAR from 2002 to 2006, and as Past President from 2006 to 2008.

Unfortunately, Ritscher did not live to see much of this resurgence of German or international interest in Dronning Maud Land, as he died in 1963 at the ripe old age of 84. Herrmann died in 1970, aged 75. Kraul lasted for another year, dying in 1971 aged 79. Regula rose to head the first satellite observing section of the German Weather Service, and died relatively young, aged 70, in 1980. One suspects they would all have been proud of Germany's significant post-war contribution to Antarctic science in the region of their own pre-war investigation.

References

1. Lüdecke, C., 2007, Karl Maria Herrligkoffer's private „German South Pole Expedition" 1957/58: A failed initiative. In. C. Lüdecke (ed.), Steps of Foundation of Institutionalized Antarctic Research. Proceedings of the 1st SCAR Workshop on the History of Antarctic Research, Munich 2-3 June 2005, Reports on Polar and Marine Research, Alfred Wegener Institute of Polar and Marine Research, Bremerhaven, Nr. 560, 195-210.

2. Herrligkoffer, K.M., 1956, Deutsche Südpol-Expedition. Deutsches Institut für Auslandsforschung, München: 31 pp.

3. Bruns, H., 1956, Deutsche Südpol-Expedition 1956/58. Ein akutes Problem der Gegenwart. München, 15 pp.

4. Gernandt, H., 1984, Erlebnis Antarktis. Transpress, Berlin, 283 pp.

5. Borman, P. and Fritzsche, D., (eds.), 1995, The Schirmacher Oasis, Queen Maud Land, East Antarctica, and its Surroundings. Justus Perthes Verlag Gotha. 448 pp.

6. Kohnen, H., 1981, Antarktis Expedition. Deutschlands neues Vorstoß ins ewige Eis. Gustav Lübbe Verlag, Bergisch Gladbach, 208 pp.

CHAPTER 8: THE MYTHS

The Hitler Survival Myth

At the end of WW II the legend arose that Hitler's suicide had been faked. He was supposed to have escaped Germany on a submarine convoy that had deposited him and his entourage, including Martin Bormann, either at a 'New Berchtesgarden' in Dronning Maud Land, Antarctica, or - some say – in Argentina. Ladislas Szabo, a Hungarian journalist living in exile in Argentina, started the Antarctic myth in a newspaper article in the Argentine newspaper *La Critica* on 16 July, 1945, shortly after a stray U-Boat showed up unexpectedly in Argentina, on 10 July 1945, two months after the war with Germany had ended [1]. The story was too good to miss, and it hit the world press almost immediately, for example under the headline 'Hitler's on Ice in Antarctic' in the Toronto Daily Star of 18 July 1945. Much to everyone's amazement, yet another U–boat showed up in Argentina on 17 August 1945 [1]. This was all grist to Szabo's mill, and by 1947 he had expanded his tale into a book 'Hitler is Alive' [2], stimulating a conspiracy theory industry that is flourishing today with the myth being repeated in books published as recently as 2005, and in many articles on the Internet.

The key elements of the myth, which has been comprehensively detailed and analysed by Summerhayes and Beeching [1], and also examined by Schön [3], are: that the 3rd German Antarctic Expedition of 1938-39 set up a base in Neu-Schwabenland (Dronning Maud Land); that the Nazi government continued to expand the base during the war; that the base comprised huge caverns in the mountains, capable of storing aircraft and submarines, and manned by large numbers of personnel; and that key personnel were taken there after Germany's surrender, to prepare for an eventual Nazi resurgence. Even wilder elements of the Nazi base theory claim that the Germans had developed new secret aerial weapons systems (flying saucers), and were flying them out of this base after the war, thus accounting for the many reports of UFOs that began to appear after the flying saucer craze started in mid 1947. One version of the legend has it that the US government was determined to wipe out this 'vipers nest', and dedicated the US Naval Operation 'Highjump' to that end in 1946/47. According to that version of the legend, the US attackers were beaten off by superior German arms (for which read flying saucers). Undeterred, the US launched a nuclear strike against the German base in 1958.

By that time, however, so the story goes, the inhabitants of the base had already, and very conveniently, moved to South America [1]. A more recent version of the legend has it that the British government was equally determined to eliminate the German base, and launched an attack on it by Special Forces from the Falkland Islands around Christmas 1945. That attack was not completely successful, and the American forces of Operation 'Highjump' were supposed to finish the job.

The Facts: U-Boats and Antarctic Bases

Looking at the real events, there were indeed two U-boats. They fled the North Atlantic theatre believing that they would be safer in German-friendly Argentina than in surrendering to the Americans. It took them a long time to plough their way south because they were short on fuel for such a long and unplanned voyage, and they had to submerge during the daylight hours, all of which slowed them down. That they had no nefarious purpose was clearly established by their interrogators: first the Argentine navy, then the United States navy, then the British Royal Navy. Knowing the type of submarine and its capability, and bearing in mind the need to be submerged during daylight for much of the journey, it is easy on the back of an envelope to calculate that they could not have got from where they were in the North Atlantic, when the war with Germany ended on May 8, to Mar del Plata in Argentina via the Antarctic coast of Dronning Maud Land in the time available, unless they were making top speed. Speeding to Antarctica in a Second World War submarine was not on the cards, and there is no evidence at all to support the notion that these two submarines were somehow special – photographs taken at their surrender in Argentina show they were not.

Could World War II U-boats have reached the coast of Dronning Maud Land in July or August of 1945? These months are now, and were then, at the heart of the southern winter, when sea ice 1-2 m thick forms a vast plain 1000 km wide around Antarctica that prevents access to the coast for anything but a first class ice-breaker. Only an armchair theorist from the northern hemisphere who knew nothing about the Antarctic winter would dream up such a ridiculous idea and expect people to believe it. And to get there and back to Mar del Plata meant making faster times than would have been possible under the circumstances. Besides, these World War II U-boats had to come up for air frequently – they could not travel far and fast whilst submerged and breathing through their snorkel tubes – which they could not use anyway from beneath sea-ice. In any case they were not strengthened for use in ice-covered seas. In 1947 Admiral Byrd took the US World War II submarine *USS Sennet* to the Antarctic in Operation 'Highjump', and it had to be towed to safety because it was being so battered by ice floes. And that was in the southern summer, not the southern winter, when conditions would have been vastly worse. The *USS Sennet* was not much different from those two German U-boats.

How about the base that Szabo speaks about? He implies [2] it was the aim of the German expedition to build a base there. All the published documents as well as the papers from the private estates of the participants show that the *Schwabenland* carried no equipment

U530 in the harbour at Mar del Plata, Argentina, 1945

for setting up a land base – its goal was aerial reconnaissance not construction [1]. An interview with a survivor, Siegfried Sauter, confirms that not only did the ship not carry any construction materials, it was not equipped for transporting such materials, most of its deck space being taken up by the enormous catapult required for launching the reconnaissance aircraft [3]. There was a plan to establish a base on Antarctica if a suitable place could be found, but that was for a follow-up expedition, not this first one. And all plans for the follow-up expedition that might have established a land base were cancelled due to the higher priorities of the war in Europe, which broke out 4 ½ months after the *Schwabenland* returned to Hamburg. As the records show, *Schwabenland* was assigned to naval duties from 1940 on – it did not visit Antarctica again. Besides, even in 1939 the *Schwabenland* was not on the Antarctic coast long enough for a base to be built in the nearby mountains, despite ill-informed claims to the contrary. It takes considerable time, effort and means, including extensive land transportation, just to set up a base quite close to an unloading ship, let alone to move everything 200 km inland over previously unmapped terrain full of crevasses to mountains whose existence was not even known when the expedition left Germany. Building a huge base of the type suggested by the conspiracy theorists would have required setting up a construction site including facilities to produce electricity, not forgetting the heavy equipment needed for digging into the mountains, including railway lines and wagons typical of mining operations, and the need for the production of large amounts of concrete. Perhaps such an effort might have been feasible as part of a second expedition, after the first expedition had returned to Germany with the maps that would have been needed as the basis for planning. But such operations have never been carried out anywhere in Antarctica by any nation in the past 100 years – not least because of the enormous logistical difficulties involved. To think otherwise is to confess to quite complex fantasies.

Were there secret British military operations in Antarctica during and immediately after the war as some claim? Yes. The British established a few small military bases in their territory in the region of the Antarctic Peninsula in 1944, as part of a classified Operation named 'Tabarin'. But these were tiny establishments for just a few men whose publically stated task was to keep an eye out for German surface raiders and to call in the Royal Navy if needed, although an underlying reason was to secure the British claim to sovereignity over the area. These men started the scientific and geographical exploration that continues to this day as the British Antarctic Survey. They did so because among the requirements in support of territorial claims at that time were occupancy and exploration. Were they associated with Special Forces? Again, the answer is yes, but only indirectly and after the war. The British Army's Special Air Service (better known as the SAS) was disbanded in October 1945 and its leaders were looking for exciting challenges. Three of their demobilised officers answered an advertisement calling for experienced adventurers to help to man and expand the network of bases set up under Operation 'Tabarin', which had by then been converted from a military operation into the civilian Falkland Islands Dependencies Survey (FIDS), the forerunner of today's British Antarctic Survey. These tiny pre-existing bases, and those three SAS men did not constitute a military force sent down south to oust non-existent German soldiers from a non-existent German base in the Norwegian territory of Dronning Maud Land in Christmas 1945, seven months after the war with Germany had ended, as claimed by one misguided source (see Summerhayes and Beeching for that and related sources [1]). The number of Britons in the region was, in fact, tiny – as the now public records

U977 in the harbour at Mar del Plata, Argentina, 1945

show. They simply did not have the capacity to get to or achieve anything in neighbouring Dronning Maud Land, which lay on the opposite side of the infamous ice-bound Weddell Sea, where Shackleton's ship *Endurance* and Nordenskjöld's ship *Antarctic* had been crushed by the ice and sunk some decades before. Indeed, the tiny British bases were hard-pressed to survive where they were, on the faraway Antarctic Peninsula.

Operation Highjump

And what of the Americans who mounted a major military expedition to Antarctica? The USA's Operation 'Highjump' in 1946-47 was indeed a major military operation that was (initially) classified. It involved 4700 men, 13 ships and 33 aircraft. What was it doing in Antarctica? The answer is readily available from the published literature, the declassified naval and army reports, the film of the expedition, the thousands of press and radio stories filed by the 11 journalists aboard, and the various books people wrote about it afterwards [1,4]. We have to remember that the Cold War began right at the end of Word War II. The US was worried by the expansion of communism and by the growth of Soviet power, and had begun to conduct naval exercises in Arctic seas as early as the fall and winter of 1945 in preparation for a possible Arctic war with the Soviet Union. By 1946 it felt that it needed to hold a training exercise that would be so large that it could pose a destabilising threat to US-Soviet relationships if it were held in the Arctic. Given the pre-eminence of retired Admiral Richard Byrd, then America's greatest living Antarctic explorer, it is hardly surprising that the Navy was persuaded to hold this exercise in southern rather than northern polar seas, where it would pose no geographical threat to the Soviets. Aside from training men to operate under frigid conditions, 'Highjump', with Byrd in charge of the scientific part, was supposed also to [1]:

- consolidate and extend United States sovereignty over the largest practicable area of the Antarctic continent (this was publicly denied as a goal even before the expedition ended);

- determine the feasibility of establishing, maintaining and utilising bases in the Antarctic and investigating possible base sites;

- develop techniques for establishing, maintaining and utilising air bases on ice, with particular attention to later applicability of such techniques to operations in interior Greenland, where conditions are comparable to those in the Antarctic;

- amplify existing stores of knowledge of hydrographic, geographic, geological, meteorological and electro-magnetic propagation conditions in the area;

- meet supplementary objectives of the Nanook expedition. (a smaller equivalent operation conducted off eastern Greenland in July-September 1946).

Note the two references to Greenland, which give away the true goal of the exercise – preparation for an Arctic war.

It is no coincidence that while 'Highjump' was at sea, on 12 March 1947, President Truman launched the Truman Doctrine, to help prevent the spread of communism. It is also no surprise, given the background to the expedition, that the scientific part was small (almost the last objective). 'Highjump' was not a one-off operation; it was not only preceded by several other naval polar operations in the Arctic, but also followed in the Antarctic by Operation 'Windmill', with two ships, in the summer of 1947-48 [1,4]. There was nothing 'sinister' about 'Highjump'; it did precisely what the Navy said it would do, with the world watching openly through the eyes of the journalists aboard the ships and on the ice sheet in the Ross Sea.

Unfortunately for the conspiracy theorists, who needed the mighty 'Highjump' fleet to attack the supposed German base in Dronning Maud Land, the 'Highjump' ships almost missed that part of Antarctica completely. The fleet started in the Ross Sea, because that's where Byrd went to establish his land base, Little America IV, on the Ross Ice Shelf. Note that this is on the opposite side of the continent from Dronning Maud Land. The fleet then split into three: one to stay in the Ross Sea; one to sail east around West Antarctica and the Antarctic Peninsula to Dronning Maud Land, surveying the coast and flying over and photographing the adjacent land en route; and one to sail west through the southernmost Indian Ocean to Dronning Maud Land, doing the same things. Owing to a combination of heavy workload and bad weather, the eastern fleet didn't get to the Dronning Maud Land coast until 1 March 1947, and found the land too covered in cloud to permit aerial surveying. After waiting a day or so to see if conditions might improve – they didn't – they sailed for home on 3 March 1947 to avoid being trapped by the rapidly forming sea ice (these were normal naval ships, not ice breakers, and no attempt had been made to strengthen their thin steel hulls against the shock of meeting sea ice). The western fleet also had so many other interesting things to do en route to Dronning Maud Land that it managed just one flight over land there, by a lone aircraft on 22 February 1947. At its westernmost extent, this flight just reached the easternmost edge of the Wohlthat Massif discovered by the Germans in 1939. That was more than 100 miles east of the hypothetical German base in the Mühlig-Hofmann Mountains. This fleet too then left for home. Given that one of Byrd's primary aims was geographical discovery, and that he knew that the Germans had already mapped Dronning Maud Land from the air between 10°W and 20°E, it would seem highly likely that neither fleet saw any reason to dally to map what had already been photographed and mapped in great detail by the Germans (and was already noted on the 1943 US Hydrographic Chart of the region), especially as the sea ice was closing in. So it is hardly surprising that both eastern and western fleets were off the Dronning Maud Land coast for no more than about a day each and did not bother to land. We fail to see in the records of this well-reported expedition the basis for a believable

108

US military offensive against a mythical German base. This is confirmed by the lack of any attempt by the preceding US Antarctic Expedition of 1940-41 or the following US Expedition of 1947-48 (Operation Windmill) to visit or spend any significant amount of time in Dronning Maud Land, a point the conspiracy theorists have missed.

Nuclear Explosions and UFOs

But there were those nuclear explosions too, weren't there? Again, the answer is yes. The US military did indeed explode three nuclear warheads in the general region in 1958. These then secret experiments (which were swiftly unclassified) were part of Operation 'Argus', a contribution to the International Geophysical Year of 1957-58 [5]. They were designed to see how the charged particles and radioactive isotopes released by the explosions would interact with the Earth's magnetic field, which in turn would help scientists to understand how disturbances of the field might potentially interfere with radar tracking, communications, and the electronics of satellites and ballistic missiles. Were the warheads exploded over Antarctica as conspiracy theorists claim? No. They were all between 160 and 750 km high in the upper atmosphere over the South Atlantic, and none was closer than 2280 km from the Dronning Maud Land coast. There is no support for these being part of a nuclear attack on a hypothetical Antarctic base defended by determined Nazis. Besides, analyses of radioactivity trapped in the Antarctic ice clearly show no major peak in chemical fallout of the kind that ought to be there if atomic weapons had been used in Dronning Maud Land [1].

Finally, there is the widespread belief amongst the conspiracy theorists that Admiral Byrd is supposed to have said something about being attacked by UFOs (for which read flying saucers, or German secret weapons), thought – by the conspiracy theorists – to have been piloted by Germans from the 'base', following which Byrd gave the sudden order to abandon the Highjump expedition. First of all there is no evidence that the expedition was abandoned. It was shorter than hoped, but that was because it arrived late, not because it left early. In fact all those involved knew it would have to leave as soon as winter conditions approached, simply because steel-hulled ships without ice strengthening, could not risk being around at a time when growing sea-ice would start to form a major hazard. According to the conspiracy and UFO theorists, Byrd is also reported to have said that 'in case of a new war the continental United States would be attacked by flying objects which could fly from pole to pole at incredible speeds.' This turns out to have been a mistranslation from an article in Spanish in a Chilean newspaper [6]. What the article actually said [translated by J. Guzman of Darwin College, Cambridge – see full translation in Summerhayes and Beeching [1]] was this: 'Admiral Richard E. Byrd warned today that the United States should adopt measures of protection against the possibility of an invasion of the country by hostile planes coming from the Polar Regions. The Admiral explained that he was not trying to

USS *Sennet* in
Antarctic sea
ice, 1947 High-
jump expedition

USS *Sennet*
on tow from
icebreaker USS
Northwind in
Antarctic sea
ice, 1947

scare anyone, but the cruel reality is that in case of a new war, the United States could be attacked by planes flying over one or both poles.' Byrd was, of course, referring to the Soviet Union and the growing Cold War, which might turn hot. He did not refer to these planes flying at 'incredible speeds', but did use the phrase 'fantastic speed' in the same article, when referring to the way in which the modern world was shrinking thanks to modern communication and the growing use of commercial aircraft [1].

Summary

In summary, careful analysis shows that the conspiracy theorists have operated like giant vacuum cleaners, sucking up all manner of unrelated bits and pieces of information, which they have subsequently stitched together into a patchwork quilt to create a myth of secret wars and secret bases covered up by governments. Information that did not fit has been left out. Gaps have been filled by speculation. Evidence has been falsified. Fantasy has provided the rest. We are left not with history, but with a script for a 'B' movie.

References

1. Summerhayes, C.P., and Beeching, P., 2007, Hitler's Antarctic base: the myth and the reality. Polar Record 43 (224), 1-21. This work contains a comprehensive list of references to the facts and to the legends.

2. Szabo, L., 1947, Hitler est Vivant. SFELT, Paris, 209 pp. The legend begins here. Published in several languages.

3. Schön, H., 2004, Mythos Neu-Schwabenland für Hitler am Südpol; die deutsche Antarktisexpedition 1938/39. Bonus-Verlag, Selent. 176 pp.

4. Sullivan, W., 1957, Quest for a continent. McGraw-Hill, New York: 372 pp.

5. Sullivan, W., 1961, Assault on the unknown: the International Geophysical Year. New York: McGraw-Hill, New York 460 pp. Sullivan visited Antarctica with Byrd during the IGY and, as a science writer for the New York Times, had participated in the Highjump Expedition.

6. El Mercurio, Santiago de Chile, miércoles 5 March 1947, El almirante Richard E. Byrd se refiere a la importancia estratégica de los polos, 23. The article was provided by a US reporter, Lee Van Atta, aboard the USS "Mount Olympus", one of the "Highjump" ships, on the high seas.

IV
SCIENTIFIC OUTCOMES

CHAPTER 9: GEOGRAPHICAL MAPS

Making the Maps

The aerial photographs were taken using top quality cameras and film. Using oblique rather than downward looking photography, and taking overlapping images, enabled mapmakers to use 3-D stereo-projection to estimate heights and distances. Crude maps were prepared aboard ship, but comprehensive and detailed maps were not prepared until after the return to Germany, by Hansa Luftbild GmbH and by Gruber (Zeiss).

Prominent mountain peaks were named after German explorers or dignitaries like Alexander von Humboldt (explorer), Georg von Neumayer (promoter of German Antarctic research), Erich von Drygalski and Wilhelm Filchner (both Antarctic polar explorers), or

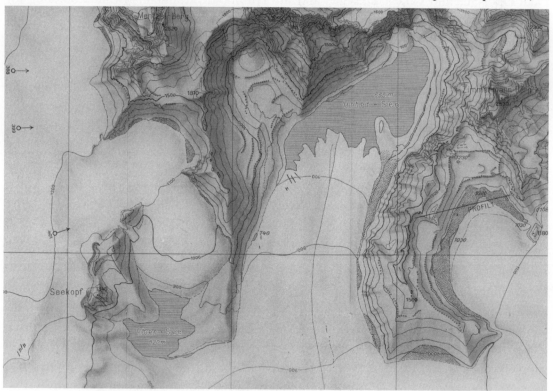

Detail from map of Wohlthat Massif (Wohlthat Mountains) in the scale 1:50.000 showing
Lake Ober-See (left) and Lake Unter-See (top centre)

for members of the expedition. Among them were the pilots, some scientists and two brave seamen Emil Brandt and Karl Hedden, who had saved the lives of others who had fallen into the icy waters between ice floes. For no apparent reason, the people in charge of radio communication were not acknowledged by having their names allocated to distant peaks. Feeling aggrieved, Erich Harmsen, the ship's radio controller, asked that he not be mentioned in Herrmann's popular account of the expedition [1]. The list of names was confirmed and approved by the Commissioner for the Four-Year Plan, Hermann Göring.

When the cartographers in Germany started their work they had no idea whether or not there would be a follow-up expedition that might enlarge the survey area. That made it rather hard to decide what kind of projection should be used for the maps. In order to make progress, they assumed that the investigations might later be expanded towards the South Pole, so as to make the survey area the same kind of pie-slice claimed by other nations in different parts of the continent, with the point of the slice fixed on the pole.

They also assumed that detailed maps would be made for special areas, such as the Wohlthat Mountains (at a scale of 1:500,000), the Central Wohlthat Mountains (scale 1:50,000) with Lake Ober-See and Lake Unter-See, and the Humboldt Mountains (scale 1:50,000), for publication in the first volume of the expedition's results [2]. The cartographers decided that these various demands and assumptions could best be met by the use of a conformal cylinder projection in transversal position.

Besides plotting the positions of the aircraft and the photographs on the base map, the height of the ground also had to be determined. That was a huge task, given that the photographed area was a full 250,000 km^2 – about half the size of Greater Germany. Each long distance flight into the unknown Antarctic and back would be like flying from the Baltic Sea to the Alps. Determining the height of the mountains was difficult, because all they could use to calculate flying altitude was the reading on the plane's barometer. As the planes only flew during good weather, pressure variations caused by changes in weather during the flight should only result in negligible errors. Nevertheless, without ground control in the mountains, estimates of land height were inevitably going to be approximate at best.

Determining geographic position was also going to be difficult, given that they had only three ground control points at the seaward edge of the ice shelf, and a number of positions for the ship, all of them rather close together near the coastline. Inland, away from those coastal points, navigation was mostly by dead-reckoning along pre-set compass courses supplemented with occasional sun sights – especially at turning points, giving ample scope for error due to wind drift. In those days there was no Global Positioning System (GPS). As a result, when the mapmakers tried to combine the polygons from all flights and to turn the photographs into maps, they ran into problems, notably a lack of correspondence

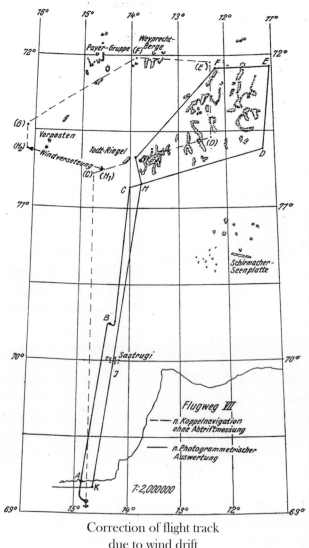

Correction of flight track
due to wind drift

between survey tracks that crossed one another. The problem had already been recognised on the ship, when the first attempts were made to match up the photographic surveys from different days. Evidently the planes had suffered more than had been imagined from wind drift and other sources of error. This problem was to haunt the expedition leader for some time to come, and devalued the work until corrections could be made after the war. Even so, despite the errors, the 1939 map was a magnificent achievement.

The German expedition was not alone in suffering from this defect. For rather obvious reasons – the land was mostly untouched by human foot - virtually all flights in Antarctica prior to this expedition had lacked ground control points to anchor their aerial photographic surveys, starting with the first Antarctic flights of Hubert Wilkins over the Antarctic Peninsula in 1929, and continuing through the aerial surveys carried out by the US Navy during Operation Highjump, in 1947 [3,4]. The very few and rather small well-surveyed areas were mostly over and around the Ross Ice Shelf, where all three of Byrd's American expeditions (1929-30, 1933-34, and 1940-41) had used extensive ground transportation as well as aircraft, something he repeated in that same area during Operation Highjump (it was the US Navy's surveys away from the Ross Sea area during Operation Highjump that lacked ground truth) [5,6].

For a time it appeared, as in the case of Wilkins and of Byrd's Highjump operation, that most of the German work had been wasted in terms of making accurate maps. Nevertheless, the mapmakers realised that crude adjustments to the aircraft tracks could be made from careful examination of the photographs – by matching physical features seen on different flight paths [7]. That realisation allowed Hans Richter from Hansa Luftbild, working in a race

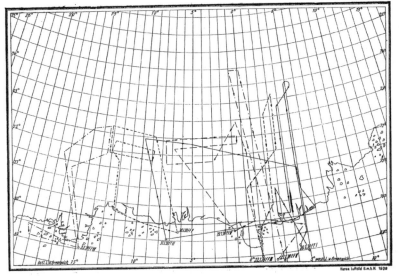

Flight tracks over Neu-Schwabenland as constructed
by Hansa Luftbild in 1939

against time, to produce within six weeks, in May and June 1939, a preliminary map of Neu-Schwabenland at a scale of 1:500,000, which was reduced to 1:1,500,000 for publication in a 1939 supplement of *Annalen der Hydrographie und Maritimen Meteorologie* of the German Maritime Observatory less than 2 ½ months after Ritscher had placed the order with Hansa Luftbild [8]. This map was the most important result of the expedition.

Why the rush? The map was of highest priority for Wohlthat to present at the International Whaling Conference, which was scheduled to take place in London on 17-20 July 1939. Wohlthat did indeed attend the meeting [9,10], but the report of the meeting gives no indication of his unveiling the new German map, and no record of it being handed out there to the assembled IWC delegates could be found. However we now know the map was not produced in time for that meeting.

Twenty 3-D photos (anaglyphes) and 3-D glasses with a red (left) and green (right) transparency were provided with the official expedition report in 1942 to give the reader a stereo impression of the mountain ranges discovered by air [11]. The next step was intended to be the construction of the final map of Neu-Schwabenland at a scale of 1:250,000, with some maps at a scale of 1:50,000 for areas of special interest. With the outbreak of World War II in September 1939, the work was stopped and it did not restart until the 1950s.

In spite of their inaccuracies, the published German maps were the only data available on the topography of this section of Antarctica, and they started to be incorporated into Antarctic atlases as early as 1939 by Australia [12,13], and into Antarctic charts in 1943 by the US Hydrographic Office [14]. The Australians got their information on the locations of the mountains seen by the German planes from a sketch map published in May 1939 [15]. After Word War II other nations began visiting this part of Antarctica [16]. Not only did they use the German maps, they fed back to Germany ground control information that could be

116

Mountains of Dronning Maud Land shown on the Australian Antarctic map of 1939

used to correct the maps. Eventually, satellite data provided the key to deciding precisely where the various named features were [17].

Aside from the aerial photographs, thousands of pictures were taken by expedition members, including stills and movies, colour and black and white. These include the first ever colour photographs from the Antarctic, some of which were published by Herrmann [18]. That publication, and the widespread use of colour film on the expedition, gives the lie to reports suggesting that the first Antarctic expedition to return home with coloured photographs was Byrd's third US expedition [19]. The Americans landed in two places – West Base on the Ross Ice Shelf (January 1940) and East Base on the Palmer Peninsula (March 1940), and left in 1941 (1 February from West Base, and 22 March from East Base). By then coloured photos of Antarctica had been available in Germany for almost 2 years – since mid-April 1939.

The German Maps in the Post-War Period

Not long after the war the preliminary German map of Neu-Schwabenland was used to guide the planning of numerous subsequent operations in Dronning Maud Land. First of these was the US aerial mapping of Antarctica on 'Operation Highjump', which took place in the southern summer season of 1946/47 under the command of Rear-Admiral Paul Cruzen and the scientific leadership of Rear-Admiral Richard Byrd [20,21]. The US Navy had already placed the Neuschwabenland details on its 1943 hydrographic map of Antarctica. The American expedition, which began its activities around Antarctica in late December 1946, made no sustained attempt to fly over Dronning Maud Land, most probably because it had already been mapped from the air by the German expedition and there was not much point in duplicating that work when time was of the essence. In any case, the US naval surveying exercise began in the Ross Sea on the opposite side of the continent from Neuschwabenland and ran out of time to include Neuschwabenland before 'Highjump' had been fully completed [21].

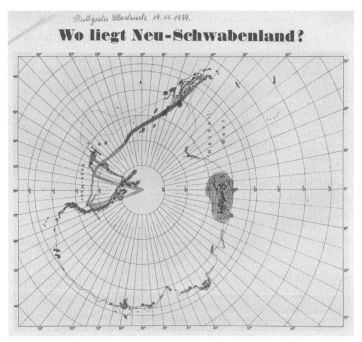

Wo liegt Neu-Schwabenland?

Mountains of Dronning Maud Land shown in a German
magazine in 1939

Next to use German information was the Norwegian-British-Swedish Expedition of 1949-52 (NBSX), which was based at the Maudheim station on the east coast of the Weddell Sea between 10 February 1950 and 15 January 1952, and at the western edge of the terrain mapped by the German expedition [22]. The initiator of the NBSX, the Swedish geographer Hans Wilhelmsson Ahlmann (1889-1974), was an expert on climate change in the Arctic. He wanted to see if evidence for climate change could also be found in Antarctica, for example from changes in the positions of glaciers with time that could be determined from the distribution of glacial moraines [22,23]. In 1943 or 1944 (the date is uncertain), during World War II, he managed to obtain some maps and original paper prints of aerial photographs from the German *Schwabenland* expedition. While it appears that these items may have been smuggled to Sweden from Germany [24], it is worth bearing in mind that, firstly, the preliminary results had been published in 1939, while Herrmann's popular book followed in 1941, and Ritscher's report in 1942 [25], and, secondly, that Sweden was a neutral country not at war with Germany. It would be surprising if Sweden did not have access to this information, not least since it had already appeared on the Australian Antarctic map of 1939 and the US Naval Antarctic chart of 1943. Nevertheless, Ahlmann never disclosed who in Germany had provided him with these items [24]. From the photographs he was able to identify glaciers ending on land and substantial moraines showing that the glaciers had retreated (or to put it another way, the ice level had gone down, exposing the moraines) – probably in response to climate warming [23]. This phenomenon had not been noted in the German reports. Its discovery by Ahlmann - an expert in observing such things - led him to begin planning a post-war scientific expedition to the German working area. The plan was launched in 1945 with Norway taking the lead and Britain and Sweden as key partners [22].

118

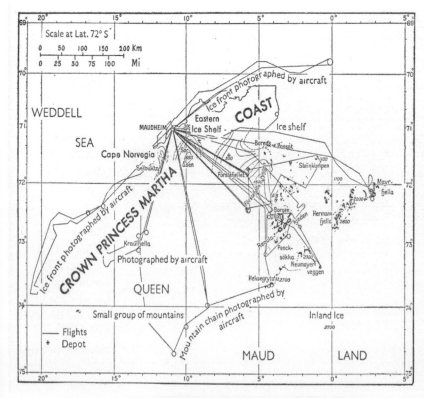

Flight tracks of the Norwegian-British-Swedish Expedition
in Antarctica, 1952

Ritscher helped the organisers of the NBSX by sharing with them his private experiences, the still existing pictures, and the maps, during their visit to Hamburg in November 1948 [26]. In due course, the NBSX set up their base at Maudheim on the Quar ice shelf. They had a field party of glaciologists, geologists and geophysicists along with aircraft to undertake aerial surveys, and managed to penetrate by land and air to around 350 km to the east from their base, as far east as Mayr-fjella (the German 'Mayr-kette') at the western end of the Mühlig-Hofmann Mountains on the eastern side of the Penck Trough (Penck Sökka). In addition, they investigated in depth by foot and by plane the mountains on the western side of the Penck Trough or Penck-Mulde, which they called the Borg Massivet, and which had been mapped in less detail by the *Schwabenland* Expedition [27,28]. While carrying out their survey they looked for some of the German metal arrows in this area, but in vain [29].

Initially, as recorded by Roots (1954), they found it difficult to match the terrain to the German aerial photographs [28]. But eventually Roots and his geological field party were able to make the connection. They camped on the western side of what they came to call the Hoegfonna peak located on the eastern side of the Borg Massivet and on the western side of the Penck Trough, and climbed to set up trigonometric station 18 on the peak of Hoegfonna (at 2579 m). This peak is located at 72° 44.7'S, 3° 35'W. It was one of the highest points in the area, and from there they were finally able to match Ritscher's photos with what they could see on the ground [28].

119

Central Part of
Wohlthat Massif.
The moraines
leave a sort of
'bathtub ring'
on the side of
the mountains,
showing the levels
to which ice
formerly reached

Breischüsseln in
the western part
of Alexander
von Humboldt
Mountains

The LANDSAT satellite map of the same area shows that Hoegfonna peak lies in the mountains originally named Schubertgipfel by the Germans [30]. A comparison of the satellite picture with Ritscher's original map confirms that many of the features surveyed by the *Schwabenland* expedition were mapped out of position – something that Ritscher was well aware of, though unable to control in the absence of ground control points. During their survey the NBSX team found that some of the mountain locations on the German map were out of position by up to 30 miles, and that heights were too high by up to 1000 m [32].

A second comparison of Brunk's LANDSAT photo with Ritscher's Photo Tafel 55, originally labelled as showing the Seilkopfberge, shows that the mountain chain in the foreground (named Hoegfonna by the NBSX) is the Schubertgipfel, and that the mountains in the background are the Seilkopfberge. The Seilkopfberge appear on the NBSX map as Seilkopf-fjella, within the Borg-Massivet. The Hoegfonna peak at which Fred Roots' Station 18 was located is the sharp peak in the centre of the Schubertgipfel. An almost identical photo to Ritscher's was taken in 1952 by the Swedish NBSX plane, and appears as Plate 10b in Schytt (1961)[23]. This interpretation was confirmed in an e-mail to CL from Fred Roots on 28 March 2010.

Later the Germans were able to use that information to revise their Neu-Schwabenland map[33,34]. News of the NBSX results was widely broadcast in German newspapers, where Ritscher was referred to as a 'tour guide of Antarctica', who knew all about Drottning-Mauds-Land [sic] [35,36].

The use of the combined name 'Neu-Schwabenland' was forbidden by the 'Regulations for the publication of maps in the British Zone of Germany' of 14 April 1949 [37,38]. The paragraph in question said. 'Polar regions shall not represent German claims, f.e. "Neues Schwabenland" [New Swabia Land] in Antarctica, because Swabia was a region in southwest Germany'. This led Johannes Georgi of the German Maritime Observatory (Deutsche Seewarte), who had been a member of Alfred Wegener's expedition to Greenland in 1930-1931, to address the question of naming features in the Neu-Schwabenland area, which he did in the well-known national German newspaper Die Welt, on 23 July 1949 [39]. According to Georgi's account, his article and his accompanying petition to the occupying power led to the annulment of the 'Regulations' on 23 November 1950 [38]. Georgi later went on to discuss the right to name features, the technical procedure for it, and the process for the international acceptance of new names. He was particularly critical of naming features in Antarctica after people who had held prominent positions in the national-socialist bureaucracy, and suggested that the names proposed by Ritscher for the topographic features of Neu-Schwabenland be 'de-nazified': the Mühlig-Hofmann-Gebirge should be renamed Alfred-Wegener-Gebirge, after the German meteorologist and polar researcher Alfred Wegener; the Kurze-Gebirge should be renamed Meinardus-Gebirge, after the geographer Wilhelm Meinardus; the Conrad-Gebirge should be renamed Dallmann-Gebirge after captain Eduard Dallmann of the "Grönland" expedition to the

Antarctic Peninsula; and the Wohlthat-Massiv should be renamed Nansen-Massiv, after the Norwegian explorer Fridtjof Nansen.

Having read Georgi's paper, Wohlthat felt sufficiently offended by Georgi's suggestions that on 18 August 1951 he asked the senior prosecutor of Hamburg to prosecute Georgi for defamation [40]. Following discussions between the two men's lawyers, a printed correction appeared in the next issue of Petermanns Mitteilungen, saying that Wohlthat's name shall not be understood as belonging to names of high political members of the National Socialist regime [41]. Wohlthat said that at that time (meaning the time of the expedition) he was not a member of the National Socialist Party – which rather implies that later he did become a member. Ritscher's own response to Georgi's suggestion - a six page manuscript - was not published, because Petermanns Mitteilungen, printed at Gotha in the German Democratic Republic, preferred anti Nazi stories and not a clarification of the facts [40,42]. To support his point of view, Ritscher sent his response to various German geographers, pointing to the fact that the naming of features had been done according to international guidelines, and names of high-ranking persons of the Third Reich had not been used. Only names of especially active supporters of the expedition, like Admiral Conrad or Admiral Kurze, as well as deserving expedition members, had been considered, along with distinguished German explorers, and, of course, the inspiration for the expedition – Wohlthat himself [42].

Wohlthat had good connections to the new government of the Federal Republic of Germany, and used his leverage to discuss the problem of naming with the Federal Chancellery and the Minister for the Department of Foreign Affairs. This paved the way for official approval of Ritscher's proposal for the expedition's list of German names in Antarctica to be sent to the Federal Chancellery in December 1951 [43]. There was no reply, so Ritscher repeated his request on 31 July 1952, pointing out that delay in obtaining an official German government position on

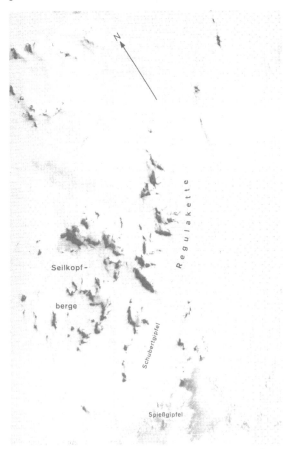

Borg Massivet depicted by LANDSAT and renamed after the corrected positioning of the aerial photographs of the *Schwabenland* expedition

naming could well mean that German names would be excluded from the new 1:4,000,000 scale map of Antarctica that was being constructed by German geographer Hans-Peter Kosack [44]. This map was to include the latest discoveries from various sources, along with a new map of Neu-Schwabenland with corrected positions and heights derived from the NBSX and reproduced in a map in 1951[45]. It was to be financed by the French Polar Institute in Paris [44]. After many meetings in Paris, Kosack had been informed in mid-June 1952 that after three years of negotiations by Bryan Roberts from Cambridge, F. Cooper from the Australian Joint Intelligence Bureau in Melbourne, Sir Cecil Day from the government of New Zealand, as well as H. Sverdrup and H.E. Nansen from Norway, and Paul Victor from France, the decision had been made to use only official British, French, and Norwegian names for the new map. The American's Bureau of Place Names had agreed to this decision [46,47]. And in the autumn of 1952 official delegates of the geographic communities of these countries planned international negotiations on guidelines to naming of geographical features in the new map of Antarctica. Ritscher urged the Federal Chancellery to act immediately, so as to ensure that German names could be included.

Ritscher was very happy when his list of place names was officially published in the *Bundesanzeiger* (Federal Advertiser) on 5 August 1952, only one week after he had sent his letter [48]. He was especially happy that the published list retained the names originally proposed in 1939, without any omissions or changes. Despite official publication of the list of names, the Federal Republic of Germany made no claim to any territory in Antarctica[49]. The publication of the name list was only done to show official interest in the German names given by Ritscher's expedition being used in German geographical publications. Following the advice of the Amt für Landeskunde (Office of Regional Research), Ritscher then wrote to publishers of atlases, globes, textbooks and wall-maps asking them to use in new publications the newly published German names for Antarctic features [50]. In 1954 Kosack's new map of Antarctica in four sheets appeared with the German names and the status quo of 1 October 1953 [33,51]. Ritscher had been vindicated, and the expedition's legacy was assured.

As the late 1950s approached, the scientific world became absorbed in planning for the International Geophysical Year (IGY) of 1957-1958. As the planning for the IGY went on, Ritscher was busy finding new people to help to complete Volume II of the expedition results – the full scientific report. No easy task, the work was finally completed for publication in 1958, in time for it to make a major German Antarctic contribution to the mass of findings that emerged during the IGY. At the same time the German discoveries appeared for the first time in an issue of the *Times Atlas* [52].

Although Germany had no national programme in Antarctica during the IGY, the Norwegians and the Belgians, who set up scientific research stations in Dronning Maud Land for the IGY, were able to use Kosack's revised map of Neu-Schwabenland [45], and some of the aerial photographs, to guide their IGY research activities. That enabled yet

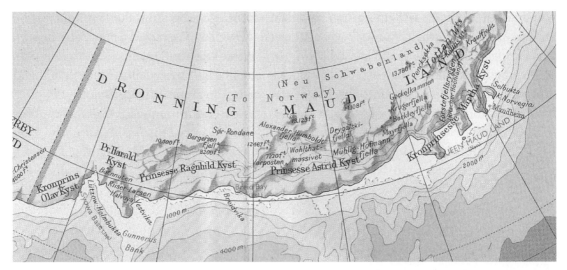

Post-war Times Atlas map from 1958 showing details of Neu-Schwabenland

more of the locations of the topographic features seen from the air to be fixed by ground control, supplementing the data already provided by the NBSX. Kosack used their new data to modify the Neu-Schwabenland map yet again, for publication in the second volume of the expedition results published as preprint already in 1954 [33,34].

As Germany had decided not to counter Norway's 1939 claim to ownership of this part of Antarctica, the territory of what Germany still referred to as Neu-Schwabenland had become internationally accepted as Norwegian, with the name Dronning Maud Land. That state of affairs persisted through the 1950s, until the opening for signature of the Antarctic Treaty in 1959, and its ratification in 1961. Under the Treaty it was agreed that all territorial claims would be set aside.

While the Norwegians had been happy to use the German map, they had given Norwegian names to many of the mountain features discovered and first named by the Germans. Nevertheless, some of the original German names remain e.g. the Wohlthat Massif, the Mühlig-Hofmann Mountains, the Schirmacher Oasis etc - a legacy of the influence of the Third Reich on this faraway continent. When Ritscher died in 1963, a paper in *Kartographische Nachrichten* (Cartographic News) focussed on his contribution to the improvement of maps of Antarctica and of the South Atlantic Ocean [53]. Even in South Africa, a detailed obituary was published in the *Antarktiese Bulletin* giving credit to the leader of the investigation of the Atlantic sector of Antarctica, where the South African expedition teams worked from their base SANAE [54]. In 1983, Paraguay issued a stamp celebrating the *Schwabenland*, but as a celebration of the German-South American mail service that *Schwabenland* had been part of, rather than in celebration of the expedition.

Towards the end of his career, Kosack produced a large wall map of Antarctica [55]. At the time of writing, one of these maps was still hanging in the Lecture Theatre of the Scott Polar Research Institute in Cambridge, UK. It depicts the location of Neu-Schwabenland, with the Wohlthat-Gebirge and Penck-Mulde as important features.

Further significant improvement in relating the German names to real features on the ground in Dronning Maud Land came with the arrival of a new technology – the orbiting NASA land observation satellites named Landsat. Landsat 1 and 2 images of Antarctica had become available in the period 1972-1976. When the Alfred Wegener Institute of Polar Research was founded in 1980 in Bremerhaven, the German Science Foundation sponsored work on a digital name database of the Antarctic initiated by Professor Schmidt-Falkenberg of the Institute for Applied Geodesy (IfAG) in Frankfurt/Main, with the aim of collecting all German names given to Antarctic features [56]. A better interpretation of the expedition map became possible, when some 600 of the 11,600 18 cm x 18 cm paper prints of oblique photographs were discovered by chance in December 1982. Using the newly found aerial photographs, the satellite images, various historical sources and the plethora of ground control points established by post-war expeditions, Karsten Brunk of IfAG was able to determine the positions of the original aerial survey tracks with some precision [57].

Having accurately established the survey tracks, together with the points from which the oblique photos had been taken, Brunk was able to identify precisely those topographic features that had been named on the Neu-Schwabenland map, thus removing the uncertainty about what names went with what features. One key result was the use of the aerial photographs and satellite images to produce the first accurate topographic map of the region [57]. Another key result of his investigation was that 96 names connected with the *Schwabenland* expedition could be entered into the Digital Name Data Base Antarctica of about 600 names in the year 1982, 427 of which referred to Antarctic topographic or geographic features named by German expeditions in the period 1873-1945 [56,58,59].

During the 1980s, efforts continued to preserve the German names, for example the Symposium on Antarctic research at Garwitz (GDR) in 1986, where there had been a presentation of German naming of Neu-Schwabenland [60]. There it was apparent that the Russians had used 'Oasis Schirmachera' since 1959, adapted from the original German name 'Schirmacher Oase'. However in the American compilation of Geographic Names of the Antarctic of 1981 'Schirmacher Oasis' was translated into 'Schirmacher Hills' in contrast to 'Schirmacher-Seengruppe', which was translated to 'Schirmacher Ponds'. Schirmacher Oasis is now in general use, but the Indians prefer their own name 'Dakshin Gangotri' for this area [46].

References

1. Harmsen, E,. 4.8.1939, Harmsen's letter to Herrmann. Herrmann's estate, Bonn.

2. Gruber, O.v., 1942, Das Wohlthat-Massiv im Kartenbild. In: A. Ritscher, Wissenschaftliche und fliegerische Ergebnisse der Deutschen Antarktischen Expedition 1938/39, Hrsg. im Auftrag der Deutschen Forschungsgemeinschaft, Koehler & Amelang, Leipzig, Vol. I, 157-230.

3. Bertrand, K.J., 1971, Americans in Antarctica, 1775-1948. Special Publication. 39, American Geographical Society, New York. 554 pp.

4. Byrd, R.E., 1947, Our Navy explores Antarctica. National Geographic Magazine. 92 (4), 429-522.

5. Byrd, R.E., 1930, Little America: aerial exploration in the Antarctic, the flight to the South Pole. Putnam and Sons, New York, 422 pp.

6. Byrd, R.E., 1935, Discovery: the story of the Second Byrd Antarctic Expedition. Putnam and Sons, New York 405 pp.

7. Geßner, W., 1942, Die deutschen luftphotogrammetrischen Arbeiten in Neu-Schwabenland. In: A. Ritscher, Wissenschaftliche und fliegerische Ergebnisse der Deutschen Antarktischen Expedition 1938/39, Hrsg. im Auftrag der Deutschen Forschungsgemeinschaft, Koehler & Amelang, Leipzig, Vol. I, 115-125.

8. Ritscher, A., 1939, Die Deutsche Antarktische Expedition 1938/39. Annalen der Hydrographie und Maritimen Meteorologie. VIII, Beiheft, 9-19.

9. International Whaling Conference, 1939, Report of the International Whaling Conference of 17-20 July, 1939, London. UK Ministry of Agriculture and Fisheries.

10. Time Magazine, 31 July, 1939, Smoke and Fire.

11. Ritscher, A., 1942, Wissenschaftliche und fliegerische Ergebnisse der Deutschen Antarktischen Expedition 1938/39, Hrsg. im Auftrag der Deutschen Forschungsgemeinschaft. Vol. 1, Koehler & Amelang, Leipzig.

12. Bayliss, E.P., 1939, Antarctica. 1:10,000,000 map. Canberra: Property and Survey Branch, Department of the Interior.

13. Bayliss, E.P. and J.S. Cumpston. 1939, Map of Antarctica: handbook and index. Canberra: Department of External Affairs.

14. USHO, 1943, Antarctica; compiled from all available sources to 1943. Map 1: 11.250.000. Washington DC: US Hydrographic Office. H.O. Chart No. 2562.

15. Berliner Illustrierte Zeitung, 1939, Number 21, 25th May 1939; p. 867 (with information on the expedition) and pp. 986-987 (with photographs from the expedition, including one of the so-called Gralsburg and a sketch of the flight tracks outlining the main areas of high rocky topography; these are the same areas that appear on the Australian Antarctic map of 1939). Note that a photo Gralsburg also appears on page 51 of Nazis in Antarctica, Life Magazine, July 3, 1939, pp. 51-53, and in Die weite Welt, Nr. 28, 9. Juli 1939, no page numbers given, title page and 4 pages (Ritscher's estate folder Antarktis bis 1941).

16. Giæver, J., 1954, The White Desert. The Official Account of the Norwegian-British-Swedish Antarctic Expedition. Chatto and Windus, London, 304 pp.

17. Brunk, K., 1986, Kartographische Arbeiten und deutsche Namengebung in Neuschwabenland, Antarktis. Bisherige Arbeiten, Rekonstruktion der Flugwege der Deutschen Antarktischen Expedition 1938/39 und Neubearbeitung des deutschen Namensgutes in Neuschwabenland. Frankfurt am Main, Institut für Angewandte Geodäsie. Geodätische Kommission der Bayerischen Akademie der Wissenschaften, Reihe E, Heft Nr. 24, Teil I, II), 42 pp. + 100 pictures.

18. Herrmann, E., 1941, Deutsche Forscher im Südpolarmeer. Safari Verlag, Berlin, 184 pp.

19. Reader's Digest, 1985, Antarctica. Reader's Digest, New York, 320 pp.

20. Sullivan, W., 1957, Quest for a Continent. McGraw-Hill, New York, 372 pp.

21. Byrd, R.E., 1947, Our Navy Explores Antarctica. National Geographic Vol. XCII, No.4, 429-522.

22. Giæver, J., 1954, The White Desert. The Official Account of the Norwegian-British-Swedish Antarctic Expedition. Chatto and Windus, London, 304 pp.

23. Schytt, W., 1961, Blue ice fields, moraine features and glacier fluctuations. In: Glaciology II. Norwegian-British-Swedish Antarctic Expedition, 1949-52. Scientific results, vol. IVE, Norsk Polar Institute, Oslo University Press, 183-204.

24. Interview by C. Lüdecke with Ernest Frederick (Fred) Roots (born 1922), Canadian geologist of the NBSX, on 1 December 2009 in Washington DC.

25. Ritscher, A., 1942, Wissenschaftliche und fliegerische Ergebnisse der Deutschen Antarktischen Expedition 1938/39, Hrsg. im Auftrag der Deutschen Forschungsgemeinschaft. Koehler & Amelang, Leipzig. Vol. 1: Pictures and Maps 57 plates and 3 maps.

26. Ritscher, (27.1.1949), Letter to Meinardus. Ritscher's estate, Antarktis bis 1964. Unpublished.

27. Giaever, J., and Schytt, V., 1963, General report of the expedition. Norwegian-British-Swedish Antarctic Expedition, 1949-52, Scientific Results, Vol VI, part 3., 41 pp., plus maps.

28. Roots, E.F., 1954. Journeys of the Topographical-Geological Party. In Giaever, The White Desert, Appendix 3, pages 245-280, Chatto and Windus, London.

29. Personal communication with Fred Roots (born 1922), geologist of the NBSX, on 23. February 2010.

30. Brunk, K., 1986, Kartographische Arbeiten und deutsche Namengebung in Neuschwabenland, Antarktis. Bisherige Arbeiten, Rekonstruktion der Flugwege der Deutschen Antarktischen Expedition 1938/39 und Neubearbeitung des deutschen Namensgutes in Neuschwabenland. Frankfurt am Main, Institut für Angewandte Geodäsie. Geodätische Kommission der Bayerischen Akademie der Wissenschaften, Reihe E, Heft Nr. 24, Teil I, II), 42 pp. + 100 pictures.

31. Herrmann, E., 1939, Die geographischen Arbeiten. Annalen der Hydrographie und Maritimen Meteorologie, VIII, Beiheft, 23-26.

32. Swithinbank, C., 1999, Foothold on Antarctica. Lewes: The Book Guild.

33. Kosack H.-P., 1954a, Neubearbeitung der Übersichtskarte des Arbeistgebietes der Expedition. In: A. Ritscher (ed.) Deutsche Antarktische Expedition 1938/39 mit dem Flugzeugstützpunkt der Deutschen Lufthansa A.G. M.S. "Schwabenland". Wissenschaftliche und fliegerische Ergebnisse. Hamburg, Geographisch-Kartographische Anstalt "Mundus" Helmut Striedieck, Vol. 2, 1-15. Preprint.

34. Kosack, H.-P., 1958, Neubearbeitung der Übersichtskarte des Arbeistgebietes der Expedition. In: A. Ritscher (ed.) Deutsche Antarktische Expedition 1938/39 mit dem Flugzeugstützpunkt der Deutschen Lufthansa A.G. M.S. "Schwabenland". Wissenschaftliche und fliegerische Ergebnisse. Hamburg: Geographisch-Kartographische Anstalt "Mundus" Helmut Striedieck, Bd. II, 1-15. First published as preprint in 1954 (see 33, above).

35. A.J., 1949, "Fremdenführer" in der Antarktis – Ein Hamburger kennt sich in Drottning-Mauds-Land aus. Hamburger Allgemeine of 11 March 1949.

36. G.B., 1949, Auf den Spuren deutscher Forscher: Internationale Südpol-Expedition. Die Welt, Nr. 203, of 25. November 1949.

37. Georgi 19.7.1949, Letter to Stocks. Ritscher's estate, Antarktis bis 1964. Unpublished.

38. Georgi, J., 1951a, Zur Frage der Namengebung in der Antarktis. Petermanns Mitteilungen 95 (2), 81-88.

39. Georgi, J., 1949, Forschungsobjekt Antarktis – Neue Englisch-Skandinavische Expedition 1949/52 – Forschungsgebiet wurde 1939 von deutschen Wissenschaftlern durch Luftaufnahmen kartographisch erfaßt. Die Welt, Nr. 96, of 23 July 1949.

40. Wohlthat, 14.4.1964, Letter to Schmitt. Ritscher's estate, Antarktis bis 1964. Unpublished.

41. Georgi, J., 1951b, Zur Frage der Namengebung in der Antarktis. Ergäntung und Berichtigung. Petermanns Mitteilungen 95 (3), 186-187.

42. Ritscher, Juli 1951, Stellungnahme zum Aufsatz "Zur Frage der Namensgebnung in der Antarktis". Ritscher's estate, Antarktis bis 1964. Unpublished.

43. Ritscher, 31.6.1952, Letter to Federal Chancellery. Ritscher's estate, Antarktis bis 1964. Unpublished.

44. Ritscher, 31.7.1952, Letter to Federal Chancellery. Ritscher's estate, Antarktis bis 1964. Unpublished.

45. Kosack, H.-P., 1951, Eine neue Karte von Antarktika. Überschau über den Stand der Kartierung des sechsten Erdteils. Petermanns Mitteilungen 95 (2), 73-80, plate 6,7.

46. Alberts, F.G., (ed.), 1981, Geographic Names of the Antarctic. 1st ed., United States Board of Geographic Names. Washington D.C.

47. Alberts, F.G. (ed.), 1995, Geographic names of the Antarctic. 2nd ed., United States Board of Geographic Names, Reston, Virginia, 834 pp.

48. Hallstein, 1952, Bekanntmachung über die Bestätigung der bei der Entdeckung von "Neu-Schwabenland" im Atlantischen Sektor der Antarktis durch die Deutsche Antarktische Expedition 1938/39 erfolgten Benennungen geographischer Begriffe. Bundesanzeiger 4 (149) of 5 August 1952, 1-2.

49. Auswärtiges Amt, 6.10.1952, Letter to Ritscher. Ritscher's estate, Antarktis bis 1964. Unpublished.

50. Ritscher, October 1952, Letter to publishers. Ritscher's estate, Antarktis bis 1964. Unpublished.

51. Kosack, H.-P. 1954b, Zur Vierblattkarte der Antarktis in 1:4 Millionen. Petermanns Mitteilungen 98 (2), 81-85.

52. Times Atlas, 1958, The Times Atlas of the World. Mid-century edition Edited by John Bartholomew Vol. 1. The world, Australasia & East Asia., XXVII pp., 24 Tables, 34 pp.

53. Vetter, O., 1965, Alfred Ritschers Beiträge zur Verbesserung der Karten der Antarktis und des Südatlantischen Ozeans. Kartographische Nachrichten 13 (4), 114-116.

54. Brunn, V. von, 1964, Captain Alfred Ritscher, 1879-1963. Antarktiese Bulletin 5, September 1-2.

55. Kosack, H.-P., (ca.1965), Südpolargebiet. Wall map. Darmstadt: Justus Perthes, 2nd ed. 1978. New ed. 1993, Gotha: Klett Perthes.

56. IFAG, 1988. Digitale Namensdatenbank Antarktis. Frankfurt/Main, Institut für Angewandte Geodäsie, 75 pp + 6 pp.

57. Brunk, K., 1987, Die Rekonstruktion der Bildflüge und die Neubearbeitung des Namensgutes der Deutschen Antarktischen Expedition 1938/39 in Neuschwabenland, Antarktis. Polarforschung 57 (3), 191-197.

58. IFAG, 1986, Digitale Namensdatenbank Antarktis. In: K. Brunk, Kartographische Arbeiten und deutsche Namengebung in Neuschwabenland, Antarktis. Frankfurt am Main: Institut für Angewandte Geodäsie, Geodätischen Kommission der Bayerischen Akademie der Wissenschaften, Reihe E, Heft Nr. 24, Teil I, II). 06 pp. + 15 pp. + 6 pp.

59. IFAG, 1993,Verzeichnis deutschsprachiger Namen der Antarktis. Nachrichten aus dem Karten- und Vermessungswesen. 2nd edition of IFAG 1988, Sonderheft, Frankfurt am Main, Institut für Angewandte Geodäsie, 30 pp.

60. Richter, W., 1986, Boreasische Seenplatte – Oasis Schrimachera – Dakshin Gangotri: Über die Benutzung geographischer Namen in der Antarktis. Geodätische und Geophysikalische Veröffentlichungen, Reihe I, Heft 13, 138-144.

CHAPTER 10: ROCK, ICE AND LAKES

Rocks

Topography is the first clue to underlying geological processes. Ernst Herrmann, the geologist who served as the expedition's geographer, was responsible for the preliminary analysis of topographic information and any geological samples that might be obtained. He had been selected not only for his geological experience, much of it concerned with volcanoes, but also because he was an experienced Arctic researcher.

It struck Herrmann that here and there north-south oriented valley glaciers broke the several parallel ranges of the east-west mountain belt into sections [1,2,3]. Ice poured through these valleys from the Polar Plateau to feed the ice sheet between the mountains and the sea. Knowing that rivers or glaciers often cut valleys along lines of weakness, he surmised

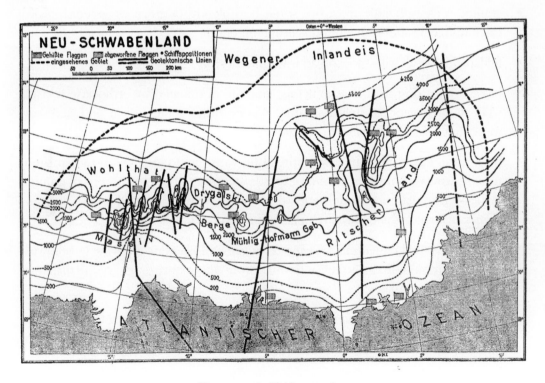

Herrmann's 1941 tectonic map

that these glacial valleys followed a series of underlying north-south trending faults and fractures, and that the Penck-Mulde (Penck Trough) was probably a fault-bounded graben. The Norwegians call this the Jutulstraumen graben. Herman's assumptions were reasonable; later work shows tectonic structures trending NE-SW and NNE-SSW across western Dronning Maud Land parallel to the Jutulstraumen graben [4], and other work shows major faults trending NNE-SSW cutting the exposed rocks of the Schirmacher Oasis [5,6].

The rocks and minerals of Herrmann's nine 'penguin pebbles' [2]

- red-brown micaceous quartzite – a sort of metamorphosed sandstone with mica flakes;

- coarser quartzite with small sericitized mica flakes (sericite is likely to reflect hydrothermal alteration);

- granitic rock with little mica but some hornblende (a green or greenish-brown calcium-magnesium-iron aluminosilicate mineral);

- feldspathic basalt with widespread iron minerals;

- basalt with widespread iron minerals; granitite dominated by orthoclase feldspar with some plagioclase feldspar, quartz and fresh biotite (mica) and accessory magnetite (a black magnetic iron oxide);

- plagioclase basalt containing widespread brownish and partly chloritised augite (a usually brown calcium-magnesium-iron silicate mineral) with inclusions of ilmenite (a black iron-titanium oxide), and with ophitic texture (laths of plagioclase in a matrix of augite); the chlorite is an alteration product.

- plagioclase basalt containing widespread augite and occasional olivine (a yellowish-green magnesium-iron silicate), and with porphyritic texture (large crystals dispersed in a fine-grained matrix);

- a diabase-like stone containing abundant augite (diabase is a term for the basaltic rocks commonly found in intrusive dikes and sills associated with basaltic volcanism).

Herrmann was disappointed that the scientific party were unable to sample any of the exposed rocky outcrops seen from the aircraft, but much to his surprise and delight he managed to find some small rock samples in the stomachs of penguins. It appears that the local penguins like to pick up pea-sized stones to aid their digestion. The key question was: 'where did they get them?' The nearest mountains were around 200 km distant, an unlikely trip for a penguin hungry for pea-sized bits of rock. But they might not have had to walk that far. Fragments of rock were constantly being eroded from the mountains and deposited in moraines on the surfaces of the glaciers pouring through the mountain range and down towards the sea. But as the moraines near the coast they tend to become buried by snow. Given that penguins are astounding swimmers, it seems likely to us that the birds picked up small stones from the seabed close to the shore, where they had been dropped from melting icebergs carrying fragments of glacial moraine out to sea. Alternatively they might have picked them up from rocky moraine material exposed on icebergs, on which penguins could often be seen taking a ride.

Herrmann realised that it would be unwise to infer much about the geology of the hinterland from these few tiny samples, not least because they had been selected by the birds and so were unlikely to be representative. Nevertheless, they did suggest that the mountains of the interior might contain old sedimentary rocks (sandstones) that had been metamorphosed into quartzite, along with deep-seated intrusive igneous rocks (granite and granitite), and volcanic rocks (basalt and diabase). Subsequent geological research has proved him right.

Looking at the aerial photographs Herrmann thought that in some of the shots of mountains he could see signs of the kind of streakiness seen in metamorphic rocks known as migmatites in the Scandinavian Arctic [2]. He also thought he could see possible signs of jointed granites, some areas of faulting, folding and fracturing, and some pronounced layering. His observations led him to speculate that the rocks of Neu-Schwabenland might well be rather like the rocks mapped in the Ross Sea embayment on the other side of the continent, where Precambrian gneisses, schists and granites followed by Tertiary basalts had been identified, for example by Scott's and Byrd's expeditions. Herrmann speculated that some of the layers might be volcanic in origin. Subsequent geological investigations of the mountains of Dronning Maud Land by Russian, German, Norwegian, Japanese, and Indian scientists show that the rocks there are Precambrian high-grade metamorphic rocks, largely between 1000-1400 million years old, which were considerably modified by the Pan-African Orogeny 500-570 million years ago [6,7,8,9,10,11,12,13,14]. Pure granite is rare, but granitoid rocks are quite common and there are layered gneisses. The age and nature of these rocks suggest that Dronning Maud Land's main East-West mountain chain is a southward extension of the East African Orogen, a major African mountain belt formed by the continent-to-continent collision of East and West Gondwanaland to form the Gondwanaland super-continent around 550 million years ago. Following subsequent erosion, the ancient rocks of the interior were overlain by Permian sediments including thin coal seams [15]. The Antarctic part of the Orogen was cut off from its northward part, which lies in east Africa, around 170-150 million years ago during the break-up of Gondwanaland that separated Antarctica from Africa in Jurassic times [8]. During that split, parts of the area were intruded by basalt dykes [8,16,17] – which explains Herrmann's pebbles of basalt and diabase. The later history of Dronning Maud Land is one of uplift associated with faulting. There is no evidence for recent volcanic activity like that typical of the Ross Sea with its Mounts Erebus and Terror.

Herrmann's notion that the north-south trending groups of massifs within the east-west mountain chain owed their lineation to underling structural control by deep-seated faults was eminently sensible. But that was not enough for him. In search of a theory to match his data, and perhaps because he had recently been thinking about the many volcanic islands of the Atlantic with which he had become acquainted on his journey south, and because he had an avowed deep interest in volcanism, he convinced himself that some of the rock strata seen in the aerial photographs might be layers of volcanic ash [1]. He was wrong - the layers are mostly those of sedimentary rocks that were later metamorphosed, for example into quartzites. Attempting to link his basalt rock samples with what appeared to him to be volcanic structures seen in aerial photos, and bearing in mind the young age of the volcanoes in the Ross Sea area, he speculated that the deep faults beneath the troughs and valleys in his study area might well have been associated with deep-seated magma chambers filled with hot lava that might have given rise to local volcanic activity, perhaps 1-2 million years ago. He recalled that the active volcanoes of Antarctica's Victoria Land, Mounts Erebus and Terror, lay on a north-south line formed by the Trans-Antarctic Mountains that mark the western edge of the Ross Sea, and speculated that the Penck Trough might be a down-faulted block like the Ross Sea, in which case it might be expected to be associated with similar volcanism to that in the Ross Sea area and even connected to it.

Magnetism

Leo Gburek, a student of geophysics at Leipzig, was responsible for measuring the Earth's magnetic field in the Antarctic [18,19]. Measurements like these were essential for establishing not only magnetic field intensity but also slow changes with time in the position of the Earth's south magnetic pole, a matter of considerable importance for mariners dependent on compasses for navigation.

MAGNETIC FIELD MEASUREMENTS

Gburek's equipment to determine the properties of the Earth's magnetic field from ice floes included a Schulze 542 magnetic travelling theodolite and two quartz horizontal magnetometers (QHM) No. 53 and 54. He planned to use one of the magnetometers to measure the variation in the azimuth direction of the magnetic field and to use the other to determine the declination and horizontal intensity of the field. On 3 February 1939, on a floe at 69°8.5'S and 14°41'E, 2nd officer Karl-Heinz Röbke and 3rd officer Hans Werner Viereck used the gimbal-mounted fluid compass from the bridge of the ship to determine a declination of 27 °W, while Gburek measured a declination of 25 °W with a Fuess hand compass. On 30 January 1939, on the solid and stable ice shelf at 70°17'S and 4°22'E, Gburek determined the magnetic declination to be 18.6°W and the horizontal intensity to be 0.1939 (Gauss). The declination value for this position given in the German nautical chart No. 1061 used on Schwabenland was 20.4°W, which differed by only 1.8° from his measurements, probably due to the constant movement of the magnetic pole. Gburek did not offer any explanation for the difference of about 6 degrees between the declination measurements on the ice floe and those on the ice shelf; perhaps the highly sensitive theodolite used on the ice shelf gave a more accurate measurement than the instruments used on the ice floe. During the observation period on the ice shelf there were no strong variations in the magnetic field - it had been a quiet day in respect to earth-magnetic activity. This implied that Gburek's measurements were typical for the area, and not disturbed by special magnetic effects derived from the solar wind and its associated magnetic storms, which can be detected as rapid variations in the Earth's magnetic field after solar flares. Confidence in the accuracy of the instrument came from calibration measurements made at the geophysical observatories in Wingst west of Hamburg, and Niemegk southeast of Berlin, before and after the expedition, and also at Cape Town during the return journey. Drawing on his experiences, Gburek recommended that future investigations of the Earth's magnetic field on expeditions like this one should use the gimbal-mounted hand compass along with Bidlingmaier's double compass to measure the horizontal intesnity of the magnetic field of the earth. The double compass had been constucted by Friedrich Bidlingmaier (1875 - 1914) from two compass roses fixed one above the other, on the basis of experiments he had carried out during the first German Antarctic Expedition (1901 - 1903). Gburek guaranteed that reliable results would be obtained by using both instruments even in unfavourable ice conditions (i.e. from wobbly ice floes).

Gburek's plan to make his magnetic measurements from nearby ice floes proved to be impracticable. When the weather conditions were good enough for him to have taken the motorboat to visit a suitable ice floe (one that was large and stable), they were also good for flying, so the motorboat had to stay close to *Schwabenland* for the safety of the air crew in case of accidents during take-offs and landings. This severely limited the possibilities for Gburek to perform magnetic measurements from a drifting ice floe, and in the end he was only able to make four excursions. The first two showed that the small floes within reach of the ship were so unstable that measurements with his travelling theodolite were impossible. So Gburek decided to leave the very sensitive instrument aboard *Schwabenland* and instead to use an ordinary gimbal-mounted fluid compass from the bridge of the ship to measure the declination of the magnetic field (see Box text). Preparation for a fourth measurement was interrupted by cloudiness and squally winds. Luckily Gburek was allowed to fly with Schirmacher on Boreas to investigate the shoreline of Neu-Schwabenland. They landed close to the shelf-ice edge on 30 January 1939, and disembarked. There, on the solid and stable ice shelf at 70°17'S and 4°22'E, Gburek was able to determine both the declination and intensity of the magnetic field (see Box text).

Unfortunately most of Gburek's geophysical data were destroyed by fire and explosive bombs, which devastated the Geophysical Institute in Leipzig during the Second World War. His surviving magnetic data were transferred to the German Hydrographical Institute in Hamburg, the successor of the German Maritime Institute, but it turned out that the material was not complete enough for further analysis. That is a pity, as magnetic measurements in the Southern Ocean and on the Antarctic Continent were still rare, and the results would have been useful not only for further scientific investigations, but also for the correction of magnetic information on nautical charts used for whaling and other purposes.

Glaciers, Ice Sheets And Ice Shelves

Herrmann connected the north-south trending glacier in the Penck Trough with a glacier tongue that protrudes beyond the edge of the ice shelf into the waters of the Southern Ocean on the Greenwich Meridian at 0° [20,21]. This massive glacier, now called the Jutulstraumen or Jutul's Stream, after a Norwiegan folk figure, is one of the largest in Antarctica. It's deepest parts are situated more than 1500 m below sea level close to the coast [22]. It flows through the lower part of the Penck Trough and out onto the Fimbol Ice Shelf, eventually forming the Trolltunga Ice Tongue. This pattern is typical of large valley glaciers that move much faster than the surrounding ice sheet, to form glacier tongues at the coast. Herrmann assumed correctly that this glacier system lay in a north-south down-faulted depression - in effect a fault-bounded graben [4,21]. He used similar reasoning to explain the origin of the glacier tongue at 15°E, assuming that the parental glacier (named the Musketova glacier in its upper reaches and the Entuziasty Outlet Glacier near the coast [21,23]) lay in a depression east of the uplifted block represented by the Wohlthat Massif. He went on to suggest that this underlying depression was connected in some way to a trough in the seabed at 8-9°E, which he had mapped from the Schwabenland's sonar data. However, one glance at the map suggests that this proposed connection is tenuous at best.

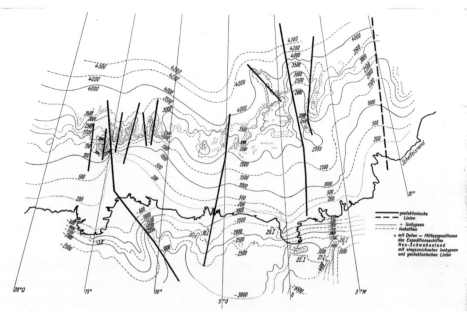

Map of mountain distribution with presumed north-south fracture zones showing Penck Trough in the west

Herrmann used studies in Greenland and earlier work on Antarctica to develop a cross section showing Antarctica as a thick ice sheet overlying a central rocky core depressed by the weight of the ice and bounded by mountain ranges. This was a reasonable guess at the time, since nothing was then known of the thickness of the ice sheet in the interior, which we now know to average 2000 m, to exceed 4000 m in places, and in some areas to extend below sea level. Radio echo-sounding profiles from aircraft operating across western Dronning Maud Land confirm the existence of a thick ice sheet penetrated by buried mountain chains, and show that the inland ice of the Polar Plateau is 2 km or more thick there [22]. Herrmann correctly envisaged the thick ice sheet as flowing away from its high core on all sides 'like hard dough', the mountains of Neu-Schwabenland acting as no more than small reefs that are washed around by the slowly moving ice mass [1]. In among the mountains he envisaged small glaciers arising in the same way that they do in the Alps and other mountain areas, before flowing down the flanks to feed into the ice streams pouring down from the polar plateau through broad gaps in the mountains, like the Penck Trough. En route the ice became distorted, forming fields of crevasses, and in places its path was marked by lines of rock fragments – the moraines. Except in the mountains, where steep slopes or winds prevent snow from settling, everything was covered in snow and ice. As Herrmann noted, that is because whereas in the Alps the snow line is at a height of 2800 m, in Antarctica it lies at sea level.

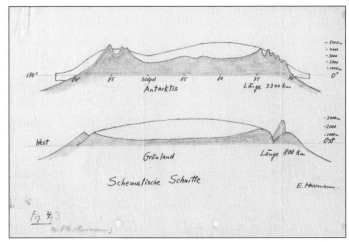

Herrmann's 1939 cross-section through the Greenland and Antarctic ice sheets

Herrmann clearly appreciated the fundamental differences between Antarctica and the Arctic – the one being a continent surrounded by sea, and the other a sea surrounded by continents – and what that meant for the climate. The Arctic water mass kept the Arctic relatively warm. In contrast, both the existence of a southern continent and its substantial height conspired to keep the south polar region much colder. Not surprisingly the flyers on long distance flight VII recorded an air temperature of −35°C over the polar plateau, on what was otherwise a warm summer's day at sealevel. The *Schwabenland* had departed for Hamburg by the time the austral winter arrived, but Herrmann knew that during the 24-hour mid-winter darkness on the Ross Ice Shelf Amundsen had recorded temperatures as low as -59°C, and Byrd as low as -62°C. Similar temperatures, reaching -65°C, had been recorded from the Greenland ice cap in winter. Herrmann was full of wonder at the 100°C difference across the sole of a boot between the blood and the ice at times like that [1]. We now know that temperatures on the polar plateau can fall as low as -89.2°C, which would make for a difference of 125°C between blood and ice.

All in all, Herrmann did not make as much as perhaps he might have done of the glaciological information in the aerial photographs – but then he was not a glaciologist, and neither was anyone else on board. Full-scale glaciological studies would be left to later research teams, starting with the Norwegian-British-Swedish Expedition (NBSX) of 1949-1952 to the westernmost part of Dronning Maud Land, and followed by the research teams of the International Geophysical Year of 1957-1958.

Antarctic Lakes - The Strange Case Of The Schirmacher Oasis

One of the most unusual features of the geographical discoveries was the Schirmacher Oasis, a long narrow strip of land covering about 34 square kilometres and centred on latitude 70° 45'S and longitude 11° 37'E. First to set foot there were the Russians and some East German scientists, in 1959 [24,25,26]. The lakes freeze in the winter but melt in the summer. They contain algae, which flourish in the summer warmth, but are surrounded by barren, dry and dusty rocky outcrops and moraines – there is almost no vegetation save lichens and mosses [25]. The oasis has been the subject of extensive scientific study, and Peter Bormann from German Geoforschungszentrum (Potsdam) and Dietrich Fritzsche glaciologist from the German Alfred Wegener Institute (Postdam) compiled a substantial book about it in 1995 [26].

The small brown rocky exposure with its blue lakes was first named Boreasische Seenplatte (Boreasic Lake District) after the aircraft that first flew over it, and later Schirmacher Seenplatte (Schirmacher Lake District) after the pilot. The term 'oasis' for Antarctic rock deserts was generally accepted after the discovery of major rocky areas with lakes further east along the coast in 1947 during Operation 'Highjump'.

View south across the dry exposed rocks of the Oasis to the downward thinning edge of the Polar Plateau in Summer 1978/79

Not being able to measure the properties of the air or the water in the oasis, Ritscher's expedition members puzzled over the possible origins of its ice-free freshwater lakes. Two schools of thought quickly developed. One, championed by those who had seen the lakes, called for a volcanic influence; the other, championed mostly by those who had not seen the lakes, rejected volcanic influence. Remembering the intellectual duels of the late 1700s between opposing experts regarding the origins of rocks in the Harz Mountains in the middle of Germany, Herrmann called those who favoured volcanic influence the 'plutonians' (after those who argued that the rocks of the Harz were magmatic intrusions – i.e. 'plutonic' rocks, named after Pluto, the Roman god of the underworld), and those who favoured non-volcanic influences the 'neptunians' (after those who argued that the rocks of the Harz were deposited from a watery solution – i.e. in the realm of Neptune, the Roman god of the sea) [1]. In the case of the oasis, the 'plutonians' pointed to lakes associated with hot springs in Iceland, and recalled that there were prominent volcanoes in Antarctica – notably Mount Erebus. The 'neptunians' took a different tack. Carefully examining the aerial photographs they identified next to the oasis all the characteristics one would expect to see at the snout of a melting glacier, except that in this case the glacier was an enormous ice sheet. But they were at as loss to explain why the ice sheet had chosen to melt where it did.

In the end the 'neptunians' were right. The oasis and the dry valleys of the Wohlthat Massif in the nearby mountains are both parts of an 'ablation zone', where evaporation exceeds precipitation [15,27]. Temperatures in the oasis average -0.6°C in January, but for 65 days between October and February temperatures hover around the freezing point. In response to these conditions, as the ice sheet approaches the oasis from the south it thins rapidly before ending abruptly in an ice cliff, much as a mountain glacier does on descending into a warm valley. On the ice sheet

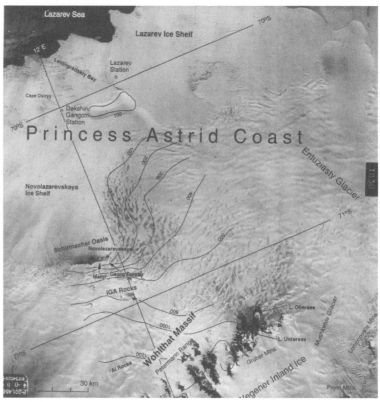

Satellite map of the Schirmacher Oasis and Wohlthat Massif and associated glaciers and ice sheet

side of the cliff, melt water erodes cracks and crevasses into much photographed ice caves and tunnels [23,24]. A melt-water tunnel up to 12 metres high and 5 metres wide runs along and under the front of the inland ice sheet on the south side of the oasis [28]. During summer the melting ice feeds the many small lakes dotting the exposed rocky surface of the oasis. To either side of the oasis the ice sheet flows inexorably towards the sea. The eastern and western ice flows curve round to meet each other in the Novolazarevskaya Ice Shelf on the seaward side of the oasis, isolating the oasis and its dry rocks from the ocean.

We now know that there are two kinds of lakes in the oasis. The southernmost ones, close to the melting edge of the ice sheet, are fed by melt-water streams emerging from beneath the ice, and occupy rocky glaciated valleys mostly with an ENE-WSW trend controlled by

140

the underlying tectonics. Drainage continues northward beyond them down the sloping surface of the exposed rock towards the coast, where water accumulates at the northern edge of the oasis in large so-called 'epishelf' lakes that sit on the floating ice shelf rather than on rock [5]. The work of the Indian Geological Survey on the Schirmacher Oasis [5] shows that its topography is characterised by glaciated valleys. This glaciated terrain is likely to be found everywhere beneath the ice.

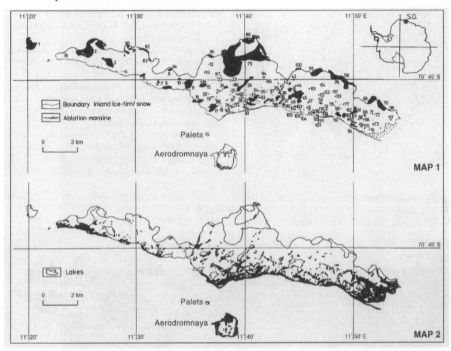

Schirmacher Oasis at 70° 45'S and 11° 37'E, showing distribution of lakes and areas of snow accumulation

Although not mentioned by Herrmann, the expedition also found small blue-ice lakes in the Wohlthat Massif, notably the Untersee and the Obersee, which are marked on the 1939 1:50,000 map of the Wohlthat Massif. These are glacial valley lakes dammed by glaciers that cross the valley mouth. They are up to 40 m deep and covered permanently with around 3 m of ice [28]. Lake Untersee is the largest surface freshwater lake in East Antarctica, at about 6.5 km long by 2.5 km wide, and its icy surface serves as a landing strip for aircraft.

In the far west of the German survey area, the glaciologists of the later NBSX expedition found a 1 km wide by 4 km long blue ice field south of Borg Mountain (at 72°32'S and 3°30'W). They explained this as old blue glacier ice exposed by strong winds and sublimation of the snow [29], and - based on that interpretation - suggested that perhaps the "lakes" described in the German expedition report [3] might also be exposed lower levels of the ice sheet. We were reminded of this suggestion in 2010 by Fred Roots, a member of the NBSX expedition [30]. However, in 1961, Walter Schytt - the NBSX glaciologist - noted that

Ice tunnels
under the edge
of the ice sheet
bounding the
south side of
the Schirmacher
Oasis

142

In a previous article ...... the author suggested that the "lakes" described in the German expedition report (Ritscher, 1942) might also be of the same nature as the ice fields - i.e. exposed lower levels of the ice sheet. This is probably not so. A further study of the German report and the accompanying pictures has convinced the author that at least the "Obsersee" and the "Untersee" ...... are real lakes [31].

References

1. Herrmann, E., 1941, Deutsche Forscher im Südpolarmeer. Safari Verlag, Berlin, 184 pp.

2. Herrmann, E., 1942, Die geographischen Arbeiten. In: Ritscher, A. (ed.), Deutsche Antarktische Expedition 1938/39. Wissenschaftliche und fliegerische Ergebnisse. Vol 1, Koehler and Amelang, Leipzig, 282-304.

3. Ritscher, A., 1942, Wissenschaftliche und fliegerische Ergebnisse der Deutschen Antarktischen Expedition 1938/39. Hrsg. im Auftrag der Deutschen Forschungsgemeinschaft. Koehler & Amelang, Leipzig. Vol 1: Text, 304 pp., Pictures and Maps 57 plates and 3 maps.

4. Spaeth, G., and Fielitz, W., 1987, Structural investigations in the Precambrian of western Neuschwabenland, Antarctica. Polarforschung, 57 (1-2), 71-92.

5. Geological Survey of India, 2006, Geomorphological Map of Schirmacher Oasis, Central Dronning Maud Land East Antarctica (1:25,000).

6. D'Souza, M.J., 2006, Geology of Orvinfjella, Central Dronning Maud Land, East Antarctica and its Evolutionary History, published with Geological Map of Orvinfjella, Central Dronning Maud Land, East Antarctica (1:150,000). Geological Survey of India. 10 pp.

7. Paech, H.-J., and Stackebrandt, W., 1995, Geology. In: Bormann, P., and Fritsche, D. (eds.), The Schirmacher Oasis, Queen Maud Land, East Antarctica, and its surroundings. Justus Perthes Verlag, Gotha, Petermanns Geographische Mitteilungen, Erganzungsheft Nr. 289, 59-170.

8. Tingey, R.J., (ed.), 1991, The Geology of Antarctica. Clarendon Press, Oxford. 680 pp.

9. Paech, H.-J. (ed.), 2005, International Geomaud Expedition of the BGR to Central Dronning Maud Land in 1995/96. Vol. II, Geophysical Results. Geologisches Jahrbuch B, Heft 97, Polar Issue No. 11. Bundesanstalt für Geowissenschaften und Rohstoffe, Hannover, 407 pp.

10. Engvik, A.K., and Elvevold, S., 2004, Pan-African extension and near-isothermal exhumation of a granulite facies terrain, Dronning Maud Land, Antarctica. Geological Magazine 141 (6), 649-660.

11. Jacobs, J., Bingen, B., Thomas, R.J., Bauer, W., Wingate, M.T.D., and Feito, P., 2008, Early Paleozoic orogenic collapse and voluminous late-tectonic magmatism in Dronning Maud Land and Mozambique: insights into the partially delaminated orogenic root of the East African-Antarctic orogen? Geological Society, London, Special Publication 308 (1), 69-90.

12. Baba, S., Owada, M., and Shiraishi, K., 2008, Contrasting metamorphic P-T path between Schirmacher Hills and Mühlig-Hofmannfjella, central Dronning Maud Land, East Antarctica. Geological Society, London, Special Publication 308 (1), 401-417.

13. Weber, K., and Jacobs, J, 2009, Two decades of geological mapping and research in Heimefrontfjella, Dronning Maud Land, Antarctica. Polarforschung 79 (1), 1-2.

14. Spaeth, G., 2009a, History of the geological research expeditions to the Heimefrontfjella (East Antarctica) and

chronology of the geological mapping programme. Polarforschung 79 (1), 3-10.

15. Bauer, W., 2009, Permian sedimentary cover, Heimefrontfjella, Dronning Maud Land (East Antarctica). Polarforschung 79 (1), 39-42.

16. Spaeth, G., and Schüll, P., 1987, A survey of Mesozoic dolerite dykes form western Neuschwabenland, Antarctica, and their geotectonic significance. Polarforschung 57 (1-2), 93-113.

17. Spaeth, G., 2009b, Mesozoic hypabyssic mafic intrusions and basalt flows in the Heimefrontfjella (East Antarctica). Polarforschung 79 (1), 43-45.

18. Gburek, L., 1939, Geophysikalischer Arbeitsbericht. In: Vorbericht über die Deutsche Antarktische Expedition 1938/39. Annalen der Hydrographie und Maritimen Meteorologie. VIII, Beiheft, 21-23.

19. Gburek, L., 1958. Erdmagnetische Messungen, Eisuntersuchungen, Strahlungsmessungen und Kernzählungen. In: A. Ritscher (ed.), Deutsche Antarktische Expedition 1938/39. Wissenschaftliche und fliegerische Ergebnisse, Vol 2. Helmut Striedieck (Geographisch-Kartographische Anstalt Mundus), Hamburg 97-100. (Reprint of Gburek 1939 plus an explanatory remark by the editor).

20. Herrmann, E., 1940, Zeitschrift für Erdkunde zu Berlin 8 (17/18), p. 431.

21. Herrmann, E., 1939, Die geographischen Arbeiten. Annalen der Hydrographie und Maritimen Meteorologie, VIII, Beiheft 23-26.

22. Sandhäger, H, and Blindow, N., 1997, Ice-sheet geometry in western Neuschwabenland, Antarctica. Polarforschung, 67(1-2), 77-86.

23. Hermichen, W.-D., 1995, The Continental Ice Cover in the Surroundings of the Schirmacher Oasis. In: Bormann, P., and Fritsche, D., (eds.), The Schirmacher Oasis, Queen Maud Land, East Antarctica, and its surroundings. Justus Perthes Verlag, Gotha, Petermanns Geographische Mitteilungen, Ergänzungsheft Nr. 289, 221-242.

24. Gernandt, H., 1984, Erlebnis Antarktis. (Adventure Antarctica). Transpress VEB Verlag für Verkehrswesen, Berlin. 284 pp.

25. Richter, W., 1995, Biology. In: Bormann, P., and Fritsche, D., (eds.), The Schirmacher Oasis, Queen Maud Land, East Antarctica, and its surroundings. Justus Perthes Verlag,Gotha, Petermanns Geographische Mitteilungen, Ergänzungsheft Nr. 289, 321-348.

26. Bormann, P. and Fritzsche (eds.), D., 1995, The Schirmacher Oasis, Queen Maud Land, East Antarctica, and its surroundings. Justus Perthes Verlag, Gotha, Petermanns Geographische Mitteilungen, Ergänzungsheft Nr. 289, 448 pp.

27. Richter, W., and Borman, P., 1995a, Weather and Climate. In: Bormann, P., and Fritzsche, D., (eds.), The Schirmacher Oasis, Queen Maud Land, East Antarctica, and its surroundings. Justus Perthes Verlag, Gotha, Petermanns Geographische Mitteilungen: Ergänzungsheft Nr. 289, 207-221.

28. Richter, W., and Borman, P., 1995b, Hydrology. In: Bormann, P., and Fritzsche, D., (eds.), The Schirmacher Oasis, Queen Maud Land, East Antarctica, and its surroundings. Justus Perthes Verlag, Gotha, Petermanns Geographische Mitteilungen: Erganzungsheft Nr. 289, 207-221.

29. Giæver, J., 1956, Station im Eis. VEB Hermann Haak, Geographisch-Kartographische Anstalt Gotha, 388 p.

30. Personal communication (e-mail) from Fred Roots (born 1922), geologist of the NBSX, on 23 February 2010.

31. Schytt, W., 1961, Blue ice fields, moraine features and glacier fluctuations. In Glaciology II. Norwegian-British-Swedish Antarctic Expedition, 1949-52. Scientific results, v.IVE, Norsk Polar Institute, Oslo Univ. Press, 183 -204.

Schwabenland

Table iceberg
with toy-like
Schwabenland in
front

Boreas (North Wind) on the catapult

1938 - Release
of a radio-
sonde from
Schwabenland

November,
2004 – Hartwig
Gernandt
launches a
helium-base
radiosonde
balloon from
the facilities at
Neumayer II
(To the left,
Henry Valentine
[S Africa]; to
the right, Colin
Summerhayes)

Boreas moored to the ice edge

An ice tunnel under the edge of the ice sheet bounding the south side of the Schirmacher Oasis

Expedition members on the return journey

Schwabenland run aground on a Norwegian beach close to Egersund, April 1944

(above) Alfred
Ritscher, aged
about 80

(left) Vignettes depicting the
first three German Antarctic
expeditions and Herrligkoffer's
planned 4th expedition for
decorative use on envelopes or
elsewhere

CHAPTER 11: THE SOUTH ATLANTIC SEABED

Fathoming the Mysteries of the Deep

As in the case of previous German Antarctic Expeditions, a conscious decision was taken that scientific data would be collected on *Schwabenland's* journey south to add to the global store of scientific knowledge, not just to the polar section. In the 1920s Germany had become the leader in the new technique of scientific echo-sounding, which built on advances in the use of sonar developed in the First World War. The German research vessel *Meteor* was the world's first to make scientific use of this technology, applying it on the German Atlantic Expedition of 1925-1927 to the South Atlantic. The result was the first detailed topographic map of the South Atlantic [1], a product that delighted geographers and provided physical oceanographers with the true shape of the basins in which the objects of their study swirled.

Schwabenland was equipped with two echo-sounders to enable it to make soundings at close spaced intervals while underway. The soundings had to be recorded manually, and were taken as close as 5 minutes apart where the topography changed rapidly. The process allowed a near continuous record of the shape of the seabed beneath the ship – a bathymetric profile – to be recorded along the ship's track. The accuracy of the profile depended primarily on two things: the depths along the track, which in turn depended on the scientist's knowledge of the velocity of sound in seawater (which was rather primitive in those days), and the position of the track, which in turn depended on how good the ship's navigators were at sun and star sights.

Given its Antarctic priorities, *Schwabenland* had no time to detour to follow up on the *Meteor's* results, but all being well it would provide novel supplementary echo-sounding data along its course that would help to improve the bathymetric maps of the South Atlantic produced from *Meteor's* data.

The only other ship undertaking scientific echo-sounding in the South Atlantic at that time was the British research ship *Discovery 11*, which did so from 1933-1939, mostly south of the latitude of Cape Town [2]. Byrd had used a sonic depth sounder in the Antarctic in December 1928 [3], but there it does not appear to have been used to derive profiles of seabed topography – more likely it was used as a safety measure when approaching land.

Given the novelty of the technology and the scarcity of observations in the South Atlantic and Southern Ocean, *Schwabenland's* echo-sounding profiles inevitably provided new and fascinating high-resolution views of the topography of the seabed in the South Atlantic. The echo-sounding profiles were discussed by Theodor Stocks of the Institute and Museum of Oceanography in Berlin in 1939 [4], and published at small scale by Herrmann in 1941 [5], but owing to the outbreak of war in 1939 the data were not fully published in fine detail and at large scale until 1958 [6], by Arnold Schumacher (1889-1967) from the Deutsches Hydrographisches Institut in Hamburg, as a German contribution to the results of the International Geophysical Year of 1957-1958.

The Mid-Ocean Ridge – a Linear Volcano

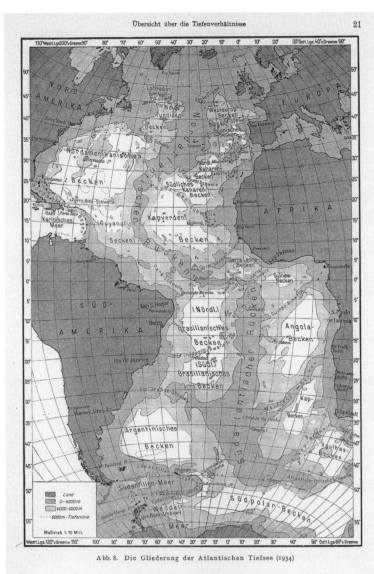

Abb. 8. Die Gliederung der Atlantischen Tiefsee (1934)

Atlantic bathymetry, based on data from the *Meteor* and other expeditions

Lead-line soundings from ships, including among others the global deep-sea expedition of *HMS Challenger* in 1872-1876 and the German Deep-Sea Expedition to the South Atlantic and Indian Oceans on the *Valdivia* in 1898-1899, had established the fact that in most of the oceans there was a broad central topographic rise that came to be known as the mid-ocean ridge. Based on these soundings, by 1912 the ridge had been defined crudely as far as 50°S in the South Atlantic [7]. In the Atlantic this ridge came to be known as the Mid-Atlantic Ridge, and was mapped in detail for the first time in the South Atlantic by the *Meteor* [8]. The *Schwabenland's* geographer, Herrmann, who was in charge of the echo-sounding programme, knew as much as anyone could at that time about the nature of this major

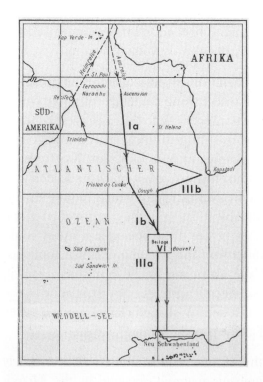

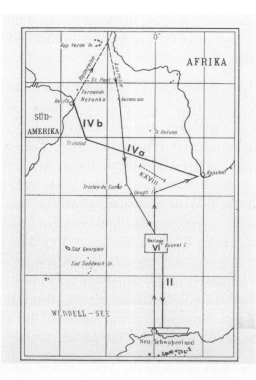

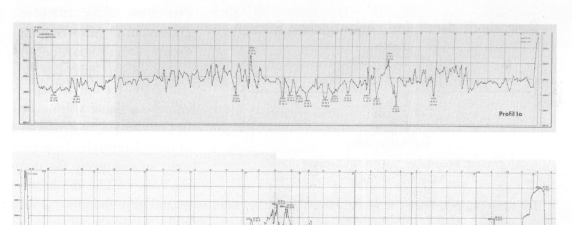

(from top) Location map of echo-sounding profiles Ia and IIIa; Location map of echo-sounding profiles II and IVa; profile 1a The first echo-sounding line down the Mid-Atlantic Ridge in the South Atlantic, from Ascension (at right) to Tristan da Cunha (at left); profile IVa SE to NW cross-section of the Mid-Atlantic Ridge (from Cape Basin at right, over the Walvis Ridge (at right) and mid-ocean ridge (centre), to the island of Trinidade off Brazil – at left)

topographic feature, not least that its southward prolongation ended at Bouvet, which he referred to as the last buttress of this undersea range [5], beyond which was a deep ocean basin.

The *Schwabenland's* sounding lines added two significant pieces of information about the ridge. One was the first ever echo-sounding transect along the length of a mid-ocean ridge anywhere in the world; this was a north-south transect close to the ridge crest between Ascension and Tristan da Cunha. The transect shows the extremely rugged topography typical of the Mid-Atlantic Ridge, which today is known to be a long high N-S trending feature cut at intervals of about 50 km by E-W trending fracture zones, many associated with narrow E-W deeps that are clearly visible cutting the N-S profile. It would require the far higher density of echo-soundings that became available in later decades, and seabed shape interpreted from gravity data collected by satellites, before these fine-scale features could be mapped with any accuracy. Secondly, *Schwabenland* also added a diagonal southeast to northwest profile across the ridge, between Cape Town and Recife in northeast Brazil, which complemented the set of east-west profiles collected across the South Atlantic by the *Meteor*. Prominent in the middle of this profile is a deep V-shaped cleft, a median valley also seen on several of the *Meteor* profiles, and as deep as the Grand Canyon.

The association of the Mid-Atlantic Ridge with volcanic islands, along with its crudely triangular cross-section and some samples of volcanic material obtained by the *Meteor* expedition of the 1920s led Herrmann - who was an expert on the geology of volcanoes - to speculate that the ridge was in effect an enormous linear volcano fed by lava rising through a fissure of some kind and debouching onto an essentially flat deep sea-floor [5]. The implication

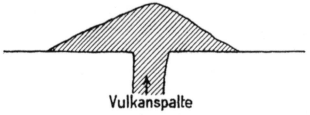

Querschnitt durch den Atlantischen Rücken

Vulkanspalte

Herrmann's model of the volcanic origin of the Mid-Atlantic Ridge

is that the youngest rocks were deposited atop the older ones and were therefore closest to the surface, as in any typical volcano. This would appear to be the first mention in the literature that the ridge was a continuous volcanic structure. The notion that the ridge had something to do with volcanism had been put forward a few years earlier by Hans Cloos, professor of geology at the University of Bonn, who had proposed in 1936 that the mid Atlantic Ridge was a gigantic graben system like those forming the Rhine Graben in Europe or the East African Rift Valley - in effect a broad and massive swell with a collapsed central rift, an example of which is visible in Iceland where the ridge protrudes above the ocean surface [9]. Cloos had observed that the Atlantic ridge system was characterised, like the other two rift systems, by being studded with volcanoes of Atlantic type. Despite the

148

evident differences between the Herrmann and Cloos models for the ridge, Herrmann did call on Cloos's conjecture to support his own idea when it was written up in more elaborate form in 1943, including a more detailed picture of the Mid-Atlantic ridge, though this work was not published until 1948 [10].

In the absence of abundant rock samples or detailed geophysical information from the ridge neither Herrmann nor Cloos could be proved right. The major oceanography text of the era, published in 1942 by Sverdrup, Johnson, and Fleming [11], and the major marine geology textbook, published in 1948 by Francis Shepard [12], show that at the time nothing was known about the geology of the mid-ocean ridge, although by 1948 geophysical data indicated that the ocean floor was underlain by basalt [12,13]. Indeed, the great American geophysicist, Maurice Ewing, pointed out in National Geographic Magazine in 1948, that the Mid-Atlantic Ridge was 'a Jules Verne world under the sea – one of the last great challenging frontiers of geography' [13].

Ewing was the first to confirm from rock samples that the Mid-Atlantic Ridge was at least partly volcanic. Like Shepard, he seems to have been unaware of Herrmann's ideas, and indeed of the *Schwabenland* expedition. Ewing had noticed that most Atlantic earthquakes occur along the ridge crest, where the topography seemed to be most rugged; there he surmised that the crust of the Earth was being deformed and broken, while the surrounding ocean basins remained undisturbed. On 16 July 1947, he set sail from Woods Hole on the *Atlantis* to probe the secrets of the mid-ocean ridge in the North Atlantic for the first time with deep-sea cameras, robust deep-sea rock dredges, and coring tubes. He reported that the steep slopes and a deep trench running down the axis suggested a fault scarp and rift valley [13]. His coring tube recovered olivine gabbro and his dredge hauled to the surface anorthosite gabbro, serpentine, and pillow basalts. The pillow basalts were formed by lava spewing onto the seabed in volcanic eruptions, while the gabbro represented the deep-seated magma chambers from which the lavas had come, and the serpentine was a product of the alteration of such rocks.

Later, during the 1950s, measurements of the gravity, heat flow, magnetic properties, and geology of the Mid-Atlantic Ridge, especially in the North Atlantic, confirmed its volcanic character [14,15]. By 1960 scientists realised that the Mid-Atlantic Ridge was part of a 75,000 km long world encircling mid-ocean ridge system [16]. But was it the kind of super-giant volcanic structure implied by Herrmann's sketch? Or was it closer to the model of Cloos – a giant swell topped by a rift?

The mechanism Herrmann proposed – volcanic lavas pouring out onto a deep sea floor and building up to form a ridge - is what builds volcanic island chains, like the Hawaiian chain in the Pacific. But it is not what built the Mid-Atlantic Ridge. In 1962, Harry Hess, professor of geology at Princeton University, proposed that mid ocean ridges arose through a process that came to be known as sea-floor spreading, which is a key component of the theory of plate tectonics, the driving force for continental drift [17,18,19]. According to the theory, the Earth's crust consists of a set of thin rigid plates that ride on a hot fluid sub-crust, the Earth's mantle, in which convection takes place to dissipate heat from the Earth's core. The plates are moved around by this convection in such a way that in some places the edge of one plate will sink beneath another in a process known as subduction, while in other places two plates will move apart from another potentially creating a gap. The creation of that gap and the process by which it is filled constitutes sea-floor spreading. In the Atlantic, the spreading taking place along a crack (the plate boundary) beneath the crest of the Mid-Atlantic Ridge. The rigid sea-floor forming part of the European and African Plates on the east side of the ridge is moving away from the rigid sea-floor forming part of the North and South American Plates on the west side of the ridge, at about the rate a fingernail grows. As the plates move apart, long linear fissures begin to appear through which lava rises to the surface to form small volcanic cones. The lava in the fissures then cools and solidifies to form basalt dykes. A new set of cracks then forms and the process repeats itself. In the process the earlier dykes are split longitudinally and moved off to either side. Thus the newest rocks are always found along the line of the plate boundary, while progressively older ones are found as one moves away to east and west. The younger, hotter rocks along the plate boundary rise high, forming the crest of the Mid-Atlantic Ridge. The older rocks that have been moved off to either side become cooler and denser, and so sink to form the ridge flanks. Eventually they sink to the average depth of the ocean basin, which is floored by the oldest rocks that have been moved furthest to east and west away from the ridge crest by the continuous sea-floor spreading process. Thus instead of the young rocks being at the surface of the pile and the old rocks at the bottom of the pile, as in Herrmann's model, the young rocks lie along the crest of the ridge, and the old ones down the flank; the gradient in age is horizontal, not (as in a single volcano) vertical. And instead of the ridge being made mostly of volcanic lavas extruded onto the seabed, as in Herrmann's model, much of it is made of magma that congealed in vertical fissures (dykes) or was extruded horizontally into the crust (as sills).

Considering that Herrmann lacked the benefit of advanced geophysical tools or even dredge hauls of rock, he could be said to have made an insightful guess and got it partly right. Unfortunately, because his hypothesis about the possible volcanic origin for the ridge was first published only in a German travel book and at the outbreak of war, when international scientific communication broke down, it was completely overlooked by the wider scientific community, and is not referred to in the international scientific literature [15,16]. By the time Herrmann's second paper on this topic appeared in1948, Ewing had already sampled the ridge and proved its volcanic character. If Herrmann's paper had been published when written, in 1943, and there had been no war, he might have got the credit for proposing the volcanic character of the ridge.

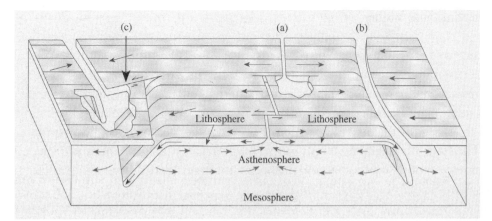

Simplistic sketch map of the mechanisms of sea-floor spreading and plate tectonics; arrows on the crust represent relative motions between pairs of plates; arrows in the asthenosphere represent complementary flow in the mantle. Mid-ocean ridges form where the crust moves apart, as in the centre of the diagram; (a) = sea-floor spreading; (b) = subduction zone where plates descend; (c) = transform fault or fracture zone

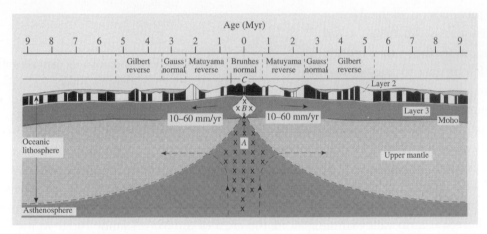

Sea-floor spreading. Magma (**XXX**) rises at A into magma chamber B, which cools to form oceanic crust (Layer 3). Pillow lavas and dykes extruded at C together form layer 2. The rocks at C take on the polarity of the Earth's magnetic field (N or S directed) as they cool. Sea-floor spreading pulls the crust apart at C (leading to formation of a median rift valley), separating rocks of the same polarity and age. As the Earth's magnetic polarity flips from time to time, the moving seafloor takes on the form of a tape that records these reversals through time. Youngest rocks are closest to the ridge crest; oldest ones are furthest from it. Sediments deposited on top (thin grey layer) of the moving crust are thinnest at the ridge crest. Further away from the crest they thicken as young sediments are deposited on older ones deposited originally near the ridge crest

151

The Median Rift Valley

The process of sea-floor spreading is not just volcanic. Tectonic processes are also at work. As the crust pulls apart in the sea-floor spreading process, and as the mid-ocean ridge slowly rises, some of the stress is relieved by faulting that commonly in the Atlantic creates a steep-sided, fault-bounded, median rift valley, or graben, along the ridge crest . It is in this graben that most of the active volcanic processes associated with sea-floor spreading take place. The floor of the graben is commonly littered with small volcanoes and sheet flows of lava in the form of pillow basalts, and harbours hot water (hydrothermal) vents that support strange communities of deep-sea animals.

This valley was first visible to the scientific world on the echo-sounding profiles made across the Mid-Atlantic Ridge by the *Meteor* in 1925-1927 and the *Schwabenland* in 1939. However, because the valley does not occur on all the *Meteor* profiles across the ridge, it did not occur to those interpreting the *Meteor* data to suggest that the ridge was characterised by

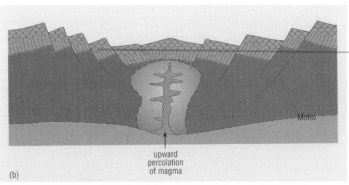

Simplistic sketch map of the formation of a median rift valley at the crest of the Mid-ocean Ridge

a continuous median valley, nor that the valley was a fault-bounded graben. That there were parallel ridges and valleys running along the crest of the mid-ocean ridge was first identified for the North Atlantic by Dietrich in 1939 based on the results of the German North Atlantic Expedition of the *Meteor* in 1938 [20a and b]. Dietrich connected ridges and troughs on adjacent echo-sounding profiles across the ridge to suggest that the axis of the ridge comprised a set of parallel folds. But he did not specifically point out a median valley. That there was a rift valley running along the crest of the Mid-Atlantic Ridge in the North Atlantic (as had been implied by Cloos in 1936 based on an offshore projection of the rift valley in Iceland [9]) was first proposed by Ewing in 1948 [13] and confirmed not long after by the British marine geophysicist Maurice Neville Hill as a result of investigations in 1953[21,22].

Re-analysing the *Schwabenland* and *Meteor* profiles in 1958 in the light of the British and American discoveries, Schumacher proposed that the deep valley seen on the German echo-sounding profiles at the crest of the Mid-Atlantic Ridge in the South Atlantic was also a median (rift) valley of the kind discovered in the north [6]. Ewing and one of his students, geologist Bruce Heezen, had seen this median valley on the *Meteor* profiles and elsewhere on the world-encircling mid-ocean ridge, and named it a 'rift valley', thinking of it as a more or less continuous feature of a more or less continuous ridge [16]. Schumacher's proposal that the cleft in the South Atlantic was a median (rift) valley appeared too late to be used by Ewing and his student Heezen in the late 50s and early 60s in their papers on the character of the mid-ocean ridge, and his work is effectively ignored in the international literature.

Not everyone agreed with the concept that the valley was continuous, notably Shepard [15], who recalled that while some of the *Meteor* profiles in the South Atlantic showed the rift valley, others did not. We now know that profiles across a mid-ocean ridge may not show a median valley, even where one exists, because the ridge is cut into segments by transverse faults (fracture zones) in which local uplift may obscure or block the median valley. An east-west echo-sounding profile at such a spot would miss seeing the valley that stretched away along the ridge crest to north and south.

Herrmann's Line

Herrmann wondered if there might be some tectonic and volcanic connection between the active volcanoes of the Ross Sea (Mounts Erebus and Terror) and the north-south structures of Neu-Schwabenland [5,10]. But he was not content to stop at the edges of the continent. Having surmised that the mid-Atlantic ridge was volcanic in origin, Herrmann wondered if his presumed Antarctic volcanic connection might continue north from Neu-Schwabenland up the axis of the Mid-Atlantic Ridge, connecting the volcanoes of Bouvet, Gough, Tristan, Ascension, the Cape Verdes, the Azores, Iceland and Jan Mayen. Similarly, working north from the Ross Sea, he

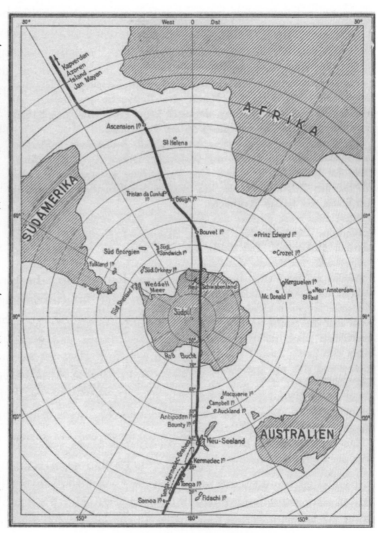

Herrmann's volcanic line

153

thought he could detect a volcanic line extending from Mount Erebus to Samoa, and passing through the volcanoes of New Zealand, and of the Kermadec and Tonga Islands. He was convinced he had discovered a major crack in the Earth's crust. Where the crack cut into magma chambers, volcanoes spawned, he surmised.

In some ways Herrmann was right. Most of his tectono-volcanic line in the Atlantic was a real tectono-volcanic line - the divergent or constructive plate boundary running along the mid Atlantic Ridge, and most of his line in the Pacific was another such line – this one the convergent or destructive boundary between the Pacific and Australian plates (a subduction zone). Unfortunately for his theory, firstly there is no geological connection between Bouvet and Neu-Schwabenland, just a very deep, flat-bottomed ocean basin interrupted near the Antarctic coast by the Maud Bank; secondly, there is no volcanic lineament running across the centre of Antarctica from Mount Erebus to Neu-Schwabenland - instead it runs from Erebus through the length of West Antarctica then north into the Antarctic Peninsula and the South Shetland Islands, where we find the active volcano of Deception Island, then out through the Scotia Arc and finally up into the Andes; and thirdly there is no simple geological connection linking the volcanoes of Erebus, Antipodes, New Zealand's North Island, Kermadec, Tonga and Samoa, although some of these are indeed connected along the line where the Pacific Plate dives beneath the overlying Australian Plate. Samoa is part of a different structure, being one of the WNW-ESE trending mid-plate volcanic lineaments typical of the Pacific Plate. The continuity of the volcanic line turns out to be mostly speculation based on a very few data points and projected into a region with no data at all – namely the Antarctic interior.

New Banks and Seamounts

En route from the ice edge to Cape Town along the Greenwich Meridian (Profile IIIb), *Schwabenland* discovered a hitherto unknown shallow bank at 45° 58'S 00° 11'E, with a depth of 1575 m. It now bears the name Schwabenland Seamount, in honour of its discoverers. They had wanted to name it Behm Bank after the German inventor of scientific echo-sounding, but that name was later given to another Antarctic bank, near the southern end of the Weddell Sea. Schwabenland Seamount is part of a small group of seamounts. Its main partner is Herdman Seamount, at 45° 20'S 00° 30'E, discovered by *Discovery 11* and named for the ship's Chief Scientist Henry Herdman.

Not far away, at around 41° 58'S on the Greenwich Meridian, *Schwabenland* also crossed another significant seamount, which they named Discovery Bank, knowing that the bank had been crossed by *Discovery 11* in May 1936. Herdman subsequently mapped Discovery Bank from various sounding lines made across it by *Discovery 11*, and showed it to be an E - W trending feature at least 150 km long [2]. It is now known to be part of a large ENE

-WSW trending chain of submarine volcanoes that was named Discovery Tablemount in 1963, and renamed the Discovery Seamounts in 1993, according to the Gazetteer of the General Bathymetric Chart of the Oceans (GEBCO)[24]. It no longer carries the name Discovery Bank, which is now given to a shallow volcanic bank in the Scotia Sea. The Discovery Seamounts are younger than the sea floor on which they sit, and so are thought perhaps to be the volcanic outpourings from an underlying hotspot in the Earth's crust [23].

It seems odd that the report of the German naming of Discovery Bank appeared in the published text of George Deacon's address to the Royal Geographical Society on 9 January 1939 on the subject of the investigations of *Discovery 11*[25], because at that time the *Schwabenland* had not begun its return journey and so had not yet crossed the bank. The solution to this conundrum must lie in editorial changes to the manuscript of Deacon's talk made before it was published in (late) March 1939, by which time *Schwabenland* had crossed the bank (on 1 March). Evidently news of the intent to name the bank Discovery Bank had reached Deacon shortly after *Schwabenland* had crossed this feature. By the time the *Discovery 11* soundings were published in 1948 [2], the term Discovery Bank was in common use.

Quite by coincidence, *Discovery 11* almost met *Schwabenland*, in January 1939. *Discovery 11* left Cape Town on 6 January, and stopped at Bouvet on 17 January, where they managed to make a landing – a feat which had until then been rarely been accomplished [26]. They then continued south, reaching the edge of the pack ice at the edge of the Antarctic continental slope at 69° 35'S 02° 05'E on 22 January. On that day, *Schwabenland* was hove to at around 68° 40'S 00° 40'W. So the two ships were within 150 km of one another, neither knowing of the other's presence. *Discovery 11* then turned west. Had it turned east, instead, the two ships might well have met.

The two ships almost met again, on 23 February. Having returned to Cape Town from the ice edge, *Discovery 11* then left again on 15 February, once more heading south along the Greenwich Meridian, but this time fractionally to the east. By then *Schwabenland* was heading north along the Greenwich Meridian, and had just left Bouvet, where it had stopped on 14 February, though not to land. The two ships must have passed within a few sea miles of one another near 48° 30'S, at around 0400 on 23 February, one heading north, the other south. *Schwabenland* was closer to the Greenwich Meridian, at 00° 03'W, while *Discovery II* was at 01° 00'E. From March 3 to March 5 *Discovery II* surveyed the ice edge and sounded the seabed in the *Schwabenland's* work area between the Greenwich Meridian and 5°E, and between 69° 45'S and 70° 10'S, not realising at the time that this was where the Germans had been already.

Submarine Valleys, Canyons and Abyssal Plains

The detailed survey carried out by *Schwabenland* close to the ice margin revealed a sea floor of broad ridges and valleys extending out to sea. The valleys are likely to be submarine channels carved by glaciers when sea level was low during the last glacial maximum 20,000 years ago. They may now act as the upper reaches of submarine canyons funnelling glacial sediment down the continental slope and onto the adjacent abyssal plain. One such canyon, just to the east of the survey area at 66° 35'S 18°E, has subsequently been named Schwabenland Canyon, in honour of the expedition ship. Another, slightly further to the east at 33°E, has been named Ritscher Canyon in honour of the leader of the expedition. Based on a recommendation made by Colin Summerhayes in June 2010 the International Hydrographic Office agreed to name two further submarine canyons around Antarctica after members of the expedition: Herrmann Canyon, (69° 48.6'S, 2° 06.90'E), in honor of the man who was in charge of the ship's echo - sounding programme and Kraul Canyon, (69° 43.0'S, 2° 30.0'E) in honour of the ship's ice pilot.

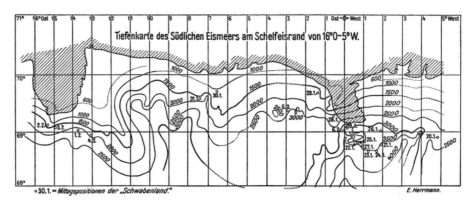

Schwabenland's bathymetric map showing troughs and ridges

In some places the floors of the deep ocean basis are covered by flat plains known as abyssal plains. The *Schwabenland* was one of the first research vessels to recover an echo-sounding profile across an abyssal plain, though at the time they did not realise that. Echo-sounding Profiles II and IIIa both cross the deep Atlantic-Indian Antarctic Basin between Bouvet and the Maud Rise, and show it to have an almost flat bottom at a depth of around 5400 m. Given that this is the largest expanse of flat seabed on any of the *Schwabenland's* profiles it is somewhat surprising that Herrmann did not speculate about its origin. Perhaps this reflects his well-known interest in mountains and volcanoes rather than the realm of sediments. Abyssal plains were first noted on echo-sounders during Ewing's 1947 mid-Atlantic ridge expedition to the North Atlantic and during the 1948 Swedish deep-sea expedition to the Indian Ocean [27]. They owe their origin to the supply of abundant sediment from the nearby land. The sediment is transported down the continental slope

156

in turbidity currents that flow down submarine canyons and then through channels that meander across the plains. From time to time the currents flood beyond their channels, depositing mud in sheets across the seabed. The implication is that regardless of its cover by a thick mantle of ice, Antarctica nevertheless manages to be a significant source of sediment, which is brought to the coast by glaciers rather than rivers, and thence makes its way to the deep sea both through submarine canyons and by deposition from melting icebergs. Examination of the GEBCO chart of the region shows that the abyssal plain crossed by the *Schwabenland* appears to be the eastern end of the Weddell Abyssal Plain. Between Bouvet and Maud Rise this plain begins to show signs of abyssal hills. We interpret these data to suggest that the Weddell Abyssal Plain is fed from the west, where its turbidity current deposits (known as turbidites) have buried the abyssal hill topography of the basin floor, and that the turbidites thin to the east, where burial of the hills is therefore not yet complete, not least because Maud Rise blocks the supply of sediment from the south that might otherwise have buried them. Given that so little was known about the deep sea floor at the time, and that abyssal plains had not yet been recognised by the reigning experts [27], Herrmann can perhaps be forgiven for not having made more of his interpretive skills on this occasion.

The Significance of Schwabenland's Echo-Soundings

Like those of the *Meteor* before it, the *Schwabenland's* echo-soundings made significant contributions to refining subsequent bathymetric maps of the South Atlantic. Even so, it would be many more years before the geological significance of many of the features there was recognised, not least because in the late 1930s little was known about the processes shaping the deep sea-floor [11,12]. *Schwabenland* contributed one piece of a picture that was completed over the years, enabling the topography of the deep sea floor to gradually emerge over time, as through a fog. Herrmann's main, though overlooked, contribution to geological understanding of the deep sea floor was his interpretation of the Mid-Atlantic Ridge as a gigantic linear volcanic construction [5]. Almost twenty years later Schumacher [6] was able to recognise that both *Schwabenland* and *Meteor* had discovered in the South Atlantic what was probably a more or less continuous median valley along the Mid-Atlantic Ridge crest like that found previously in the North Atlantic, yet the geological interpretation of that feature was left to the British and the Americans [13,21,22]. The discovery of isolated seamounts – banks, as they were then known – does not appear to have inspired the German scientists to feats of geological interpretation; these banks are now known to be submarine volcanoes. Nor did the discovery of channels around Antarctica inspire speculation about their probable causes. Today these features are recognised to be pathways that carry glacial debris from the ice sheets to the deep sea to end up on almost flat abyssal plains.

157

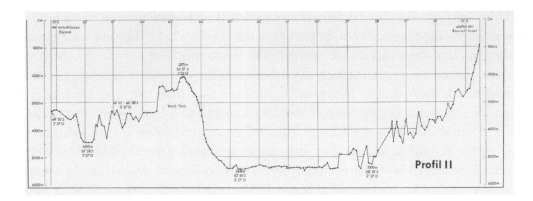

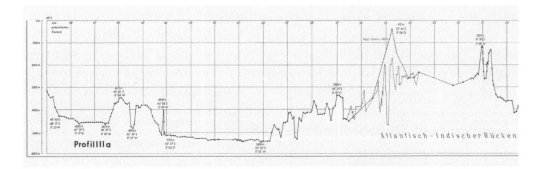

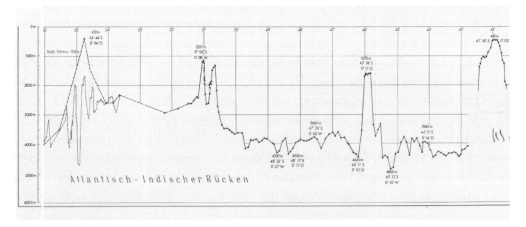

(from top) Echo-sounding profile II across the deep Atlantic-Indian Antarctic Basin and its abyssal plain, between the Atlantic-Indian Ridge (at right) and the Maud Rise (at left), ending near the Antarctic coastal ice shelf; Echo-sounding profile IIIa from the Atlantic-Indian Ridge near Bouvet (54°S) to Antarctica across the nearly flat Abyssal Plain; Echo-sounding profile IIIb from Alantic-Indian Ridge near Bouvet (54°S) across Schwabenland Seamount (near 46°S) and Discovery Bank (42°S)

158

This tale reinforces the observation that in science the meaning of measurements made with new technologies is not always clear in the early stages, when there is no hypothesis to explain them. When exploring remote and unknown regions, like Antarctica or the deep ocean floor, the data often arrive before the explanation – as in this case. It was the picture of the shape of the ocean floor built up through a multitude of ocean expeditions like this one that eventually stimulated Ewing, with new technologies forged in the furnace of the Second World War, to take the samples in 1948 that would show what the mid ocean ridge was made of, which in turn led to Hess's explanation in 1962 of how the ridge was formed. Similarly, it was the gradual realisation that there were abyssal plains all over the deep ocean basins, starting in 1947 (although we now know they were earlier found on this expedition), which led to their explanation as repositories of sediment supplied by submarine canyons [15,27]. *Schwabenland's* sounders were ahead of their time.

The sounders were ahead of their time in one other respect too. Herbert Bruns, the electrical engineer from Atlas Werke, experimented around Bouvet with a horizontal echo-sounder, presumably (though this is not recorded) as a means of detecting any rising seabed ahead of the vessel [28]. This would constitute the first example of the use of side-scanning sonar, a technique in widespread use today to map the seabed to either side of a research vessel. The earliest use of a horizontal sonar seems to be that of Fessenden, in the USA, around 1915 or so. Following the sinking of the *Titanic* [29], he used a sonar deployed from a lifeboat davit to demonstrate echoes from icebergs at some miles' range - certainly a 'horizontal' approach, though nothing to do with the seabed.

References

1. Maurer, H., and Stocks, T., 1933, Wissenschaftliche Ergebnisse der Deutschen Atlantischen Expedition auf dem Forschungs- und Vermessungsschiff "Meteor" 1925 - 1927. Vol. 2, Die Echolotungen des "Meteor". de Gruyter, Berlin, 309 pp.

2. Herdman, H.F.P., 1948, Soundings taken during the Discovery Investigations, 1932-39. Discovery Reports. Cambridge University Press, 39-106.

3. Rose, L. A., 2008, Explorer - the Life of Richard E. Byrd. University of Missouri Press, Columbia. 568 pp.

4. Stocks, T., 1939, Lotarbeiten der "Schwabenland" Dezember 1938 bis April 1939. In: Vorbericht über die Deutsche Antarktische Expedition 1938/39. Annalen der Hydrographie und Maritimen Meteorologie, VIII, Beiheft, 36-40.

5. Herrmann, E., 1941, Deutsche Forscher im Südpolarmeer. Safari Verlag, Berlin, 184 pp.

6. Schumacher, A., 1958, Die Lotungen der "Schwabenland". In: A. Ritscher (ed.), Deutsche Antarktische Expedition 1938/39: Wissenschaftliche und fliegrerische Ergebnisse, Vol. 2. Helmut Striedieck (Geographisch-Kartographische Anstalt Mundus), Hamburg, 41-62.

7. Murray, J. and Hjort, J., 1912, The Depths of the ocean: a general account of the modern science of oceanography based largely on the scientific researchers of the Norwegian steamer Micjeal Sars in the North Atlantic. Macmillan, London, 821 pp.

8. Stocks, T., and Wüst, G., 1935, Die Tiefenverhältnisse des offenen Atlantischen Ozeans. *Deutsche Atlantischen Exped. Meteor, 1925-1927*, Wiss. Erg., Bd. 3, Teil 1, l., Lief., 31 pp.

9. Cloos, H., 1936, Einführung in die Geologie. Gebr. Borntraeger, Berlin, XII, 503 pp.

10. Herrmann, E., 1948, Tektonik und Vulkanismus in der Antarktis und den Benachbarten Meersteilen. Petermanns Geographischen Mitteilungen, 1. Quartalsheft, 1-11 (note – manuscript submitted April 1943).

11. Sverdrup, H.U., Johnson, M.W., and Fleming, R.H., 1942, The Oceans, Their Physics, Chemistry and General Biology. Prentice-Hall, Englewood Cliffs, N.J., 1087 pp.

12. Shepard, F.P., 1948, Submarine Geology. 1st ed., Harper and Row, New York, 338 pp.

13. Ewing, M., 1948, Exploring the mid Atlantic ridge. National Geographic Magazine, 94 (3), 275-294.

14. Hill, M.N., 1963, The sea: Ideas and observations on progress in the study of the seas - Vol. 3. The Earth Beneath the Sea. Interscience, New York, London, 963 pp.

15. Shepard, F.P., 1963, Submarine Geology. 2nd ed., Harper and Row, New York, 557 pp.

16. Heezen, B.C., 1960, The rift in the ocean floor. Scientific American, October, 98-114.

17. Hess, H., 1962, History of ocean basins. In: A.E.J. Engel et al. (ed.): A Volume in Honour of A.F. Buddington. Geological Society of America, New York, 599–620 also Holmes, A., 1928, Trans. Geol. Soc. Glasgow 18 (3), 559-605

18. Whitmarsh, R.B., Bull, J.M., Rothwell, R.G., and Thomson, J., 1996. The evolution and structure of ocean basins. In Summerhayes, C.P., and Thorpe, S.A., (eds.), Oceanography: an illustrated guide. Manson Publishing, London, 113-135.

19. Open University, 1998, The ocean basins: their structure and evolution. 2nd edition. Open University, Milton Keynes, p. 73.

20a. Dietrich, G., 1939, Einige morphologische Ergebnisse der "Meteor"-Fahrt Januar bis Mai 1938. Bericht uber die 2. Teilfahrt der Deutschen Nordatlantischen Expedition des F.-V.-S.-"Meteor". Beiheft z. Jan.-Heft, Ann. Hydrogr. u. marit. Meteorol. 67, 20 (22)

20b Dietrich, G., 1939 (English translation of 20a), Some morphological results of the cruise of the "Meteor", January to May 1938. Int. Hydrographic Rev., 52-55

21. Hill, M.N., 1956, Notes on the bathymetric chart of the N.E. Atlantic. Deep-Sea Research 3, 229-231.

22. Hill, M.N., 1960, A median valley of the Mid-Atlantic Ridge. Deep-Sea Research. 6 (3) 193-205.

23. Thomson, G., Humphris, S., and Schilling, J.-G., 1983, Petrology and Geochemistry of basaltic rocks from Rio Grande Rise, South Atlantic: Deep Sea Drilling Project Leg 72, Hole 516F. Reports of the DSDP, Washington DC, doi:10.2973/dsdp. proc. 72.115.1983.

24. GEBCO, 2003, South Atlantic sheets. General Bathymetric Chart of the Oceans Digital Atlas, 3rd release, British Oceanographic Data Centre (BODC), Liverpool http://www.bodc.ac.uk/projects/international/gebco

25. Deacon, G.E.R., 1939, The Antarctic voyages of R.R.S. Discovery II and R.R.S. William Scoresby, 1935-37. The Geographical Journal 93 (3), 185-209.

26. Mackintosh, N.A., 1941, The fifth commission of the R.R.S. Discovery II. The Geographical Journal 97 (4), 201-216.

27. Heezen, B.C., and Laughton, A.S., 1963, Abyssal Plains. In: The Sea. Vol. 3, John Wiley, Chichester, 312-364.

28. Hallstein, 1952, Bekanntmachung über die Bestätigung der bei der Entdeckung von "Neu-Schwabenland" im Atlantischen Sektor der Antarktis durch die Deutsche Antarktische Expedition 1938/39 erfolgten Benennungen geographischer Begriffe. Bundesanzeiger 4 (149), 5 August 1952, 1-2.

29. Schlee, S, 1973, The Edge of an Unfamiliar World: A History of Oceanography. E.P. Dutton and Co., 398 pp.

CHAPTER 12: WEATHER, CLIMATE AND ATMOSPHERIC COMPOSITION

The Meteorological Measurement Programme

Following the tradition of previous German Antarctic and South Atlantic expeditions, it was decided that en route to and from the Antarctic the meteorologists would use the very latest meteorological technology – in this case the radio-sonde (an instrument with a transmitter deployed beneath a hydrogen-filled balloon) - to contribute to what would be a unique North Sea-to-South Pole cross-section through the atmosphere. The data would also contribute to the first comprehensive analysis of the atmospheric circulation in the southern hemisphere.

The meteorologists were the busiest scientists on the ship, with a constant succession of things to measure at regular intervals. Herbert Regula, the leader of the meteorological party, and Heinz Lange, his principal assistant, had two different jobs to fulfil. Regula was the resident meteorologist, responsible for making daily weather observations, constructing weather charts for 12:00 GMT, and preparing weather forecasts for the pilots for their long distance flights. On the return journey he had to provide meteorological advice to the biologist and the oceanographer for their investigations along the Greenwich Meridian section between Antarctica and South Africa. Lange's work was more akin to scientific research without immediate practical application. Between the Bay of Biscay and Antarctica he was responsible for releasing radio-sondes to make vertical measurements, through the atmosphere, of temperature and relative humidity, along with pressure - from which the height can be calculated. These balloon ascents were designed to provide a north to south cross-section through the weather elements in the troposphere, where clouds form and weather happens, as the basis for improving understanding of how the global atmosphere works. As well as radio-sonde ascents, so called 'pilot balloons' (hydrogen filled balloons which did not carry instruments) were released to determine the strength and direction of the winds of the upper atmosphere. The balloons did not go on forever. As they rose gently into the sky the air around them thinned, allowing the hydrogen in the balloons to expand until eventually they burst. That was the end of the ascents, unless clouds hid the balloons from view first.

Regula's and Lange's scientific programme of special investigations included [1]:

1) Expanding the climatology for aircraft flights – which meant acquiring enough meteorological data so as to provide or enhance statistical averages of weather conditions

for use by aircraft in the regions crossed by *Schwabenland*;

2) Determining the height and change of height of the Antarctic tropopause, the boundary between the troposphere and the overlaying stratosphere (which today is well known as the region of the ozone layer that protects us from too much ultra-violet radiation);

3) Determining the occurrence of cold air from Antarctica and the extent of its invasion of surrounding areas during the austral summer;

4) Analysing air-masses to distinguish between cold air-masses from Antarctica and subtropical warm air-masses at the Antarctic Polar Front, or to allow further subdivision of air-masses between Antarctica and the Tropical Front.

Along with these were two additional optional tasks:

5) Determining the vertical temperature gradient in the air above drifting ice and open water; and

6) Determining the vertical gradient of wind speed in the air above drifting ice and open water.

Observing the Weather

Schwabenland had left Hamburg in a stiff wind from the southeast that was blowing in cold air from the Russian steppes. The scientific party would be surprised to find that the air temperature of -13°C was the lowest measured at sea level during the whole journey to Antarctica and back.

Regula's work started at midnight, when he made the first weather observations of the new day, including pressure, temperature, relative humidity, wind direction and speed, precipitation, and radiation, which were followed by similar observations at 0600, 1200 and 1800 [2]. The data from these so-called 'term' observations were transmitted to Quickborn, the German overseas radio station. They also were written down in a notebook on board together with notes on other remarkable phenomena, like waterspouts, or halos around the sun. These weather logs were collected by the Deutsche Seewarte (German Maritime Observatory) in the tradition of the American oceanographer Matthew Fontaine Maury (1806-1873), to extract the data so that they could be used for determining the best routes for shipping. Besides making his standard instrumental readings, Regula also used special registering instruments, like an 8-day barograph and a 2-day barograph with higher resolution, to detect tiny changes in the conditions that might be relevant to understanding the development of the weather en route. He also tested two 'remote' thermometers, which were placed at the peak of the foremost mast and close to the bow and connected electrically with the weather station on the boat deck, where he could compare their measurements with his other readings. These 'remote' measurements would enable him to detect small-scale changes in atmospheric conditions close to the ship.

Weather data were also collected by German whaling ships in the Antarctic, and by German merchant ships from elsewhere in the South Atlantic, and radioed to Quickborn. Regula used the *Schwabenland* data, plus the information from these other sources provided by the German weather service via Quickborn, to construct a daily weather chart of the region for 12:00 GMT. Once the ship arrived at the Antarctic coast on 19 January 1939, he prepared more detailed weather charts for briefing the pilots of the two aircraft before they set off on their long distance flights into the interior of the icy continent. To construct these detailed maps he also used additional weather data received directly by radio from South America and from the German Antarctic whaling fleet [3]. The state of the weather was a critical limitation for both flying and photography, for which few clouds and good visibility were a must. In addition, safe landings called for wind speeds less than Beaufort Force 4-5 (11-21 knots or 20-38 km/h) at the position of the catapult ship [4]. To obtain information about high-level winds for these flights, Regula sent up pilot balloons [2]. Their track was followed by two observers using theodolites positioned at the ship's bridge and on the after deck, a base-line distance of about 100 metres, which enabled Regula to determine balloon heights up to the stratosphere. Wind speed and wind direction were calculated from the three-dimensional co-ordinates of the balloon positions in the air, the times of observation of these positions, and the measured rate of ascent.

Altogether 125 pilot balloons were sent up and the results from 112 of them were analysed before the ship returned to Hamburg. The balloons reached a mean height of 6,270 m and a maximum of 25,725 m; within the Polar Circle the record was 22,500 m. Aside from these investigations of the upper air, Regula arranged for Gburek and the 1st officer Amelang to make a long series of observations on the height, wavelength and direction of ocean swells, for comparison with wind measurements made by an anemometer fixed to the top of the ship's mast at a height of 35 m [4].

While the ship was operating off the Antarctic coast there were only three periods of weather good enough for flying. The first of these lasted from 19 to 22 January, and the second from 29 to 31 January. The third one allowed only one long distance flight, on 3 February, and two short reconnaissance flights along the coast on 4 and 5 February . Ritscher had hoped to launch a long distance flight to the south-east already on 2 February 1939 14:00 GMT, for which Regula had got everything ready to brief the pilots on the weather [5]. His report reads as follows:-

Weather situation: A large high is situated about 1500 nautical miles north-north-west of *Schwabenland*. Observations from *Schwabenland* and *Wikinger* show that the pressure rises slightly towards the southwest sector of this high. This will lead to the weather stabilising gradually, with an increased chance of showers.

Flight weather outlook: *Wind*: Measurements from *Schwabenland* show that wind speed is 30-35 km/h. Direction: around 110°. Based on measurements of the higher level winds, which increase in strength upwards to a height of 1000 m, no significant drop in wind speed is expected in the next few hours.
Clouds: There are several layers of clouds: there is quickly changing stratus at heights of 150 to 300 m, and there are chains of large cumulus clouds, all beneath a cover of high-level stratocumulus.
Precipitation: At the moment I estimate that the flight may run into small snow showers in places extending around 10 – 20 km along the flight path. Close to the mountains more clouds can be expected, as well as more precipitation (i.e. larger snow showers).
Visibility: More than 20 km away from the snow showers.

In general the forecast is for decreasing cloudiness and precipitation. Nevertheless, where it is cloudy the flight may find low visibility and experience some icing, and snow showers will have to be taken into account." [5]

In the end that flight was cancelled, because there was too much uncertainty about the cloud cover and snow showers, and the pilots had to wait another day before they could fly again.

With the advancing season, the length of daylight available for a long distance photo flight became progressively shorter, limiting their ability to survey large areas. Average daily air temperature decreased steadily from about 0°C to –6°C during the three weeks stay, while new ice began developing in the open water between the drifting ice floes. Flying conditions were best around 20 January. Unfortunately, the weather log containing the 6 hourly observations, the weather charts, and other details was lost during the war, so Regula could only deliver a rough weather description for publication in 1954 [4].

After the expedition returned to Germany, Regula summarised his experiences [6]. Flight conditions were unfavourable when humid maritime air masses were transported south by northerly winds. Under these conditions, extensive areas of fog developed over open water and the adjacent land, which would lead to icing on the aircraft. Conditions most favourable for flying arose after the passage of the centre of a low pressure air mass, when cold south-east or south-west winds originating in Antarctica advanced over the open sea. The cold air blowing off the continent could be gusty over the sea, where the interaction between the relatively warm water and cold air could generate sea fog. But, over the continent there would be few clouds and very good visibility, which was up to 100 km over the polar plateau [4].

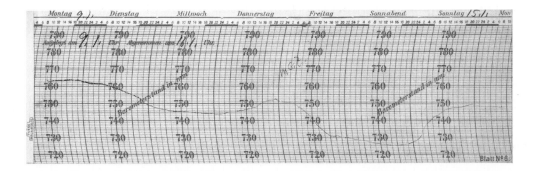

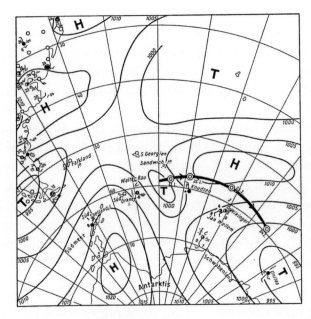

(above) Pressure diagram of the *Schwabenland* expedition from 5 to 16 January 1939 with lowest pressure at about 725 mmHg (966,54 hPa) close to Bouvet Island on Saturday 15 January;

(left) Surface weather chart of 20 January 1939, and track of a depression from 20 to 24 January 1939;

(below) Sketch of weather development (representing air pressure) at the coast of Neu-Schwabenland between 19 January and 6 February 1939. Above the line = flying weather; below the line = no flying weather.

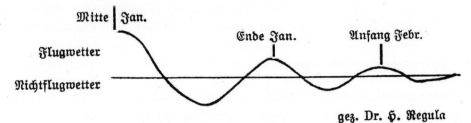

gez. Dr. H. Regula

Abb. 31. Schematische Darstellung des Wetterverlaufs im Arbeitsgebiet von Mitte Januar bis Anfang Februar.

Before World War II, the flight level of airships at first and later of Lufthansa aircraft crossing the oceans was mostly below 500 m. For that reason, the sea flight group of the German Maritime Observatory considered the measurement of wind speed above the ocean surface and up to 500 m as very important. To meet the need for these data the ship's meteorologists measured those winds on the transect between Antarctica and Bouvet Island, and occasionally between Cape Town and Pernambuco. Measuring winds from a ship is a tricky business, because the superstructure distorts the air currents. To escape such distortion, Regula mounted the anemometer measuring wind speed on top of the mast, at a height of 35 m above the level of the ocean.

Regula also managed to devise an original method for measuring wind speed for the first time in the open sea at just 60 cm above sea level. He fixed a contact wind speed meter onto a wooden cross mounted on a life buoy and connected to *Schwabenland* by a mooring rope; this makeshift apparatus was allowed to drift about 60 m away from the ship when the vessel was hove to, so as to avoid the effects of the superstructure on the local air currents. A waterproof electrical cable connected the instrument to a registering device aboard *Schwabenland*. Measurements of wind speed in m/s were made at Beaufort wind strengths of between 2 and 8, and at each measuring station were taken 17 times over a period of 24 hours. They could not make any measurements in storm conditions, when wind speeds were higher than strength 8 (74 km/h), because the makeshift raft overturned in the high seas. Although the data were lost during war, Regula remembered that wind speeds 60 cm above sea surface proved to be 60 to 70 % of the wind speed measured at 35 m. This result confirmed the expected logarithmic increase of wind speed from near zero (due to friction) at a flat surface, to what is referred to as the wind speed of the undisturbed atmosphere, which is measured on land at a height of 10 m.

Information on the winds above the ship and up to 500 m height was obtained by observing the progress of the slowly ascending pilot balloons [4,7]. They were released one after the other within a short time interval and tracked by theodolites to give precise details on wind strength and direction. The technique could only be used when *Schwabenland* was in calm seas, because observers could not keep the balloons in the crosshairs of their theodolites while the ship was pitching and rolling.

The knowledge gained about the changes in wind strength and direction with height at low levels was important not only for low flying aircraft, but also for understanding air-sea interactions. Where the wind meets the sea the wind speed is retarded by friction with the ocean surface, and the air delivers kinetic energy to the sea, creating a broad range of sea states. In the late 1930s it was important to understand these interactions not least as a first step in understanding the generation of cyclones, especially tropical cyclones, as the basis for forecasting their behaviour. Unfortunately, Regula's low level wind data, which could have helped to address this important question, were burnt and lost forever during the war.

A New Look at the Upper Atmosphere

Lange's balloon-borne radio-sondes probed the atmosphere, making observations for the study of the meteorological conditions of the upper air, a topic known in the meteorologist's trade as 'aerology'. Radio-sondes were a new technology, having been introduced only six years previously during the 2nd International Polar Year of 1932-1933 (see BOX). Each radio-sonde was a disposable instrument transmitting pressure, temperature, and relative humidity data to a receiver on the ground. In contrast to them, pilot balloons were used just to determine wind speed and direction. By using theodolites to track the balloons, observers could calculate not only horizontal but also vertical winds, the upward and downward movements of the balloons registering regions of upwelling and downwelling currents of air.

RADIO-SONDES - A NEW METEOROLOGICAL TOOL

Radio-sondes heralded the arrival of a new era of meteorology. Following the 2nd International Polar Year of 1932-1933, a worldwide network of radio-sonde stations had been developed in 1935 to measure profiles of temperature and humidity through the atmosphere. In March 1937, the German meteorologist Ludwig Weickmann (1882-1961), a member of the International Aerological Commission, collected all the available information about radio-sondes [8]. Seven countries (Finland, France, Germany, Japan, The Netherlands, USA, and USSR) had designed and built their own models. Apart from the United States, which had produced five different types, Germany was the leading country in making radio-sondes: Paul Duckert (1900-1966) had invented a radio-sonde in 1930, which was produced by Telefunken in Berlin [9]; the Askania-sonde was tested during the airship expedition with Graf Zeppelin in 1931 [10]; the Kölzer-Graw-sonde was developed by Josef Graw in the years 1931-1933 (later used by the German Army) [11]; and the Lang-sonde was constructed by the Reich Weather Service in the years 1935/36 (later used by the German Air Force) [8]. In 1936 G. Becker and W. Hey developed a different type, by order of the Naval Observatory in Wilhelmshafen (later used by the German Navy)[11], which was released during the *Meteor* expeditions of 1937 and 1938 and during the international Gulf Stream investigation in 1938 [9]. It became well known under the name Marine-sonde.

Lange used two different types of sondes during the *Schwabenland* expedition: Lang-sondes and Marine-sondes [12]. A comparison of both types would show which sonde was more reliable under Antarctic conditions. By comparison with measurements made from calibrated instruments fixed to an aircraft, it was known that Lang-sondes recorded temperatures that were slightly too high (by +0.5 to +1.0°C), whereas Marine-sondes were constantly 2 to 3°C too cold. These calibrations enabled sonde data to be corrected when they were analysed [13]. Given that prior calibration, it was somewhat surprising to find that during the expedition the temperature measurements made by Marine-sondes were about 3°C too high in the troposphere up to about 10 km.

The humidity measurements also had to be calibrated, because the two types of sondes were equipped with different methods to measure relative humidity. Lang-sondes used a mechanical hair-hygrometer, in which the length of hair changes according to relative humidity (e.g. expanded longer hair indicated more humid air), while Marine-sondes used a psychrometer consisting of two electrical contact thermometers, one of them being moistened by a wet stocking. The difference between the two temperature measurements provided a measure of the relative humidity of the air, which could be determined by use of a special psychrometer table. At low temperatures both instruments showed growing errors due to either the inertia of the hygrometer hair, or to there being too small a temperature difference between the two thermometers of the psychrometer. Bearing the relative accuracy of the two instruments in mind, humidity data from Lang-sondes were accepted up to heights of 5 km, and from Marine-sondes up to 8 km. Above that height neither of them were accurate enough for their humidity data to be seriously considered.

Altogether 119 Lang-sondes and 65 Marine-sondes were launched on 106 days between 20 December 1938 and 7 April 1939 at various points between Brest on the French coast and Neu-Schwabenland [12]. Lang's model was cheap (100 Reichsmark) and light (675 g with batteries, parachute and antennas) [8]. The instrument was easy to handle, and measured the meteorological parameters mechanically and independently from each other. The data were registered automatically, which excluded any influence from the observer. The balloons were filled with hydrogen inside the ship and released through a hatch 2 m in diameter between the two rails of the catapult on the quarterdeck, a process that worked very nicely [4]. Each balloon trailed a 40 m long radio antenna. To prevent it becoming entangled in the ship's superstructure during the launch, the antenna was coiled so that only the bottom one meter was left dangling – the rest unrolled later automatically. Only one sonde was destroyed by collision with the supporting beams of the catapult, although they only were released at wind speeds up to 20 m/sec.

Within the Polar Circle, 21 Lang-sondes and 15 Marine-sondes were launched. Usually the first sonde was launched after breakfast, between 0900 and 1000, and the second one in the afternoon between 1600 and 1700. In the tropics some sondes were started after sunset to check for mistakes in measurements caused by the sun's radiation, which could result in too high a temperature being recorded (the thermometers were not shielded, and exposure to the sun could raise their temperature considerably above that of the ambient air). In those days the analysis of the ascents took some time, and the results were rarely available for immediate use; i.e. they were too late to be considered for weather forecasts for flights starting within a few hours of the balloon launch. 73 radio-sonde analyses were finished just in time to be transmitted as so-called 'radio-temps' to the German Maritime Observatory in Hamburg. Some of the data were published in the *Täglicher Wetterbericht* (Daily Weather Report) of the maritime observatory, and thus survived the effects of war in several libraries [4,7].

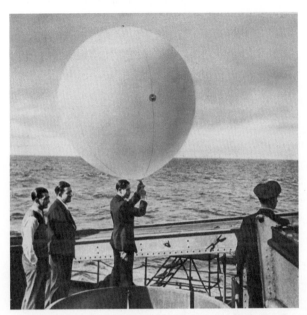
Release of a radio-sonde from the quarterdeck of *Schwabenland*

Ninety-five analysed radio-sondes reached the stratosphere, with a mean height of 17,880 m. Thirty-nine of the sondes flew over 20 km high [12]. Only 14 sondes failed to reach a height of 24 km. This was a great achievement for the new meteorological measuring techniques. For comparison, the instrumented kite and balloon ascents of the 2nd German Antarctic expedition to the Weddell Sea in 1911-1912 reached a mean height of only 2,400 m. The good results were due to the new free-flying radio-sonde technique and the use of an excellent radio receiver, which was usually able to follow the transmission of the measured data from the ascending instruments until the balloons exploded. The lowest temperature measured was -74.4 °C, found at a height of over 16 km at about 6°N, north of the Island of St. Paul in the equatorial Atlantic on the morning of 27 March 1939. [9]

The north-south cross section of aerological ascents by radio-sonde over the Atlantic had the potential to provide exceptional data for maritime meteorological studies. Unfortunately, most of the data were lost during World War II, and those who would have been most likely to work up the data, meteorologist Lange and geophysicist Gburek, died in the war. Just by chance, some hand written copies of the original data survived in the hands of the eminent German climatologist Hermann Flohn, who had been given the data to analyse for a publication [13]. Luckily, Flohn had partly extracted data from 102 out of 119 Lang-sonde measurements (the rest of the data was seen as questionable and not considered

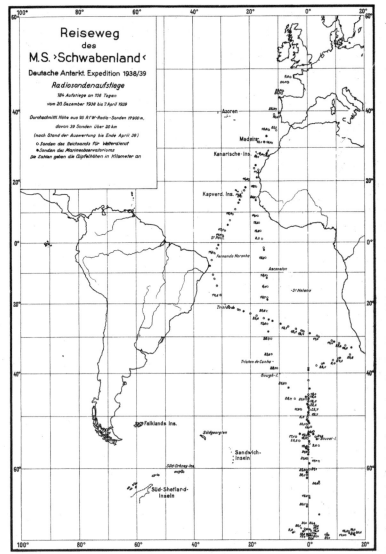

Position and maximum height of radio-sonde ascents from *Schwabenland*

in his analysis), before the original material was burnt in a freight car in 1944 while being transferred to a safe place. The most distinctive data of 56 out of 65 Marine-sonde ascents had subsequently been found in the debris of the Maritime Observatory in Hamburg. Regula published these aerological results in 1949 [7]. Between them, Flohn and Regula produced the first ever north-south radio-sonde section through the Atlantic from the North Sea to the equator and up to a height of 7 km [4,7], to which Flohn added his analysis of a collection of radio-sonde data from the southern hemisphere between the equator and the South Pole [13]. These aerological north-south cross sections were a novel achievement in meteorology, with widespread implications for understanding atmospheric processes at the global scale. We note in passing that the first comparable oceanographic north-south cross-sections of the Atlantic and the Indian Ocean were also provided by German scientists, on the first two German Antarctic expeditions led by Drygalski and Filchner [14].

In the regional context, Regula's analysis of the meteorological data from the meridional cross-section along the ship's route between the Bay of Biscay at 50°N and the equator showed that during 20-26 December 1938 there was a low centred over Corsica, and a high over the north central Atlantic and stretching east as far as the Sahara and northeast as far as Great

170

Britain [7]. Sailing southwards, they were not surprised to find that the temperature increased steadily at heights below 5000 m. At the sea surface the air temperature between the Bay of Biscay and 9°N warmed from +3°C to +25°C, while at 5000 m it warmed from -26°C to +2°C. Ascending upwards temperatures decreased until the height of the tropopause was reached. The tropopause divides the atmosphere into the troposphere (below) and the stratosphere (above), and marks an inversion where the temperature conditions change from decrease with height (below) to increase with height (above). Along the ship's track from north to south Regula found the temperature of the stratosphere cooling from -52°C at 44°N to -69°C at 15°N, nicely following the general law of compensation (when the troposphere cools, the stratosphere warms by a corresponding amount). These unique observations provided the first practical confirmation of the general law, enabling meteorologists to demonstrate with their data what had been surmised from theoretical considerations.

Combining the data from radio-sonde ascents with his observations of clouds and precipitation from the *Schwabenland*, Regula was able to determine the distribution of vertical air movements. He distinguished four different regions):

1. Convection in lower layers
2. Zone of descending air movement
3. Area of continuous ascending air
4. Large scale convection in the doldrums.

Starting from the northern Bay of Biscay at 48°N, there was an inversion layer at 3600 m height where the temperature decreased sharply upwards. This layer acted like a ceiling, below which a zone of convection or turbulence with alternating upward and downward winds resulted in the formation of cumulus and cumulonimbus clouds that gave rise to snow [4,7]. Towards the south this inversion layer decreased in height down to 1600 m at 35°N and to 400 m at 23°N, then remained at that height as far as 9°N, where it received the name Trade Wind (or "Passat") Inversion. At a height of only 400 m high, the inversion layer was too low for the development of clouds - given the prevailing humidity and temperature.

Regula's findings about the height of the Passat Inversion contradicted those of Heinrich von Ficker, who had summarised what was known about this phenomenon prior to 1936 [15]. Most of Ficker's data came from kite ascents and pilot balloon ascents made during the famous German *Meteor* expedition of 1925-1927. Ficker found the lowest inversion layer at 1,110 m height at 15°N, which was some 700 m higher than Regula found it on the *Schwabenland* expedition. The discrepancy between the two data sets may be explained by the *Meteor* data having been collected during a different season and in a different year.

Proceeding on southwards, Regula's next two radio-sonde ascents at 5°N and 1°N showed a remarkably different pattern. The inversion at 400 m was missing, and the air between 500 m and 5000 m was colder than it had been further north. Regula realised that this

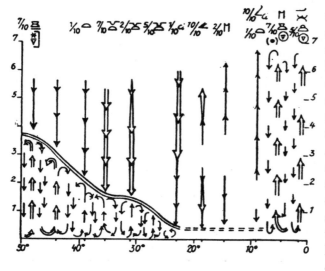

(left)Vertical movement of the air on a cross section between the Bay of Biscay and the Equator. Scale in km height at left. Along the top is weather data from *Schwabenland*; numbers are degrees of cloudiness, e.g. 7/10 = 7 tenths of the sky covered by cloud. Symbols represent the types of cloud, such as cumulonimbus. At top left the * and inverted triangle symbols represent snow showers. The arrows indicate the direction and strength of vertical movement; the thicker the arrow, the stronger the motion. Towards the north a prominent inversion layer separates rising air below from descending air above.

(middle) Meridional vertical section showing the distribution of temperature in the southern hemisphere in summer. The indication of the Passat (trade wind) inversion originated in the *Meteor* data of 1925-1927;

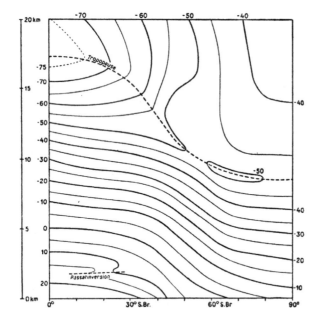

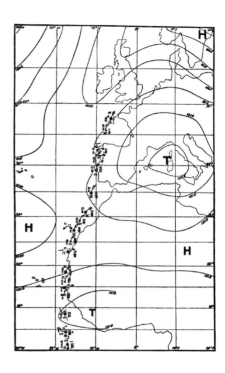

(right) Mean pressure chart from 20 to 26 December 1938, and weather observations of *Schwabenland*

172

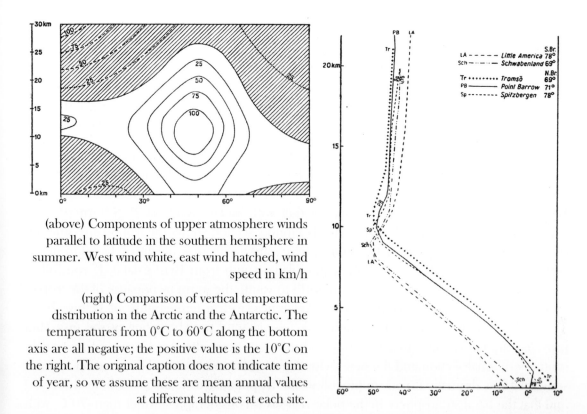

(above) Components of upper atmosphere winds parallel to latitude in the southern hemisphere in summer. West wind white, east wind hatched, wind speed in km/h

(right) Comparison of vertical temperature distribution in the Arctic and the Antarctic. The temperatures from 0°C to 60°C along the bottom axis are all negative; the positive value is the 10°C on the right. The original caption does not indicate time of year, so we assume these are mean annual values at different altitudes at each site.

change documented their arrival in the 'doldrums', the Inter Tropical Convergence Zone close to the equator, where the northeast and southeast trade winds converge resulting in ascending currents of air. His data showed that the warm, rising, humid air quickly cooled, its temperature dropping by 0.52°C/100 m between the sea surface and 1500 m. Relative humidity was mostly higher than 70 %. In this area he knew that there was strong convection connected with rising air currents. Very tall cumulonimbus clouds form by rapid condensation as the rising air cools, bringing the showers and sheet lightning typical of the region. Not surprisingly, the signals from the ascending radio-sondes showed highly variable up and down movements reflecting the turbulence typical of this environment.

From observations made on just two of the radio-sonde ascents in the tropics off the African coast, Regula was able to speculate about the role of ozone in warming the stratosphere [4]. He noticed that as the sondes ascended into the lower stratosphere, where temperatures can fall to -80°C, the thermometer fluid, a mixture of mercury and thallium, froze. The fluid melted again at a height of about 20 km, where the stratosphere began to warm. A strong easterly wind was measured at this height, confirming observations made by pilot balloons launched by the *Meteor* expedition of 1925-1927 (radio-sondes had not then been invented). Regula knew that a similar freeze-thaw pattern had been observed during measurements made by V2 rockets in America after World War II. There the melting of the thermometer fluid had taken place in response to a rapid increase of temperature from -40°C to more than +30°C. This temperature increase is caused by the absorption of ultra-violet light by ozone, a naturally occurring gas that is concentrated in the lower stratosphere between 20 and 25 km above ground. Unfortunately the resolution of the thermometers of both types of radio-sondes on the expedition was not high enough to allow a detailed investigation of the phenomenon, thus leaving open for further research the question of ultimate cause.

Flohn was able to expand on Regula's work by adding data on the vertical distribution of temperature in summer with latitude along a line between the equator and the South Pole[13]. He used data from the expedition's Lang-sondes, plus single radio-sonde ascents made from Batavia, South America and Australia, together with ascents made at 79°S during Byrd's expedition to the Ross Ice Shelf in1940/41. Flohn's section shows the tropopause (the top of the troposphere or base of the stratosphere) sinking from a height of 17.5 km at the equator to 8.5 km at the South Pole (extrapolated south from Byrd's data). If you follow the same height level (say 17.5 km) from north to south, the warm tropopause of the tropics corresponds to a cold stratosphere over Antarctica, with a temperature of below -70°C. These observations confirmed the rather sketchy general understanding of the time, but provided the information in a new way and in much more detail by means of the north-south meridional section and the new technology - radio-sonde data. The situation appears somewhat less dramatic if you simply follow the tropopause as it sinks southward, for you find that the basal stratosphere in the polar regions is considerably warmer than -70°C, with temperatures of -40 to -50°C. The sharpest temperature contrast along the north-south section occurs in the region between 35°S and 65°S, where the surface air temperature falls from +20°C to the freezing point. This strong meridional temperature gradient is present at all levels of the troposphere. For instance, at 8 km height the gradient still amounts to a difference of 23 degrees. Similarly, the 0°C boundary, which lies at 5000 m at the equator and has only dropped to 4000 m at 36°S, sinks to the surface at 65°S. Flohn's findings for the summer conditions in Antarctica fit well with all year round data from Admiral Byrd's expeditions to the Ross Sea in 1940-1941[16] and in 1946-1947 (the 'Highjump' expedition) [17]. In preparation for Antarctic expeditions during the International Geophysical Year (IGY) of 1957-1958, the South African Weather Bureau published a handbook on the meteorology of the Antarctic including weather data from the German whaler *Jan Wellem* from the 1937/38 season and of the *Schwabenland* expedition 1938/39 [18], referring to Regula's radio-sonde measurements off the coast of Dronning Maud Land.

To determine the speed and direction of the upper level winds, Flohn could not use the pilot balloon measurements from the *Schwabenland* expedition, because the detailed information about their ascents were burned in a fire at the Geophysical Institute in Leipzig during World War II [13]. Instead he had to take wind data from other Antarctic expeditions. Using pressure measurements at the surface, extrapolating the vertical temperature distribution up to 30 km, and applying the so-called gradient wind equation he was able to estimate upper level winds parallel to latitude; in meteorological terms these are called zonal winds. Thanks to this approach, he discovered significant new features of the atmospheric circulation of the southern hemisphere. Close to the equator, the Trade Winds were manifest as an easterly current of low speed reaching from the surface up to 10 km. Above them, roughly between 10 and 17 km, was a layer of westerly winds reaching a maximum speed of over 25 km/h at 13 km. Above that, the stratospheric winds were once again easterly. Towards the pole the westerly wind layer thickened until it extended from the surface up to heights of 20 – 25 km, i.e. the lower boundary of the overlying stratospheric easterlies between 43°S and 58°S. At 50°S, roughly in the core of this westerly wind layer, between heights of 7 to 15 km, maximum westerly wind speeds of over 100 km/h were recorded. There the stratospheric easterlies were displaced upward to 27 km. A comparison with data from comparable latitudes in the northern hemisphere showed that northwesterly wind currents in the north only reached up to 18 km, while their maximum speed at the boundary between the troposphere and stratosphere was much lower than in the south. This difference between northern and southern conditions was explained by the abrupt opposition in the South Atlantic, discussed above, between the cold temperatures of southerly latitudes influenced by Antarctica and the warm temperatures of the subtropics. South of 60°S, Flohn was able to show that easterly winds dominated over the Antarctic continent at lower levels and also above 10 to 15 km, with westerly winds in between.

Finally, Flohn compared Antarctic radio-sonde ascents with Arctic radio-sonde ascents. First he noted that in the troposphere, temperatures measured by sondes from Byrd's Little America station on the Ross Ice Shelf at 78°S were slightly cooler than measurements made from *Schwabenland* at 69°S, but that the opposite was true in the stratosphere, where temperatures were warmer at 78°S than at 69°S, as would be expected following the law of compensation. Comparing these data with Arctic data Flohn found a significant difference between both hemispheres. In general the troposphere in the Arctic was 10 degrees warmer than it was in Antarctica, whereas the stratosphere was 10 degrees cooler. This Flohn attributed to the fact that the northern polar region was covered by an ocean, and hence had a relatively low and thus warm troposphere, while the southern polar region was covered by a 3000 m high continent that naturally had a higher and hence cooler troposphere. His findings were not new, but confirmed earlier results from an aerological point of view. However Flohn's basic analysis of the atmospheric circulation of the southern hemisphere was an important contribution to his becoming one of the world's most famous climatologists after World War II.

Several of the radio-sonde measurements made from the *Schwabenland* along the Greenwich meridian between the shelf-ice at 69°S, past Bouvet Island and up to 39°S between 6 February and 2 March 1939 detected a boundary layer close to the ocean surface [4,7]. Within that layer the temperature was fairly constant within a range of only 3 degrees, reflecting the influence of the constant temperature of the open ocean. The variation in temperature increased upward away the ocean surface, reaching temperature ranges of 7 degrees at 500 m height, 12 degrees at 1000 m, and 19 degrees at 3000 m. This is due to different air masses encountered at different heights originating from warmer or colder regions.

As another sign of the profound difference between northern and southern hemisphere climate, Regula noted that during summer, the surface air temperatures at Bouvet were around +2°C, compared with the +15.6°C yearly mean value of the Island of Helgoland, which is situated at about the equivalent latitude in the North Sea. Evidently the cold fingers of Antarctica reach further to the north than the cold fingers of the Arctic reach to the south. In part this reflects the northward penetration of the North Atlantic Current, a branch of the Gulf Stream, which brings heat to NW Europe and the Arctic, as compared with the blocking by the Antarctic Circumpolar Current of any equivalent southward penetration of oceanic heat towards Antarctica.

As one might imagine, Regula was very disappointed that most of the meteorological data had been lost before it could be processed fully, and that so much time had passed before the eventual analyses were finally published. He would have loved to compare the *Schwabenland* data with the data collected by the second German Antarctic Expedition in 1911-1912, but the loss of his data during the war made that an impossible dream.

Nevertheless, the data that had survived and that were unearthed after the war proved extremely useful to the international meteorological community. They provided the basis for the very first north-south cross section through the atmosphere from the North Atlantic to the South Pole, which, among other advances, led to a practical confirmation of the law of compensation. With these and other data Flohn was able to investigate the general circulation of the southern hemisphere, where he discovered a wind maximum with speeds of over 100 km/h at 10 km height at 50°S: today this is known as the southern hemisphere jet stream. Meanwhile Regula had pioneered the new technique of making wind measurements 60 cm above the sea surface, which would have provided very interesting results, if the data had not been destroyed during the war.

Although many of the various meteorological results would have a significant impact on knowledge, the role of the expedition in providing them is commonly not fully appreciated.

The Clarity of the Atmosphere

The journey to the far south offered a wonderful opportunity to investigate the turbidity of the atmosphere along a north to south cross section in the South Atlantic during the southern summer, something that had never been attempted before. Atmospheric turbidity is defined as the scattering of solar radiation in the visible spectrum by particles suspended in the air. It is measured as the ratio of unimpeded incoming solar radiation in a dry and dust-free atmosphere to solar radiation passing through the atmosphere and weakened by particles like dispersed dust from the surface, or dust from combustion processes or volcanic eruptions. It varies not only from place to place, but also from day to day at a single location, depending on the local supply of dust. Because there is virtually no dust in polar air, it is very clear and has minimal turbidity values in comparison with the tropics, where turbidity tends to be high.

To describe the turbidity or opaqueness of the atmosphere one has to determine both the direct solar radiation and the particles that obscure the otherwise clear sky. Among his geophysical tasks, Leo Gburek was responsible for radiation measurements and counting dust and the so-called condensation nuclei – the very small particles on which humid air condenses to form water droplets [19,20]

MEASURING THE TURBIDITY OF THE ATMOSPHERE.

Gburek measured direct radiation from the sun with a Michelson actinometer (No. 380) improved by W. Marten in 1928 and equipped with an ocular viewfinder and the new red filter RG 2 (1.5 mm thick) and orange filter OG 1 (2.5 mm thick), which excluded incoming radiation below 623 mμ (orange) and 524 mμ (green) respectively. The actinometer is a calorimetric radiation instrument used to determine radiation by comparing measurements made in different parts of the long wavelength area of the visible spectrum of incoming solar radiation [21]. Each data set comprised several measurements with and without filters. The actinometer was calibrated at the Meteorological Observatory in Potsdam before departure [19,20]. The spacious deck of the Schwabenland had many good places with windbreaks for the operation of the actinometer. Gburek mostly made his measurements from the ship's upper bridge, helped by the aircraft radio operator, Herbert Ruhnke, who listed the observations. In total Gburek took 219 data sets on 37 days as follows:-

December 1938	8 days of observation	with 35 data sets
January 1939	15 days of observation	with 86 data sets
February 1939	4 days of observation	with 29 data sets
March 1939	9 days of observation	with 57 data sets
April 1939	1 day of observation	with 12 data sets

In addition, the founder of turbidity investigations, Professor Franz Linke (1878-1944) of the Institute of Meteorology and Geophysics of the University of Frankfurt/Main, had provided Gburek with a small instrument developed by Joachim Scholz (1903-1937) for counting condensation nuclei on Franz Joseph Land during the second International Polar Year (1932-1933) [22]. Gburek did not mention what instrument he used to count dust, nor did he list his results (most likely the data were lost during the war). After his return to Leipzig, Gburek made some comparative measurements with the Michelson actinometer at the Geophysical Observatory on Collm Mountain, east of Leipzig. These showed a low level of variance comparable with those he had determined down south [19,20,] which told Gburek that the instrument had worked well aboard the rolling platform of the Schwabenland.

Unfortunately Gburek could not fully evaluate his material before the outbreak of the war, in which he had to serve as a weather observer in an aircraft and was killed in 1940 during aerial combat. He did however manage some preliminary analyses. Using the method of Karl Feußner to calculate turbidity, Gburek found a turbidity factor of 3.6 to 4.5 in equatorial air, diminishing to a factor about 2 close to Antarctica (these values are ratios, so have no units). Later, when more measurements became available, a German meteorological dictionary cited a factor of 3.62 as typical for tropical-maritime air and 2.26 for polar maritime air in the northern hemisphere [23], confirming the accuracy of Gburek's measurements, which were the first of their kind for the tropical and south polar Atlantic. Close to the African coast, near Dakar, where offshore northeast trade winds transport a huge amount of dust and smaller nuclei offshore, Gburek measured turbidity factors up to 6; these decreased abruptly to the usual oceanic values on passing into the zone of the southeast trade winds[19,20].

Surprisingly, Gburek found that his counts of condensation nuclei over the ocean during the whole journey were quite low and relatively constant, with a mean value of 200 to 400/cm^3; the highest value was 2000/cm^3. Only in the region of the Roaring Forties were the counts of nuclei rather more variable, owing to an increase of nuclei during bad weather when there were high levels of humid air and low clouds. These values were much lower than usually found in the countryside (1000 to 3000/cm^3) or in big cities, where levels could be 10 times as high [23]. In parallel with the increase in turbidity values, nuclei counts rose to a maximum of 50,000/cm^3 in the northeast trades, decreasing to a mean value of 250 to 400/cm^3 in the southeast trades. The high values associated with the northeast trades reflect the high dust loadings of air blowing west over the ocean from the Sahara Desert, which were commonly reported in ships' logbooks.

References

1. Anlage zu Nr. 1138/38, Meteorologische Aufgaben der Antarktis – Expedition 1938/39. Bb1 Meteorologie, Ritscher's estate (unpublished). Sets out the meteorological programme of investigations.

2. Regula, H., 1939, Die Arbeiten der Expeditionswetterwarte. Teil II: Radiosondenaufstiege. In: Vorbericht über die Deutsche Antarktische Expedition 1938/39. Annalen der Hydrographie und Maritimen Meteorologie. VIII, Beiheft, 35-36. Describes the radio-sonde operations and some results.

3. Ritscher, A., 1942, Wissenschaftliche und fliegerische Ergebnisse der Deutschen Antarktischen Expedition 1938/39, Hrsg. im Auftrag der Deutschen Forschungsgemeinschaft. Koehler & Amelang, Leipzig, Volume 1: Text, 304 pp., Pictures and Maps 57 plates and 3 maps. Discusses sources of meteorological data on page 46.

4. Regula, H., 1954/1958, Die Wetterverhältnisse während der Expedition und die Ergebnisse der meteorologischen Messungen. In: A. Ritscher, Deutsche Antarktische Expedition 1938/39. Wissenschaftliche und fliegerische Ergebnisse. Bd. 2. Helmut Striedieck (Geographisch-Kartographische Anstalt Mundus), Hamburg 16-40. A preprint was published in 1954. Discusses weather and sea ice conditions, results of radio-sonde measurements, conditions for ice free lakes and measurements of winds at sea surface.

5. Regula, H., 1939, Wetterberatung für einen Flug von der "Schwabenland" in südöstlicher Richtung, 2.2.1939. Bb1 Meteorologie, Ritscher's estate (unpublished). Regula's weather report for the day, advising Ritscher on conditions preparatory to plane launch.

6. Regula H., 1939, Meteorologische Gesichtspunkte. Bb1 Meteorologie, Ritscher's estate (unpublished). Regula's summary of his experiences on the expedition, written for the expedition leader.

7. Regula, H., 1949, Einige Ergebnisse der Radiosonden-Aufstiege der Deutschen Antarktischen Expedition 1938/39. Meteorologische Rundschau 2 (7/8), 229-232. Discusses the radio-sonde data.

8. Weickmann, L., 1937, Über Radiosonde-Konstruktionen. Denkschrift. Internationale Meteorologische Organisation, Internationale Aerologische Kommission. Berlin, 85 pp. Collection of all available information about radio-sondes.

9. Trenckle, F., 1982, Die Entwicklung der Radiosonden von 1930 –1955. Interner Bericht. Deutsche Versuchsanstalt für Luft- und Raumfahrt, Physik der Atmosphäre, 97 pp. Discusses the evolution of radio-sondes.

10. Weickmann, L., 1933, Die meteorologischen Aufgaben bei der 1. Polarfahrt des "Graf Zeppelin" Juli 1931. Methoden, Material, Ergebnisse. Petermanns Mitteilungen, Ergänzungsheft Nr. 216, 48-59. Testing the Askania radio-sonde on the LZ 127 "Graf Zeppelin".

11. Weickmann, L., 1939, Über Radiosonde-Konstruktionen. Denkschrift. Nachtrag. Internationale Meteorologische Organisation, Internationale Aerologische Kommission. Berlin, 32 pp. Supplement of information about radio-sondes.

12. Lange, H., 1939, Die Arbeiten der Expeditionswetterwarte. Teil I: Terminbeobachtungen, Höhenwindmessungen, Wetterdienst, Sonderuntersuchungen. In: Vorbericht über die Deutsche Antarktische Expedition 1938/39. Annalen der Hydrographie und Maritimen Meteorologie. VIII, Beiheft, 33-35. Describes basic weather observations, upper wind measurements and some results.

13. Flohn, H., 1950, Grundzüge der allgemeinen atmosphärischen Zirkulation auf der Südhalbkugel auf Grund der aerologischen Ergebnisse der Deutschen Antarktischen Expedition "Schwabenland" 1938/39. Archiv für Meteorolgie, Geophysik und Bioklimatologie 2A (1), 17-64. Analysis of the „Schwabenland! radio-sonde data in respect to the General Circulation of the Southern Hemisphere

14. Lüdecke, C., 2007, Diverging Currents - Depicting Southern Ocean Currents in the Early 20th Century. In K.R. Benson and H.M. Rozwadowski (eds.): Extremes: Oceanography's Adventures at the Poles. Science History Publication/ USA, Sagamore Beach, 71-105.

15. Ficker, H.v., 1936, Die Passatinversion. Veröffentlichungen des Meteorologischen Instituts der Universität Berlin 1 (4), 33 pp.

16. Court, A., 1942, Tropopause disappearance during Antarctic winter. Bulletin of the American Meteorological Society 28. 220-238.

17. Chief of Naval Operation, Navaer 50-1 R-214, 1948, Aerological Observations and summaries for the Antarctic from 15.XII.1946 to 15.III.1947. A project of Operation Highjump, Task Force 68, Aerology Flight section, Washington.

18. Rooy, M.P., 1957, Meteorology of the Antarctic. Government Printer, Pretoria, South Africa, 240 pp.

19. Gburek, L., 1939, Geophysikalischer Arbeitsbericht. In: Vorbericht über die Deutsche Antarktische Expedition 1938/39. Annalen der Hydrographie und Maritimen Meteorologie. VIII, Beiheft, 21-23. Discusses measurements of direct solar radiation and dust particles.

20. Gburek, L., 1958, Erdmagnetische Messungen, Eisuntersuchungen, Strahlungsmessungen und Kernzählungen. In: A. Ritscher, Deutsche Antarktische Expedition 1938/39. Wissenschaftliche und fliegerische Ergebnisse. Bd. 2. Helmut Striedieck (Geographisch-Kartographische Anstalt Mundus), Hamburg: 97-100. (Reprint of Gburek 1939 plus an explaining remark of the editor). Discusses measurements of earth magnetism, sea ice, and direct solar radiation and dust particles.

21. Albrecht, F., 1933, Apparate und Meßmethoden der atmosphärischen Strahlungsforschung. In: F. Linke, Meteorologisches Taschenbuch. 2nd. ed. Akademische Verlagsgesellschaft, Leipzig, 46-109. Discusses the measurement of solar radiation by actinometer, on pp 59-61.

22. Kleinschmidt, E., 1939, Meteorologischen Apparate und Beobachtungsmethoden. In: F. Linke, Meteorologisches Taschenbuch. 3rd. ed. Akademische Verlagsgesellschaft, Leipzig, 34-126. Discusses turbidity measurements on pp 122-123.

23. Keil, K., 1950, Handwörterbuch der Meteorologie. Verlag Fritz Knapp. Frankfurt/Main. 604 pp. Discusses turbidity of the total solar radiation, on p 527, and nuclei counts, on p 488.

CHAPTER 13 – OCEAN AND SEA-ICE

Early Observations from the Whaling Industry

One of the important tasks of the expedition was to investigate the environment in which the whales lived - the South Atlantic part of the Southern Ocean – so as to provide information that might improve prospects for the German whaling industry. Bearing that in mind, the scientific results from the *Schwabenland* and those from the German whaling fleet in the South Atlantic have to be seen together, since they were all part of the same overall scientific programme.

Most of what was known in 1938/39 about the Southern Ocean adjacent to this part of Antarctica came from the reports of three major oceanographic expeditions, two of them German and one British. The German *Meteor* expedition of 1925-1927 vastly improved understanding of the circulation of the South Atlantic and of the origin of Antarctic Deep Water [1,2], while the British 'Discovery Investigations' on the *R.R.S. Discovery II*, provided considerable detail on the circulation of the Southern Ocean right up to the Antarctic margin. British oceanographer George Deacon used these data to describe the Antarctic Convergence, where cold Antarctic waters from the south dive beneath warmer and lighter sub-Antarctic waters at about 50°S [3,4,5]. Across the convergence, now called the Polar Front, temperatures rise abruptly from 2°C or less in the south to 2.8-5.4°C in the north. German geographer Wilhelm Meinardus had discovered the convergence when he was analysing the oceanographic data from the first German Antarctic expedition (1901-1903) [6]. In his honour it was named the 'Meinardus Line', but the descriptive name 'Antarctic Convergence' became widely preferred [7]. The seas along the Convergence, or Polar Front, are rich in nutrients and support vast numbers of seals, whales and birds.

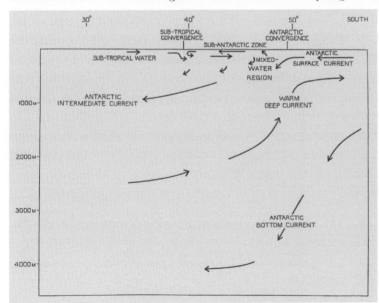

Meridional circulation in the southern Atlantic Ocean at 30° W. The Antarctic convergence is depicted at 50°S

The 'Discovery Investigations' had exactly the same aim as the hydrographic surveys planned by the German whaling industry – to establish the physical nature of the whales' home, the marine ecosystem, and to assist the biologists in understanding the seasonal occurrence of planktonic whale food, which depended on hydrographic factors[8]. The main difference was that British whaling and British whaling science was well established before the German whaling industry got started in 1936/37. Nevertheless, the German whalers lost no time in gathering this kind of information, taking a marine biologist (Dr. Nicolaus Peters) and a meteorologist (Walter Reichelt, from the German Maritime Observatory) south in the floating factory ship *Jan Wellem* in their first season[9,10].

Making meteorological and hydrographic observations from a factory ship was quite a novelty for young Walter Reichelt. Weather observations were easy, demanding no change to the ship's operations. Hydrographic measurements were a different kettle of fish, because in order to make them the ship had to stop at a so-called 'station', defined by its co-ordinates, so interrupting the routine work of whaling. Reichelt collected his water samples and measured ocean temperatures by using as a hydrographic winch an electrical Lukas-sounding machine with a 1000 m long steel cable 4 mm in diameter installed on the port side 14 m above the sea surface. He fixed water bottles and Kipp thermometers onto the steel cable at standard distances to sample and measure the conditions of different ocean layers. A complete collection of water samples and temperature measurements from pre-set depths took four to five hours and had to be aborted several times when *Jan Wellem* had to follow its six catchers to collect shot whales for the factory production line. Nevertheless, between November 1936 and April 1937, Reichelt was able to collect hydrographic data at 62 stations[9].

Reichelt's observations south of 55°S confirmed what had been observed by one of his predecessors from the German Maritime Observatory, Wilhelm Brennecke, during the drift of the *Deutschland* in the Weddell Sea on the second German Antarctic Expedition (1911-1912). Brennecke had found three different water layers at 70°S in the Weddell Sea: the upper layer comprised a warm surface sitting over colder water at 50-75 m depth that was influenced by seasonal warming; below this cold surface layer was a middle layer in which temperatures increased to a maximum at 300 m and continued positive to a depth of around 1700 m; that layer in turn overlay cold dense bottom waters[11,12,13]. The cold and low-salt surface layer was a mixture of melt-water, precipitation, and up-welling deep sea water. The warm intermediate water coincided with a weak oxygen minimum zone.

In the next season (1937/38), Karl-Heinz Paulsen became the oceanographer on the *Jan Wellem*. Because he was subsequently appointed also to participate in the *Schwabenland* expedition, he did not have time to fully analyse and publish his *Jan Wellem* results before taking part in the *Schwabenland* expedition.

In the following season from 8 December 1938 to 8 March 1939, hydrographic observations were continued aboard *Jan Wellem* by the chemist Hans Lüneburg, a member of the newly founded Institute for Whale Research [14]. Besides temperature, salinity and oxygen content he also investigated the distribution of organic and inorganic material suspended in the water column, along with the distribution of silicate, as a means of identifying different Antarctic water bodies south of Bouvet Island.

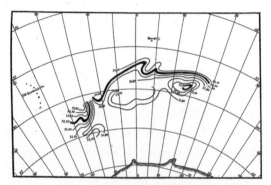

Isohalines of the ocean surface between Bouvet Island and Antarctica during the whaling season 1938/39

Lüneburg's scientific programme included daily surface measurements with chemical analysis of the water samples south and southwest of Bouvet Island, and a vertical series of hydrographic measurements at standard depths while on station every second day. In practice he could only make his vertical series of measurements every third or fourth day, so was able to complete only 26 full depth stations during the journey to add to his 63 surface measurements. His analysis of surface salinity showed a tongue of cold low salinity water south of Bouvet. The variations in surface salinity were caused by differences in the extent of ice melt. Simultaneous investigations of the plankton content of Antarctic waters aboard *Jan Wellem* underlined the connection between plankton and the different water masses as well as drift ice and icebergs.

After his experiences on the floating factory ship, Lüneburg recommended that the whole whaling fleet of seven to eight floating factory ships should undertake a programme of systematic hydrographic and hydrobiologic research including observations of ice, ocean currents, weather, distribution of plankton, krill and whales. In addition he recommended that water samples be analysed for their salinity, phosphate and silicate contents to assist the biologists in understanding the seasonal occurrence of planktonic whale food, which depended on hydrographic factors. More or less in parallel with his studies, the 'Discovery Investigations' had addressed similar problems [8]. As an end result Lüneburg envisioned the production of "reliable synoptic charts of the water bodies of the entire Antarctic whaling grounds" [14].

Schwabenland's Contribution

By the time Lüneburg had sailed south on *Jan Wellem*, the oceanographic programme of the *Schwabenland* expedition had been assigned four tasks [15]:

1. Temperature measurements and collection of water samples from the surface every four hours with the 'Sund' water bottle during the outward and return journeys.

2. Continuous underway measurements of the surface temperature with a registering thermometer.

3. Hydrographic series measurements through the water column while on station waiting for the return of the long distance flights in the work area.

4. Hydrographic series measurements through the water column on stations on traverse along the 0° longitude line from Antarctica northwards up to about 35°S.

The hydrographic series should start as close to the coast as possible, with around 120 to 150 sea miles between stations. Instruments were to be fixed at the usual standard depths. If there was not enough time, the maximum depth could be reduced to 1500 m. The equipment was organised and provided by the German Maritime Observatory and by the Institute of Marine Research in Berlin and the Marine Observatory in Wilhelmshafen.

The hydrographic winch used for the vertical sampling was positioned on *Schwabenland's* foredeck close to a small laboratory of 2 m x 2.80 m used to store boxes of thermometers and water bottles to protect them against rain and salt spray. Water samples would be titrated in a small cabin close by, to determine their oxygen content.

Surface sampling started near the Portuguese coast a little north of Lisbon at 40°36'N, 9°19'W on 21 December 1938. It turned out to be trickier than expected, because the sampling bottles oscillated sideways, which often resulted in them hitting the ship's side. After experimenting with different fastenings, Paulsen overcame the problem by the simple expedient of scooping up water with a bucket, starting on 7 January 1939. Until 5 April, when the last measurements were made halfway between the Azores and northern Portugal at 41°36'N and 19°5'W, some 337 water samples were taken from the water surface.

The electrical sensor of the registering thermometer for continuous measurements of water temperature was fixed in the entrance pipe for the engine cooling water, which lay about 6.5 m below the sea surface. Inevitably that meant that they were not measuring the temperature of the ocean surface itself. The registering thermometer worked very well, although the recording paper jammed on the rotating cylinder from time to time. The results of all surface measurements were included in Schubert's paper on whales, seals and seabirds [16].

Hydrographic measurements through the water column began on 20 January 1939, when the ship was at rest off the Antarctic coast during the first long distance flight. The periods when the ship lay still during those flights were rather short, considering that lowering and raising the sampling bottles would take 6 to 8 hours. Fortunately, there was more time available than just the flight time, as Ritscher organised a general meeting before each flight, during which the exact flight plan was discussed while the ship lay at rest. Paulsen would start lowering his water bottles as each meeting began [17]. Aside from racing to achieve his goal in the short time available, he also had to contend with the fact that Barkley, the biologist was lowering his plankton nets at the same time – though fortunately not to the same depths – with all the dangers of nets and wires and water bottles becoming entangled. It took a while to train the ship's crew to manage all this raising and lowering without hazard [15]. But before long ordinary seaman Alfred Peters was trained well enough for Paulsen to carry out the water sampling smoothly. Gburek, the geophysicist, was roped in to do the oxygen titrations when Paulsen had too little time to do all the work.

Samples were collected without problems when the weather was fine, but a rising swell and stronger winds made it impossible to hold the big ship vertically above the instruments.

At times like these the wire holding the sample bottles could extend out from the ship's side at an angle of up to 50°, a factor that had to be taken into account when determining the likely depth of each bottle on the wire. Despite the various difficulties, Paulsen managed to sample the water column at 24 stations spaced about 150 sea miles apart along the Greenwich meridian (0°) between Antarctica and Bouvet Island on the return journey. Stations 4, 6, and 10 reached down to the seabed close to the shelf ice margin. Stations 11, 13, and 16 had to be aborted due to worsening weather conditions. When the cable started to fray, measurements in the south-polar basin could be only executed down to 4000 m. Eventually, engineer Bruns managed to develop a special clamp for the wire enabling Paulsen to reach a maximum depth of 5000 m at station 23.

Besides making oceanographic measurements, Paulsen used a short coring device to collect some samples of the seabed. Given the constant pressure of time, these samples had to be collected while the biologist had his nets out, and from the leeward side of the ship, a situation fraught with potential mishaps. The tests came to an end on 23 February 1939, when the sampling tube of the coring device was lost. In the end only six samples of the seabed were collected, at stations 2, 4, 6, 7, and 15 and at

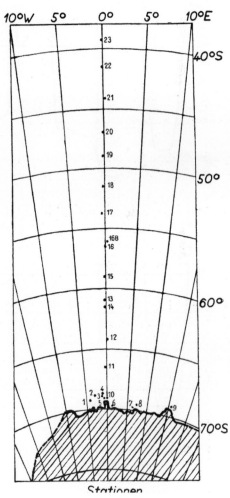

Position of oceanographic stations between Antarctica and Bouvet Island

56°23'S, 0°22'W. Unfortunately, results were never published, and the samples seem to have been lost during the war.

Salinity measurements were made on the water samples at the German Maritime Observatory in Hamburg after the return to Hamburg. The data confirm the regional picture determined by previous researchers, the sole anomaly being at station 10, in the south, where the usual layered structure of the water was interrupted by a cold-water tongue, interpreted as due to the descent of cold winter water, perhaps influenced by the bottom relief.

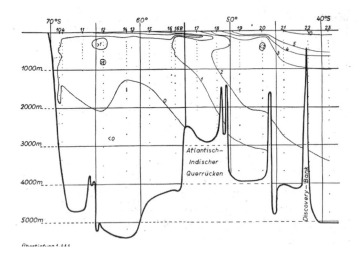

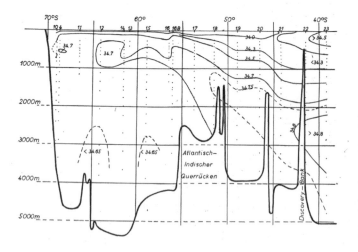

(top) Temperature cross-section of the South Atlantic Ocean between Antarctica and Bouvet Island;

(below) Salinity cross-section of the South Atlantic Ocean between Antarctica and Bouvet Island

The Circulation of the Southern Ocean

In seeking to interpret the physical oceanographic data collected by the Schwabenland in 1938/39 and by the German whaling fleet in the 1936/37, 1937/38 and 1938/39 seasons, Ritscher and his colleagues would have been standing on the shoulders of German oceanographer Georg Wüst (1890-1977) and British oceanographer George Deacon (1906-1984), the giants who had gone before [1,2,3,4,5]. The German data from the late 1930s filled important geographical gaps that existed at the time in data coverage along the Greenwich Meridian and to either side of it immediately south of Bouvet.

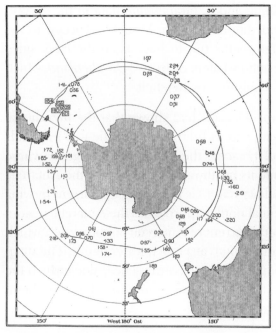

Temperatures in 2500 m depth and the location of the Antarctic Convergence (Polar Front) around Antarctica. Numbers in boxes are from 2000 m

When Paulsen died on the eastern front during World War II, in summer 1941, it was left to Ritscher and Fritz Model (born 1910), from the German Maritime Observatory, to bring together Paulsen's surface and subsurface data from the *Jan Wellem* whaling season of 1937/1938 and the *Schwabenland* expedition of 1938/39. They published this collection of data as a typewritten manuscript in the so-called unpublished series of the German Hydrographic Institute [18,19]. Model used the surface data in a paper on "Climate change or observing error?" [20], in which he compared the new data from the *Jan Wellem* and *Schwabenland* expeditions with the data given in the South Atlantic atlas of the *Meteor* expedition 1925-1927. The new results were about 0.5°C higher than the temperatures shown in the atlas, many of which came from Dutch observations made around the turn of the century. Model trusted Paulsen and the accuracy of his measurements on both expeditions, and argued that either the Dutch data were wrong due to some error of calibration, or that the ocean had warmed. Knowing as we now do that the Earth did warm significantly between 1900 and 1940, it seems reasonable to us to suppose that the global warming of those times would have warmed the surface waters over that period. Whether it would have warmed the surface of the Southern Ocean by a full 0.5°C remains to be seen. Differences in the temperature of surface waters can appear depending on where the temperature is measured (e.g. from buckets, which tend to cool as they are being recovered, or from engine intakes below the surface).

187

The typewritten reports on the oceanographic data of the *Jan Wellem* and *Schwabenland* expeditions were eventually published by Model in the second volume of the *Schwabenland* results in 1958 [21]. Had the German data been published in the internationally accessible literature in 1939, they would have been seen to confirm and strengthen the regional applicability of Deacon's circulation model for the Southern Ocean, which was based on rather few hydrographic cross sections [3,4,5]. However, the Germans were quickly overtaken by events. Quite by coincidence the *Discovery II* was collecting data from the same data gap along the Greenwich Meridian in 1939. Those data were subsequently written up by Neil Alison Mackintosh in 1947 as a follow up to Deacon's 1937 paper, when Deacon was sent to carry out war work for the Admiralty [22]. Mackintosh's paper left little for Model to add when he worked up the German whaling and *Schwabenland* data in the second volume of the results of the *Schwabenland* expedition [21]. While Model had access to the works of Deacon and Mackintosh, the reverse seems not to have been the case, since Mackintosh did not refer to the data from German whalers or from *Schwabenland*, which suggests he did not know about the papers by Paulsen [15] or Reichelt [9].

Summarising previous work, including his own, Deacon had shown that the meridional (north-south) circulation of the Southern Ocean was as follows: "Antarctic water spreads northwards in a shallow layer at the surface until it reaches the Antarctic convergence where it plunges abruptly to a deeper level to continue its northward movement as the Antarctic intermediate current." [5]. Beneath the intermediate water "is a warm deep current moving towards the south; the current is almost horizontal until it approaches the Antarctic region, but then climbs steeply towards the surface over a current of Antarctic bottom water, which sinks in the opposite direction, and then continues south at a much lesser depth. The steep slope of the deep layer decides the position of the Antarctic convergence, along which the Antarctic current sinks." [5]. These three layers, though not the connections between them, were previously identified by Reichelt [9] and Brennecke [11,12].

Surface currents sweep food towards the convergence (the Polar Front), making it a focus for fish, birds, seals and whales. In the *Schwabenland* sector it lies at about 50°S, just north of Bouvet, as shown by Deacon [5] and confirmed by Mackintosh [22]. Further west the Polar Front curves south to pass between the Falkland Islands (Islas Malvinas) and South Georgia in the north, and between Cape Horn and the Antarctic Peninsula in the south. Deacon's salinity data show that another such oceanic front forms by convergence just west of the Peninsula, where water moving north along the west coast of the Peninsula from the Bellingshausen Sea meets the waters of the northern Weddell Sea southwest of South Georgia . Model recognised this same secondary front in the data from the German whaling fleet, naming it the Bellingshausen Front [21].

In the *Schwabenland* study area, Deacon had discovered that cold Antarctic surface water spreads east and north away from the Weddell Sea in what he called the Weddell

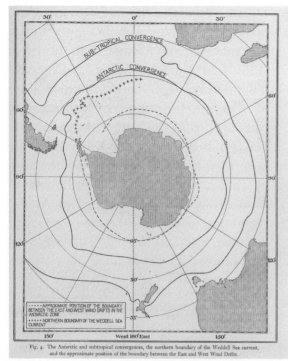

(from top) Polar Front (Antarctic Convergence) between the Falkland (Malvinas) Islands and South Georgia in the north and between Cape Horn and the Antarctic Peninsula in the south; the northern boundary of the Weddell Sea Current (++++) is the same as Model's Bellingshausen Front

Bathymetry of the Southern Ocean in metres, showing also the Bellingshausen Front north of the Weddell Sea (thin dark wavy line from 60°S 20°W to 53°S 10°E);

Fig. 4. The Antarctic and subtropical convergences, the northern boundary of the Weddell Sea current, and the approximate position of the boundary between the East and West Wind Drifts.

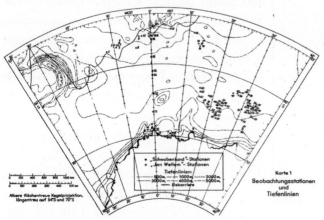

Karte 1
Beobachtungsstationen und Tiefenlinien

Sea current, which had a core at about 60°S and passed just south of Bouvet [5]. This feature appeared to extend all the way to the deep sea floor, where it was the path for Antarctic bottom water exiting the Weddell Sea. Deacon thought that this tongue of cold water and the warmer westward moving surface water to the south of it were part of a broad gyre (now called the Weddell Gyre) extending from the Antarctic Peninsula in the west to about longitude 30°E. In February 1939, surface temperatures in the tongue warmed to about 1°C [22]. The change of surface temperatures from 16 January to 15 February 1939 in the working area of *Schwabenland* showed a similar effect. Based on the German data from the late 1930s, Model confirmed the existence of the gyre and its vertical extent [21]. This gyre led Deacon to suggest that there might be two belts of pack ice in the region south of Bouvet – one moving east in the core of the Weddell Sea current, and one moving west along the coast. He thought it might even be possible for there to be open water between them in winter, but modern satellite data indicates that is not the case.

189

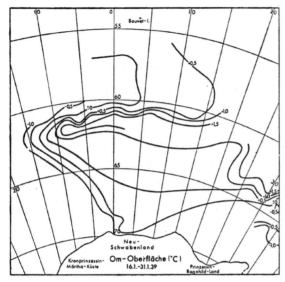

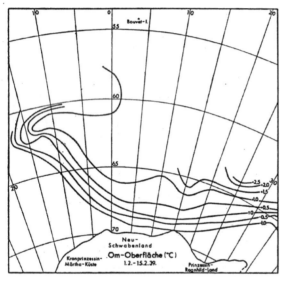

(top) Surface temperatures in the working area of *Schwabenland*, 16-31 January 1939;

(below) Surface temperatures in the working area of *Schwabenland*, 1-15 February 1939

Deacon found that the surface water south of Bouvet was typical of that elsewhere in the Antarctic, with a temperature of -1.8 to -1.9°C [5]. In summer, patches of warm water 2-3°C warmer than the surrounding water were likely to form and float on the surface without mixing with the colder waters beneath. Reichelt and Model observed the same unimodal distribution of temperature in winter and bimodal distribution in summer [9,21]. Both Deacon and Model found the surface waters to be more saline in winter, when the formation of ice caused salt to be excreted as brine [5,21].

Had the German data from the late 1930s been made more widely available, no doubt they would have made a significant contribution to understanding the oceanography of the Southern Ocean in the South Atlantic sector, building on the published work of Deacon, which contained a number of significant geographic gaps [5]. And they would have been referred to in the standard reference work on the oceans, published in English in 1942 [23]. As it was, the intervention of the war left the initiative with the British, who had quite by chance used *Discovery II* to collect data from almost the same line (close to the Greenwich Meridian) at almost the same time as the *Schwabenland*. Consequently it is Mackintosh, who published those British data in 1947 [22], and his predecessor, Deacon [5], rather than Reichelt, Paulsen, or Model, who are most remembered for their contributions to understanding ocean circulation in the region. Such is life in science, where precedence in widely acknowledged publication is all.

190

Sea-Ice and Icebergs

Whalers needed to know the northern ice limit of the sea ice, because that's where whales gathered and where a lot of money could be made. Up to the late 1920s, when Norwegian whalers began pelagic whaling in the Antarctic, there were no ice charts [24]. Eventually, Norwegian whalers began to make charts of the ice edge between 40°W and 110°E by using the information in the logbooks of factory ships [25,26]. When whaling expanded and more nations took part, the pack ice limit could be determined more accurately from year to year. For example, Reichelt charted ice conditions in the whaling area from *Jan Wellem* during the 1936/37 season, including the seaward limit of pack ice, and depicted different forms of ice in the marginal ice-zone [9]. These maps gave valuable information on the variable conditions of the whaling area. Comparing the charts with the experience of the whalers showed that the seaward limit of the pack ice was much further south than normal in that season. Based on these various sources, Kapt'n Kraul, the experienced whaling captain and ice pilot, had a good idea where to expect pack ice as they steamed south, as did Regula, the meteorologist [27].

Leaving Bouvet Island behind, *Schwabenland* encountered the first iceberg at 58°15'S. The bergs break off from the edges of the ice shelves around the margins of the continent. In this region they may rise up to 30 m above sea level, and can extend down to 200 m below sea level, making them a grave potential danger to ships passing too close, not least because these giants of the seas may become unstable and turn over without warning. Kraul counted 239 icebergs during their cruise south. He knew the area of the so-called Bouvet sector very well from his earlier whaling trips, and was astonished that they did not meet pack ice or drift ice and were able to sail strait south from Bouvet Island as far as the edge of the Antarctic ice shelf in open seas. Usually there would be two zones of pack ice here: an outer zone, centred on 58-60°S, with ice drifting eastward from the Weddell Sea, and an inner zone with a westward drift along the coast, both being part of the Weddell Gyre recognised by Deacon and Model between the South Shetland Islands and Enderby Land (at around 50°E), and having some 400 sea miles of clear water between them. Between around 20°W and 20°E, ships with ice protection could move through the outer belt of pack ice until they found more or less open water at 60 to 61°S. East of 20°E the pack ice limit would be located some degrees further south. Once through the outer belt of pack ice, it could be dangerous to approach the coast through the inner belt of coastal pack ice anywhere between 10°W and 90°E, but undoubtedly the most dangerous area was the southern and western Weddell Sea, as shown by the entrapment and drifting there of the *Deutschland,* and the crushing and sinking of Nordenskjöld's *Antarctic* and Shackleton's *Endurance.*

Normally, due to strong solar radiation, the ice of the outer zone started to melt and break up in December, and disappeared around the turn of the year. The melting process was accelerated by warm northerly and easterly winds. Kraul supposed that the favourable conditions encountered by the *Schwabenland* were caused by prevailing warm easterly and northerly winds, an assumption confirmed later by meteorological data from the observatory at Cape Town.

Compared with the expeditions of earlier years in this area, the *Schwabenland* expedition had been remarkably lucky to see very little sea ice during the summer of 1938/39. Charts published in 1940 showed the seasonal variations in the position of the edge of the pack ice, including *Discovery II* data up to January 1939 [28]. The pack ice in the *Schwabenland* study area is shown as furthest south on average in February-March, and was less than average in January, confirming Kraul's suspicions [24]. About ten years later, in 1949/52, when this area was again visited by scientists - on the Norwegian-British-Swedish Expedition - sea ice conditions were very heavy. Looking back with today's knowledge of the way in which temperatures changed globally during the 20th century, it is possible to see the reason for this change in the global warming peak of the late 1930s and early 1940s, which was followed by a marked cooling that reached its nadir around 1950.

Based on the wind conditions and the ice-blink (i.e. a light area in low clouds illuminated by sunlight reflected from the ice below), Kraul predicted that they would find heavy ice conditions at 5°W. They were duly found during the first test flight on 19 January 1939, when a huge amount of pack ice was seen with a 'lead' extending to the southwest deep into the pack ice. Ritscher wanted to start the first long distance flight from 5°W, so *Schwabenland* sailed into this lead, anticipating a very early morning start on the next day. At the time, Kraul did not object, but it soon turned out to have been a bad idea. By 0900 the lead was contracting, and Ritscher had to ask Captain Kottas to move the ship out of the lead to avoid the risk of being crushed by the closing ice. Kraul searched the sky for a 'water-blink' in the low clouds (a dark cloud base as opposed to the light cloud base of 'ice-blink'), which would tell him where there was more open water in the pack ice. He deduced that the next lead was somewhere northeast of their actual position. Kottas tried to steer that way at slow speed, but the ship did not obey the rudder well at slow speeds, and there was a danger that they would collide with lumps of pack ice rising about 7 m out of the sea, which had been broken from some ice shelf ice or small iceberg. Between the large bits of pack ice there were many big and small icebergs. Given this situation they decided to stay in the open lead and to wait for the return of *Boreas* from its flight. In the meantime *Passat* carried out a reconnaissance flight. With the help of a sketch of the view of the pack ice from the aircraft, they found a way out of the pack through a small meandering lead that had been invisible from the ship. It took them five hours to get back into the open water again. This adventure might well have ended in a catastrophe. They had learnt their lesson, and never took such risks again.

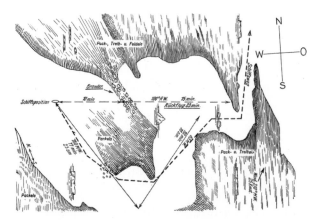

Sketch of navigating Schwabenland through pack ice leads close to the Antarctic ice shelf ice at 69°10'S 4°25'W on 19 January 1939; dashed line is ship's track

Later they saw a remarkable natural spectacle close to the ice shelf. As usual, the ocean current was moving the bigger icebergs westwards because it gained a purchase on their deep keels. Quite by contrast, the westerly wind was blowing small pieces of ice in the opposite direction, along the surface. Where the small pieces moving east met the large bergs moving west they piled up against the cliffs of the bergs like a bow wave, which much crashing and banging. *Schwabenland's* crew had constantly to be on the lookout for big moving icebergs, because this was no place for a ship without an ice-strengthened hull.

SAFE HAVENS IN THE ICE

Kraul passed on to the ship's crew some of his valuable experiences as ice pilot. If you had to seek for a safe place for your ship during a heavy storm parallel to the ice edge, he observed, you would find good protection against swell or wind within the pack ice. This might even be a good place for repairing the plates of the ship's side, or the ship's propeller, because within the pack ice the surface water has almost no swell and the wind speed is only half of the speed outside the pack. Drift ice (meaning large bits of fast drifting ice in open water) on the other hand carries significant danger for a ship with an unprotected hull. Kraul also knew that if you were caught in a fog in loose drift ice, you would find more or less clear water and clear air in the lee of tabular bergs, which offered shelter from drift ice that might otherwise damage the ship. Hunting for bergs in a fog was a risky business, and one where Kraul used his ears to detect the sound of the surf pounding on the cliff-like sides of these great ice masses, thus enabling the ship to avoid them even when they could not be seen because of poor visibility, or to find them and hide behind them.

Schwabenland reached her most southern position at 69°46'S 6°28'E on 30 January 1939. Her most easterly position was at 69°9'S 15°32'E. Further east, on longitude on 15°35'E, they could see thick and heavy sea ice stretching far to the north. Luckily for them, the prevailing westerly winds stopped this ice from advancing west into their work area. This enabled the ship to navigate without any problems with ice for the last six days before they finally turned north for home. Before they did so Gburek made several measurements of the properties of ice floes. On the return trip they saw about 200 icebergs. Kraul noted that such favourable ice conditions were rare and should not be considered as common in planning new expeditions to the Bouvet sector.

THE CHARACTER OF SEA ICE

While aboard *Jan Wellem*, Lüneburg made observations on the distribution and character of sea ice [14]. Noting that various expressions like "pack ice" or "drift ice" were defined differently in English and German, for instance, he pointed to the need for an international standard sea ice nomenclature. On *Schwabenland*, Gburek, the geophysicist, was responsible for observations on sea ice [29,30]. He noted that the sea ice along the Antarctic coast took the form of small patches of drifting ice containing floes up to 25 m long, which were often stacked one above the other. Each floe comprised a lower part made up of ice, which was covered by a thin layer of snow that had already compressed to form 'firn' (or névé); the thicker the floe, the thicker the layer of firn. On the bigger floes Gburek measured up to 60 cm of snow, while the smaller floes were only covered in a thin layer of snowy slush. Using ice probes, Gburek found that the density of the ice below the water line was 0.86 kg/m^3, while it was 0.77 kg/m^3 above the water line below the snow. The ice both above and below the water line had a pronounced granular structure, and was extremely strong and solid and difficult to break even by smashing it with a boathook. Gburek's additional notes were lost in the war, but Model reported that the surface water around the ice floes had a temperature close to -1.75°C, and salinity values close to 33.8% [21].

References

1. Wüst, G., 1926, Bericht über die ozeanographische Untersuchungen der Deutschen Atlantischen Expedition. Zeitschrift der Gesellschaft für Erdkunde zu Berlin, 24-45.

2. Wüst, G., 1936, Schichtung und Zirkulation des Atlantischen Ozeans: Das Bodenwasser und die Stratosphäre. Wissenschaftliche Ergebnisse der Deutschen Atlantischen Expeditionauf dem Forschungs- und Vermessungsschiff "Meteor" 1925-1927, vol. VI, part 1, Walter de Gruyter & Co. Berlin, 1-288.

3. Deacon, G.R., 1934a, Die Nordgrenzen antarktischen und subantarktischen Wassers im Weltmeer. Annalen der Hydrographie und Maritimen Meteorologie 62 (4), 129-136.

4. Deacon, G.R., 1934b, Nochmals: wie entsteht die antarktische Konvergenz? Annalen der Hydrographie und Maritimen Meteorologie 62 (12), 475-478.

5. Deacon, G.E.R., 1937, The hydrology of the Southern Ocean. Discovery Reports XV, Cambridge Univ. Press., 1-124.

6. Meinardus, W., 1923, Meteorologische Ergebnisse der Seefahrt des "Gauss" 1901-1903. In: Deutsche Südpolar-Expedition 1901-1903 im Auftrage des Reichsamtes des Innern, Verlag Georg Reimer, Berlin, III, Meteorologie. Bd. 1 Heft 3.

7. Schott, G., 1926, Die Tiefenbewegungen des Indischen Ozeans. Zugleich zur Besprechung von E. von Drygalski "Ozean und Antarktis". Annalen der Hydrographie und Maritimen Meteorologie 54 (12), 417-431.

8. Clowes, A.J., 1938, Phosphate and silicate in the Southern Ocean. Discovery Reports, 19, Cambridge University Press. 120 pp.

9. Reichelt, W., 1941, Die ozeanographischen Verhältnisse bis zur warmen Zwischenschicht an der antarktischen Eisgrenze im Südsommer 1936/37. Nach Beobachtungen auf dem Walfangmutterschiff "Jan Wellem" im Weddell-Meer. Aus dem Archiv der Deutschen Seewarte und des Marineobservatoriums 61 (5), 30 pp. + 55 pp.

10. Henkel & Cie (ed.), 1939, Der wiedererstandene deutsche Walfang dargestellt an der Entwicklung der Ersten Deutschen Walfang-Gesellschaft in Verbindung mit einem Reisebericht über die 2. "Jan Wellem"- Expedition von Dr. Wolfgang Frank. Henkel & Cie, Düsseldorf, 146 pp.

11. Brennecke, W., 1913, Ozeanographische Arbeiten der Deutschen Antarktischen Expedition, V. Bericht. Annalen der Hydrographie und Maritimen Meteorologie 41 (3), 134-144.

12. Brennecke, W., 1921, Die ozeanographischen Arbeiten der Deutschen Antarktischen Expedition 1911-1912, Archiv der Deutschen Seewarte 39 (1), 1-192.

13. Lüdecke, C., 2007, Diverging Currents - Depicting Southern Ocean Currents in the Early 20th Century. In: Extremes: Oceanography's Adventures at the Poles. K.R. Benson and H.M. Rozwadowski (eds.). Science History Publication/ USA, Sagamore Beach, 71-105.

14. Lüneburg, H., 1940, Über die hydrographischen Untersuchungen südlich Bouvet in der Walfangsaison 1938/39. Zeitschrift für Fischerei und deren Hilfswissenschaften, 38, Beiheft 1: Walforschung, Teil I, 37-64.

15. Paulsen, K.-H., 1939, Die ozeanographischen Arbeiten. In: Vorbericht über die Deutsche Antarktische Expedition 1938/39. Annalen der Hydrographie und Maritimen Meteorologie. VIII, Beiheft, 27-33.

16. Schubert, K., 1958, Wale, Robben und Vögel im Bereich der Deutschen Antarktischen Expedition 1938/39. In: A. Ritscher, Deutsche Antarktische Expedition 1938/39. Wissenschaftliche und fliegerische Ergebnisse. Vol 2. Helmut Striedieck (Geographisch-Kartographische Anstalt Mundus), Hamburg: 257-275.

17. Ritscher, A., 1942, Wissenschaftliche und fliegerische Ergebnisse der Deutschen Antarktischen Expedition 1938/39, Hrsg. im Auftrag der Deutschen Forschungsgemeinschaft. Koehler & Amelang, Leipzig. Vol 1: Text, 304 pp., Pictures and Maps 57 plates and 3 maps.

18. Model, F. und A. Ritscher, 1948, Walfangreise "Jan Wellem" 1937/38 und Deutsche Antarktische Expedition "Schwabenland" 1938/39: K.-H. Paulsen, Oberflächenbeobachtungen im Nord- und Südatlantischen Ozean. Unveröffentlichte Wissenschaftliche Arbeiten des DHI, Serie XII, Nr. 66, vom 24.11.1948.

19. Model, F. und A. Ritscher, 1951, Walfangreise "Jan Wellem" 1937/38 und Deutsche Antarktische Expedition "Schwabenland" 1938/39: K.H. Paulsens Serienbeobachtungen im Antarktisch-Atlantischen Ozean. Unveröffentlichte

Wissenschaftliche Arbeiten des DHI, Serie XII, Nr. 73, vom 18.12.1951.

20. Model, F., 1948, Klimaänderung oder Beobachtungsfehler? Deutsche Hydrographische Zeitschrift 1 (5/6), 220-221.

21. Model, F., 1958, Ein Beitrag zur regionalen Ozeanographie der Weddellsee. In: A. Ritscher, Deutsche Antarktische Expedition 1938/39. Wissenschaftliche und fliegerische Ergebnisse. Vol. 2. Helmut Striedieck (Geographisch-Kartographische Anstalt Mundus), Hamburg: 63-96.

22. Mackintosh, N.A., 1947, The Antarctic Convergence and the distribution of surface temperatures in Antarctic Waters. Discovery Reports XXIII, Cambridge Univ. Press., 177 -212.

23. Sverdrup, H.U., Johnson, M.W., and Fleming, R.H., 1942, The Oceans, Their Physics, Chemistry and General Biology. Prentice-Hall, Englewood Cliffs, N.J., 1087 pp.

24. Kraul, O., 1942, Die Eisverhältnisse in antarktischen Gewässern. In: A. Ritscher, Wissenschaftliche und fliegerische Ergebnisse der Deutschen Antarktischen Expedition 1938/39. Hrsg. im Auftrag der Deutschen Forschungsgemeinschaft. Koehler & Amelang, Leipzig, vol. 1, 273-281.

25. Hansen, H.E., 1934, Limits of the pack-ice in the Antarctic in the area between 40°W and 110°E. Hvalrådets Skifter 9, Oslo.

26. Atlas over Antarktis og Sydishavet, 1936, Ugitt av Norsk Hvalfangernes Assuranceforening; Anledning av Foreningens 25-Års Jublieum.

27. Regula, H., 1954/1958, Die Wetterverhältnisse während der Expedition und die Ergebnisse der meteorologischen Messungen. In: A. Ritscher, Deutsche Antarktische Expedition 1938/39. Wissenschaftliche und fliegerische Ergebnisse. Vol. 2. Hamburg: Striedieck (Geographisch-Kartographische Anstalt Mundus), Helmut 16-40. A preprint was published in 1954.

28. Mackintosh, N.A., and Herdman, H.F.P., 1940, Distribution of the pack ice in the Southern Ocean. Discovery Reports, Cambridge Univ. Press, 19, 285-296.

29. Gburek, L., 1939, Geophysikalischer Arbeitsbericht. In: Vorbericht über die Deutsche Antarktische Expedition 1938/39. Annalen der Hydrographie und Maritimen Meteorologie. VIII, Beiheft, 21-23.

30. Gburek, L., 1958, Erdmagnetische Messungen, Eisuntersuchungen, Strahlungsmessungen und Kernzählungen. In: A. Ritscher, Deutsche Antarktische Expedition 1938/39. Wissenschaftliche und fliegerische Ergebnisse. Vol. 2. Helmut Striedieck (Geographisch-Kartographische Anstalt Mundus), Hamburg: 97-100. (Reprint of Gburek 1939 plus an explanatory remark by the editor).

CHAPTER 14: MARINE LIFE: WHALING RESEARCH AND THE SCHWABENLAND EXPEDITION

German Whaling Research

Much of the marine scientific research conducted by the *Schwabenland* expedition in the Southern Ocean was part of a systematic German effort to put the exploitation of southern whale resources upon a sound, scientific basis, ensuring what in modern terms would be called '*sustainable use*'. This research began with the start of the German whaling industry in the 1936/37 season, with the aim of safeguarding the German pelagic whaling industry in the making. The biological work of the *Schwabenland* has to be seen in the context of this larger picture.

The insight that – in the interest of the industry – renewable resources such as whale stocks should not be treated like non-renewable resources such as coal mines, had led to the creation of whale research institutes in Great Britain and Norway in the 1920s. Paramount were questions of whale migration, of the seasonal and spatial distribution of whale abundance, and of whale reproduction. Systematic whale marking was conducted from the mid 1920s onward: numbered darts were fired into the whale's blubber, the time and position of marking recorded and compared to the time when and position where the whale was later killed, if the dart was recovered from the carcass. In 1930, the International Bureau for Whaling Statistics was created in Oslo, Norway. It published catch statistics of the whaling industry worldwide, giving not only data relevant for the industry to assess the production coming to market, such as the number of whales taken and the amount of oil produced, but also biological parameters, such as the composition of species in the catch, average lengths of whales in different groups of sexual maturity, proportions of males and pregnant or lactating females, and size of foetuses. The industry had grasped the fact that it needed to understand the lives of whales if it wanted to exploit them over the long term. The 1931 Geneva Convention for the Regulation of Whaling stipulated that biological data be collected on each whale taken and communicated to the Bureau for Whaling Statistics (Articles 10 and 12) [1]. The London Agreement of 1937, ratified by Germany, and the subsequent protocols, supported the application of these conservation principles.

The new German whaling operations were expected to conduct scientific whale research as stipulated in these agreements. Even before a special research institute was formally founded in Germany, a biologist was despatched with the first whaling fleet heading to the Antarctic under the German flag in the 1936/37 season. The scientist was Dr. Nicolaus Peters [2] of the Zoological Museum in Hamburg, who had already published a long paper

Dr. Nicolaus Peters (1900-1940) in the uniform of a naval lieutenant

on plankton in the Weddell Sea, based on material collected during the second German Antarctic Expedition 1911-12 [3]. Peters was destined to become the Director of the Reich-Institute for Whale Research (Reichsstelle für Walforschung), which was founded upon their return and which essentially he set up. Starting in 1937, Peters was the scientific expert on Wohlthat's delegations to the whaling conferences in London and Oslo [2,4]. Among other things the Institute was responsible for whale marking [5].

The Institute was founded, run and paid for by the Reich Ministry for Food and Agriculture. It appears that – as in other whaling nations [6,7,8] – whaling companies paid the ministry a certain fee per unit of whale oil sold, in order to finance whale research. This of course increased the price of whale oil. But since whale research was an obligation required by international agreements, the ministry retained this budgetary responsibility in spite of an offer by the Reich Institute for Dairy Products, Oils and Fats to cover the costs of whale research from their own funds, which were generated by the difference between the purchase and sale prices of whale oil fixed by the dairy institute [8,9].

The budget allocated for German whale research increased almost five-fold between the two last whaling seasons, from 21,781 Reichsmark in 1937/38 to 98,000 Reichsmark in 1938/39. This did not reflect the number of biologists despatched with the whaling fleets and *Schwabenland*, which increased by only 50% from six to nine (including a chemist) (Appendix 8, Table 3). Part of the budget increase was certainly caused by the production costs of the documentary whaling film "Kolonie Eismeer" (see Chapter 1).

Aside from studying whales, the biologists also collected plankton for studies of whale food. For plankton catches, they used a sampling net designed by Hentschel a few years earlier [10,11,12,13].

Unfortunately, very few original sources as to the scientific nature and scope of German whale and whale-related biological research have survived, because the zoological museum that housed the whale research institute was completely destroyed in the Hamburg air raids of July 1943. Luckily, some original materials survived, among them the catch diaries

198

of most shipboard biologists, and several albums with photo contact prints (Appendix 8, Table 2) that were preserved thanks to the foresight of fisheries and whale biologist Dr. Kurt Schubert [14]. These catch records were used to validate the statistics submitted by Germany to the Bureau of Whaling Statistics [15]. They were found to be quite reliable, and even included data on infractions, such as the harpooning of a 14.9 m long male Southern right whale (*Eubalaena australis*), a protected species, taken some 410 km southsouthwest of the South Orkney Islands on 1 March 1939 by whale catcher *Rau V* [5,16,17]. The anatomical samples collected from this rare whale by Dr. Fr. Zeller were probably destroyed during the war.

Results of German field research on whales and their environment were published in two special issues of the 'Zeitschrift für Fischerei und deren Hilfswissenschaften' (Journal of Fisheries and Fisheries-related Sciences) [12,18,19,20,21,22]. Barkley [11] and Schubert [13] published additional summaries on the whale research conducted on the *Schwabenland*. One of the special issue papers, by F. H. Karcher [18], dealt with diatom skin films of whales and their possible correlation with the seasonal and spatial distribution of whales, whale maturity and body condition. Although this study had potential bearing on whale management, Karcher did not arrive at any conclusions that revised previous British and Norwegian research, nor did he provide answers to the questions left open by them. The merit of his study was that he added material from whales caught pelagically in Weddell, Bouvet and Kerguelen waters, whereas previous studies had focussed mostly on the South Georgia whaling grounds.

At Heidelberg University a doctoral thesis addressing the international regulation of whaling was developed by Langberg and defended successfully in 1940; a companion thesis on territorial claims to sovereignty in the Antarctic was developed and defended successfully by Baare-Schmidt at the same time.

The *Schwabenland's* Contribution to Biological Research

Erich Barkley, biologist on board the floating factory ship C.A. *Larsen* in 1937/38 and on the *Schwabenland* in 1938/39, published a long report on the food and the anatomy of the filtering apparatus of the krill [12]. It was based not only on his own field studies, but also on those of his colleagues on board five other floating factory ships (with the exception of the *Skytteren*), who had been commissioned by Peters to collect samples for this research. The paper included his findings from material collected on board *Schwabenland* in waters off Neu-Schwabenland, which proved to be almost devoid of krill. It expanded on previous studies conducted by British scientists such as Alistair Hardy, Neil Mackintosh, John Hart, Francis Fraser and others, who had published them in Discovery Reports 8, 9, 11, 14 in 1934 and 1935 respectively.

Barkley's brief summary of the biological work he had conducted on *Schwabenland* [11]

The whale marking gun room at the Institute for Whale Research after its move to Kirchenallee in 1939

An infraction of the London whaling agreement dutifully reported by shipboard biologist Zeller: a rare southern right whale harpooned by mistake and processed on board *Walter Rau* in the Antarctic on 1 March 1939

Whale biologist Erich Barkley (1912-1944) with penguins destined for German zoos

testifies to difficulties encountered on account of the secret and strictly geopolitical agenda of the expedition, which left little opportunity for whale research. In addition to hydrographic and plankton sampling, Barkley collected data on sightings of whales, seals and birds. The biological work conducted by *Schwabenland* was not exclusively directed at whales. Seals, birds and plankton likewise were targets, insofar as their study potentially provided a better understanding of cetacean ecology. In volume II of the Expedition report, Otto Stadel of the Federal Fisheries Research Institute edited a 175-page section on the biological results of the expedition [24], which included papers on Diatoms [25], Decapod larvae [26], Salps [27], Chaetognaths [28], fish and fish larvae [29], and whales, seals and birds [13]. In his introduction, Stadel [24] pointed out that near the ice edge, south of 69°S, biological field research was significantly reduced due to other expedition priorities. Only on the return voyage was systematic plankton research feasible, and 13 samples were netted at regular intervals (150 nautical miles) along or close to the 0° meridian between Antarctica and Cape Town.

Half-hour observations of birds took place at noon on *Schwabenland* and were supplemented by similar observations from the German floating factory ships, enabling Schubert [13] to produce four distribution maps and a table of relative species abundance. Not surprisingly, bird abundance was high in the zone of the Antarctic convergence between 61° and 65°S, as was that of whales. When whales were processed, scavenging birds flocked in the wake of the floating factories, feeding on the offal. Observations of seals by *Schwabenland* were made randomly from the airplanes, and six animals were collected from ice floes, but the notes Barkley made before he was killed during the war were incomplete and yielded no insightful results. Schubert's records show that most of the shot seals were Weddell Seals, with one Crabeater Seal.

Military action during the war destroyed almost all the larger specimens deposited at the Reich whale research institute. Of the plankton samples, losses were less dramatic, but many suffered from iterative dislodgements, so that more delicate organisms such as radiolarians, appendicularians, medusas and siphonophorians were dismembered beyond recognition.

In his short papers on decapod larvae and salps and his longer piece on chaetognaths – all collected by Barkley on *Schwabenland* – Stadel [26,27,28] makes passing reference not only to the logistical difficulties that hampered meaningful scientific research in the target area of the expedition, and to the effects of war on the quantity and quality of the sampled specimens, but also to some flaws inherent in the research method itself. For instance, the mesh width of the various plankton nets used seemed to have been unsuited to representative sampling of salps.

A similar view was expressed by Hamburg biologist Wolfgang Villwock, whose note on the polychaetes had to be very short because the sampling nets used could not be closed at certain depths, thus preventing insights into the vertical distribution of these organisms in the water column [30].

The Bremen self-taught diatom expert Friedrich Hustedt examined the diatoms collected from the digestive tracts of krill and salps as well as from plankton samples netted in the Kerguelen area by the biologist of the floating factory *C.A. Larsen* in the 1937/38 season. This material was supplemented by plankton samples from the *Schwabenland* expedition. Hustedt [25] was able to describe over two dozen new diatom species and variants, as well as to re-name known forms.

Perhaps inevitably, as far as the non-cetacean organisms are concerned, the political priorities of the *Schwabenland* expedition prevented biological research in the Antarctic of any meaningful, systematic scope. In addition, there were some teething troubles with the methods applied. Finally, of all that was sampled, much was destroyed or rendered useless by the effects of war. The contribution of *Schwabenland* to whale and whaling-related research was therefore negligible, and pales by comparison with long-term studies such as that on phytoplankton periodicity in Antarctic surface waters conducted by Hart and others and published in the "Discovery Reports" [31].

Germany's General Contribution to Whale Research

The publications by the German whale scientists contributed by adding material from other parts of the Antarctic whaling grounds than those covered by British and Norwegian whale scientists, but contained no pioneering achievements, substantially revisionist methods or novel research trends. Apart from a few methodological modifications, they followed the research schemes laid out before by British and Norwegian whaling biologists such as Hardy, Macintosh, Wheeler and Hjort.

The German work suffered in another way too. Whether obtained in the field or in the laboratory in Hamburg, the results were published – if at all – in German and not in the *lingua franca* of the international scientific community, English. In addition, because the papers came off the press during the war years in probably fairly small runs (the special issues are scarce in libraries!), with much of the customary interlibrary exchange severed, their findings were not discussed in the international cetological community. German whale research of the 1930s thus seems to have had no international scientific impact; this pertains to the marine biological results of the *Schwabenland* expedition as well. However, one aspect of German whaling research did have a substantial international impact – the pioneering German Whaling Handbook [32].

The German Whaling Handbook

When the whale research institute was founded in October 1937, its director was commissioned to edit a "handbook of the historical, legal, scientific and technical background of whaling", for which there was no precedent in any of the established whaling nations. It was to serve the interests of political, administrative and entrepreneurial decision-makers involved with German whaling. Given the Reich's economic political agenda, and the goal of striving for the complete utilisation of each whale carcass, the handbook's strength lies in its several seminal chapters on uses of whale by-products such as meat (canned, frozen, pickled, as meat extract or whale meat meal), endocrine glands and organs (for hormones and vitamins), or fibre, baleen, sperm oil and ambergris [33,34]. Not everyone was happy with the handbook. For instance, the whaler owners were quite concerned that many of the technical problems, which had been successfully tackled and solved by the concerted efforts of the "section whale processing" (Fachgruppe Verarbeitung von Walen), and at a considerable cost to the industry, were thus disclosed to the public and foreign competitors[35].

The handbook also covered the current state of knowledge about whale biology [32]. Aspects of whale abundance in relation to whaling were summarily treated for each species. At the end of his original manuscript, Peters worded a lengthy warning against over-harvesting of whale stocks ('Nun noch ein Wort über den Raubbau!' :*In closing, a word about over-fishing!*). In a confidential, unpublished talk before the "section whale processing" in Berlin in October 1938, Peters also expressed concerns about the sustainability of whaling, especially regarding the fin whale catch, which had increased almost three-fold in the past three seasons, from 9,200 to 25,800 [36]. Peters regarded the complete utilisation of the whale as the crucial instrument against waste of the valuable raw material: incomplete utilisation stimulated faster catching, resulting in excessive hunting pressure on whale stocks, leading to stock depletion and ensuring higher production costs for whalers, thus making whaling uneconomic. Although he explicitly and morally criticised the "greed" of whalers, he tried to appeal to their sense of business, as others such as Bjarne Aagaard and Paul Sarasin had done before him [37,38]. But needless to say, his warning was deemed inappropriate in a handbook intended to serve the interest of a whaling industry in the making; accordingly, the entire passage was deleted by an anonymous reviewer of the Ministry of Food and Agriculture [39]. Peters' handbook "Der neue deutsche Walfang" (New German Whaling) was published in August 1938 without the editor's caveat.

Unlike the whale studies of his staff, Peters' pioneering handbook did enjoy international acclaim. Without the editor's warning against over-harvesting, and because of its indisputable value for the industry, the German whaling handbook set a pattern for other newcomers to Antarctic whaling, such as Japan, the Netherlands and the Soviet Union. In these countries, vernacular handbooks of a similar scope were produced, giving due credit to their German precursor [40,41,42,43].

The subsequent German contribution to cetacean studies was Whale Research (Walforschung) part II, released in 1942 under the editorship of Professor Alfred Willer [44], but its papers on haematology and x-ray anatomy [21,22] and on a blue whale enzyme [20] did not contain any research on the ecology or the environment.

The Impact of the Second World War

War brought an end not only to plans for two more research expeditions, but also to plans for a new whaling fleet. German whaling and whale science never completely recovered. During the war there was no German whaling. When German troops occupied Norway, in April 1940, all confiscated Norwegian whaling material was placed under the management of the EDWG (Erste Deutsche Walfang Gesellschaft / 'First German Whaling Company'), a daughter of the giant Henkel industrial trust. In the short term this helped to safeguard the supply of whale oil - which had become a staple item in Germany, as it

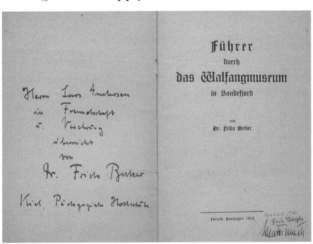

was in WWI. There were also long-term interests, with Nazi rule over much of the "Germanic" world in view. Occupying forces granted special protection to the whaling museum that had been founded in 1917 (during the previous war) in Sandefjord, then the world's whaling capital, with the purpose of advancing the technological, scientific and economic progress of the national (Norwegian) whaling industry by creating a suitable research facility with library and collections; a museum guide in German was printed in 1943 [45].

1943 German guide to a museum-type whale research institute in occupied Norway, the Christensen's Whaling Museum

Back in Germany, the whale research institute had been completely bombed out, and was formally dissolved in 1948. Its former staff member Dr. Kurt Schubert, now employed with the Bundesforschungsanstalt für Fischerei (Federal Fisheries Research Institute), summarised or edited the results of his colleagues' pre-war research that had not been destroyed [13].

References

1. Birnie, P., 1985, International Regulation of Whaling. From Conservation of Whaling to Conservation of Whales and Regulation of Whale-Watching. 2 vols., New York, London, Rome.

2. Willer, A., 1940, Dr. Nicolaus Peters †. In: Zeitschrift für Fischerei und deren Hilfswissenschaften 38 (4/5), 395-399. Obituary.

3. Peters, N., 1928, Beiträge zur Planktonbevölkerung der Weddellsee. Die Peridineenbevölkerung der Weddellsee mit besonderer Berücksichtigung der Wachstums- und Variationsformen. In: Internationale Revue der gesamten Hydrobiologie und Hydrographie 21 (1), 17 – 146. Peters's first paper on Antarctic plankton.

4. Klatt, B., 1950, Gedenken – Nikolaus Peters. In: Mitteilungen aus dem Hamburgischen Zoologischen Museum und Institut 50, 1-2. Obituary.

5. Barthelmess Whaling Archive, Cologne. Unpublished.

6. Hart, I. B., 2006, Whaling in the Falkland Islands and Dependencies 1904-1931. A history of shore and bay-based whaling in the Antarctic. Newton St Margarets: Pequena. On financing whaling research.

7. Drejer, B., 2006 a, Aukra Hval A/S –det første industrieventyret på Nyhamna. Molde: Morild. On Norwegian whaling research.

8. Drejer, B., 2006 b, Aukra Hval, forsøksdrift and the Møre investigations. In: Ringstad, Jan Erik (ed.): Whaling and history II: New perspectives (= Kommandør Chr. Christensens Hvalfangstmuseum, Publikasjon 31). Sandefjord: KCCHM, 2006, 77-83. On Norwegian whaling research.

9. 17 June 1938 and 29 June 1938 Bundesarchiv, Koblenz, R 15 V / 288. Unpublished.

10. Hentschel, E., 1938, Über quantatitatvie Seihmethoden in der Planktonforschung. In: ICES Journal of Marine Science 13(3), 304-308. Methods of plankton research.

11. Barkley, E., 1939, Die biologischen Arbeiten der Expedition. In: Deutsche Seewarte (ed.): Vorbericht über die Deutsche Antarktische Expedition 1938/39 = Annalen der Hydrographie und maritimen Meteorologie, VIII, 1939, Beiheft, 19-21. Schwabenland biology.

12. Barkley, E., 1940, Nahrung und Filterapparat des Walkrebschens Euphausia superba Dana. In: Zeitschrift für Fischerei und deren Hilfswissenschaften, 38 (Beiheft 1: Walforschung, Teil I), 1940, 65-156. Krill food and anatomy.

13. Schubert, K., 1958, Wale, Robben und Vögel im Bereich der Deutschen Antarktischen Expedition 1938/39. In: Deutsche Antarktische Expedition 1938/39 mit dem Flugzeugstützpunkt der Deutschen Lufthansa A.G. M.S. „Schwabenland", Kapitän A. Kottas. Ausgeführt unter der Leitung von Kapitän A. Ritscher. Wissenschaftliche und fliegerische Ergebnisse, Vol. 2, Geographisch-Kartographische Anstalt "Mundus", Helmut Striedieck, Hamburg, 257-275. Whales, seals and birds.

14. Barthelmess, K., 1997, Die Fauthsche Versuchsanlage auf der norwegischen Walfangstation Hestnes. Ein Betrag zu den Autarkiebestrebungen im Neuen Deutschen Walfang. In: Deutsches Schiffahrtsarchiv 20, 359-372. Autarchy of German whaling.

15. Kock, K.-H., 1996,Validation of Catch Data from German Whaling in the Southern Ocean before World War II. In: International Whaling Commission (ed.): Reports of the International Whaling Commission 46, 649-651.

16. Barthelmess, K., 2007, Der Südkaper der WALTER RAU 1938/39. In: Fluke 14, 2007, 28-30. The illegal right whale of 1939.

17. Barthelmess, K., 2008, Die Walstatt des Südkapers der WALTER RAU 1938/39 in: Fluke, 15, 2008, p. 9. The illegal right whale of 1939.

18. Karcher, F.H., 1940 Über den Algenbewuchs auf südlichen Walen. In: Zeitschrift für Fischerei und deren Hilfswissenschafte 38 (Beiheft 1: Walforschung, Teil I), 13-36. Algae. Contains a list of the German whaling shipboard biologists.

19. Knoll, W., 1940, Blut und embryonale Blutbildung bei den Walen. In: Zeitschrift für Fischerei und deren Hilfswissenschaften 38 (Beiheft 1: Walforschung, Teil I), -12. Whale hematology.

20. Bomskov, C., and Schall, W., 1942, Über den Prolaktingehalt der Blauwalhypophyse. In: Zeitschrift für Fischerei und deren Hilfswissenschaften 40 (Beiheft 2: Walforschung, Teil II), 55-66. Whale endocrinology.

21. Knoll, W., 1942 a, Beobachtungen über die Blutzellbildung bei Barten- und Zahnwalembryonen. In: Zeitschrift für Fischerei und deren Hilfswissenschaften 40 (Beiheft 2: Walforschung, Teil II), 1-29 . Whale hematology.

22. Knoll, W., 1942 b, Röntgenbefunde bei Walen. In: Zeitschrift für Fischerei und deren Hilfswissenschaften 40 (Beiheft 2: Walforschung, Teil II), 31-54. X-ray-supported embryology of whales.

23. Ritscher, A, 1942, Wissenschaftliche und fliegerische Ergebnisse der Deutschen Antarktischen Expedition 1938/39, Hrsg. im Auftrag der Deutschen Forschungsgemeinschaft. Vol, 1, Koehler & Amelang, xv, 304 pp. Vol. 1 of the Schwabenland research.

24. Stadel, O., 1958 a, Die biologischen Arbeiten der 'Deutschen Antarktischen Expedition 1938/39. In: Deutsche Antarktische Expedition 1938/39 mit dem Flugzeugstützpunkt der Deutschen Lufthansa A.G. M.S. „Schwabenland", Kapitän A. Kottas. Ausgeführt unter der Leitung von Kapitän A. Ritscher. Wissenschaftliche und fliegerische Ergebnisse, Vol. 2, Geographisch-Kartographische Anstalt "Mundus", Helmut Striedieck, Hamburg, 101-102. Biological research.

25. Hustedt, F., 1958, Diatomeen aus der Antarktis und dem Südatlantik. In: Deutsche Antarktische Expedition 1938/39 mit dem Flugzeugstützpunkt der Deutschen Lufthansa A.G. M.S. „Schwabenland", Kapitän A. Kottas. Ausgeführt unter der Leitung von Kapitän A. Ritscher. Wissenschaftliche und fliegerische Ergebnisse, Vol. 2, Geographisch-Kartographische Anstalt "Mundus", Helmut Striedieck, Hamburg, 103-191. Diatoms.

26. Stadel, O., 1958 b, Die Decapodenlarven. In: Deutsche Antarktische Expedition 1938/39 mit dem Flugzeugstützpunkt der Deutschen Lufthansa A.G. M.S. „Schwabenland", Kapitän A. Kottas. Ausgeführt unter der Leitung von Kapitän A. Ritscher. Wissenschaftliche und fliegerische Ergebnisse, Vol. 2, Geographisch-Kartographische Anstalt "Mundus", Helmut Striedieck, Hamburg, 192-198. Decapod larvae.

27. Stadel, O., 1958 c, Die Salpen. In: Deutsche Antarktische Expedition 1938/39 mit dem Flugzeugstützpunkt der Deutschen Lufthansa A.G. M.S. „Schwabenland", Kapitän A. Kottas. Ausgeführt unter der Leitung von Kapitän A. Ritscher. Wissenschaftliche und fliegerische Ergebnisse, Vol. 2, Geographisch-Kartographische Anstalt "Mundus", Helmut Striedieck, Hamburg, 199-207. Salps.

28. Stadel, O., 1958 d, Die Chaetognathen-Ausbeute. In: Deutsche Antarktische Expedition 1938/39 mit dem Flugzeugstützpunkt der Deutschen Lufthansa A.G. M.S. „Schwabenland", Kapitän A. Kottas. Ausgeführt unter der Leitung von Kapitän A. Ritscher. Wissenschaftliche und fliegerische Ergebnisse, Vol. 2, Geographisch-Kartographische Anstalt "Mundus", Helmut Striedieck, Hamburg, 208-244. Chaetognaths.

29. Krefft, G., 1958, Antarktische Fische und Fischlarven aus den Planktonfängen. In: Deutsche Antarktische Expedition 1938/39 mit dem Flugzeugstützpunkt der Deutschen Lufthansa A.G. M.S. „Schwabenland", Kapitän A.

Kottas. Ausgeführt unter der Leitung von Kapitän A. Ritscher. Wissenschaftliche und fliegerische Ergebnisse, Vol. 2, Geographisch-Kartographische Anstalt "Mundus", Helmut Striedieck, Hamburg, 249-256. Fish and fish larvae.

30. Villwock, W., 1958, Kurze Mitteilung über die Polychaeten. In: Deutsche Antarktische Expedition 1938/39 mit dem Flugzeugstützpunkt der Deutschen Lufthansa A.G. M.S. „Schwabenland", Kapitän A. Kottas. Ausgeführt unter der Leitung von Kapitän A. Ritscher. Wissenschaftliche und fliegerische Ergebnisse, Vol. 2, Geographisch-Kartographische Anstalt "Mundus", Helmut Striedieck, Hamburg, 245-256. Polychaetes.

31. Hart, T. J., 1942, Phytoplankton periodicity in Antarctic surface waters. In: Discovery Reports, Cambridge Univ. Press, 21, 261-356.

32. Peters, N., 1938 a, Der neue deutsche Walfang: Ein praktisches Handbuch seiner geschichtlichen, rechtlichen, naturwissenschaftlichen und technischen Grundlagen. Hamburg, Hansa. The pioneering German whaling handbook.

33. Hamburgische Ausstellungs-Gesellschaft (ed.), 1939, Führer durch die 1. Deutsche Fischerei- und Walfang-Ausstellung Segen des Meeres. Hamburg 1939, 28. April - 29. Mai. Bock & Schulz. Hamburg. Exhibition guide presenting German achievemnts in the complete utilisation of whale carcasses.

34. Reichsarbeitsgemeinschaft für Volksernährung (Hrg.), 1939, Lebensmittel und Rohstoffe vom Wal (= Schriftenreihe der Reichsarbeitsgemeinschaft für Volksernährung beim Reichsausschuß für Volksgesundheitsdient, Heft 9). Theodor Steinkopf Dresden & Leipzig, Food and non-food products from whales.

35. Winterhoff, 4 January 1938, Letter by Dr. Edmund Winterhoff of Walter Rau Neusser Ölwerke AG to Reichsstelle für Walforschung, archive Federal Fisheries Research Institute, Hamburg. Unpublished

36. Peters, N., 1938 b, Über den antarktischen Walbestand und die Massnahmen zu seiner Überwachung. Vortrag gehalten auf der Tagung der Fachgruppe 'Verarbeitung von Walen' am 11. Oktober 1938 in Berlin. Unpublished typescript, 6 pp. Bundesarchiv Koblenz, R 15 V / 12. On whale management and whaling control.

37. Ringstad, J.E., 2006, Bjarne Aagaard and his crusade against pelagic whaling in the late 1920s. In: Ringstad, Jan Erik (ed.): Whaling and history II: New perspectives (= Kommandør Chr. Christensens Hvalfangstmuseum, Publikasjon 31). Sandefjord: KCCHM, 167-178.

38. Barthelmess, K., 2006, An international campaign against whaling and sealing prior to World War One. In: Ringstad, Jan Erik (Hrg.): Whaling and history II: New perspectives (= Kommandør Chr. Christensens Hvalfangstmuseum, Publikasjon 31). Sandefjord: KCCHM, 2006, 47-165. On Sarasin's anti-whaling campaign.

39. MS in the Bundesforschungsanstalt für Fischerei, Hamburg. Unpublished

40. Omura H., Matuura, Y., and Miyazaki, I., 1942, Kujira. Sono kagaku to hogei no jiisai [Whale. Its science and the practice of whaling]. Tokio: Suisansha. Japanese whaling handbook after Peters's prototype.

41. Feltmann, C.F., and Vervoort, W., 1949, Walvisvaart. Biologische en technische grondslagen van de moderne, antarctische walvisvaart. Gorinchem: Noordduijn & Zoon. The Dutch whaling handbook after Peters's prototype.

42. Knudtzon, H. T., 1951, Hvalfangst – fangstnæring, part IV in: Jan Strøm (ed.): Norsk fiskeri og fangst håndbok: Saltvannsfiskeriene, ferskvannsfiskeriene, ishavsfangsten, hvalfangsten. Vol. 1 (of 2). Cammermeyers, Olso, 864-970. A handbook-like chapter. In part patterned after Peters's handbook.

43. Golovliev, I. P., 1959, Technika kitoboinogo promisla [technology of whaling]. Moscow: Pishtshepromisdat. The Soviet whaling handbook after Peters's prototype.

44. Willer, A., 1942, Walforschung, Teil II (= Zeitschrift für Fischerei und deren Hilfswissenschaften 40, Beiheft 2). Special issue on German whale research, part 2.

45. Becker, F., 1943, Führer durch das Walfangmuseum in Sandefjord. Larvik: Druckerei Preutz. The German guide through the whaling museum and research institute in occupied Norway.

if only...

If only Adolf Hoel had not been visiting Germany in December 1938, the 3rd German Antarctic Expedition could have continued on its secret way, and with its fantastic discovery of previously unknown mountain ranges – not to mention the German landings on the coast – Norway would not have rushed as it did to claim Dronning Maud Land, and the international community might well have supported instead a German claim to Neu-Schwabenland.

If only Ernst Herrmann had been able to publish in 1943, when he wrote it, his scientific paper on the volcanic origin of the Mid-Atlantic Ridge, he rather than Maurice Ewing of the USA might have won the credit for this novel concept.

If only Karl Heinz Paulsen had survived to write up the oceanographic data from the German whaling fleet and the *Schwabenland*, he rather than Neil Mackintosh of Great Britain might have been able to write a definitive follow up to George Deacon's studies of circulation in the Southern Ocean.

If only Regula's, Lange's and Gburek's data and Barkley's samples had not been destroyed by bombing, the meteorological, geophysical and biological results from the expedition would have been far more comprehensive and complete.

If only there had been a follow-up expedition in 1939/40 to establish ground truth for the aerial photographs, the maps of Neu-Schwabenland would have been more accurate soon after their first printing.

If only Germany had not invaded Poland on 1 September 1939, leading Britain and France to declare war with Germany on 3 September, the 3rd German Antarctic Expedition would likely have been far better known outside Germany, because its second volume of results would have been completed, published and widely distributed long before it eventually appeared in 1958.

If only there had been no war, Wohlthat would have approved Ritscher's plan for a follow-up expedition in 1940/41 to establish a German whaling base on the Neu-Schwabenland coast, from which it is likely that scientific expeditions might have begun to explore the hinterland 17 years before the International Geophysical Year of 1957-58 (IGY). Instead the task fell to Norway, Belgium and Japan with their three coastal stations in Dronning Maud Land during the IGY.

In reality, despite all these real and apparent 'failures', the expedition was a great success in providing maps and photographs of an enormous new mountain range – radically changing geographical perceptions about the far off continent, and stimulating the urge in German hearts as well as in others of follow-up expeditions to find out more. Knowing what we now do about the expedition from published reports and private papers it seems to us that the results are far less well known than they should be, even in German circles. Paradoxically, the influence of the expedition was much wider than might at first appear – it is just not realised today. The impact of the photographs and maps on others in Antarctic circles was substantial – not least in guiding the evolution and activities in Dronning Maud Land of the Norwegian-British-Swedish Expedition of 1949-52, of Norway and Belgium during the IGY, and of many others afterwards – beginning with the Russians and their East German colleagues working out of the Schirmacher Oasis from 1959 on. They would not have been in the oasis in the first place if Ritscher's team had not discovered those icy lakes amid the barren rocky hills. Discovery is always a stimulus to others to find out more. Too little credit is rendered to these first discoverers. Though the expedition's legacy does live on in mountain names, few appreciate their origins. All credit to Norway, nevertheless, for the initial discovery of this far off shoreline, and, indeed, for retaining so many of the German names – even if in Norwegian form.

This was a leading edge scientific expedition, using the most advanced technology of its day for aerial photographic surveys, studies of the meteorology of the upper atmosphere, and seabed mapping. Its key discoveries linger on - in mountain names, in the first north-south cross section through the atmosphere – revealing the circulation in both hemispheres -, and in some of the very first accurate echo-sounding profiles of the South Atlantic and of the Antarctic continental shelf. Who first discovered deep channels crossing the Antarctic continental margin? Ernst Herrmann. Herrmann, Ritscher, Kraul and the *Schwabenland* now have Antarctic submarine canyons named after them. Herrmann may not have appreciated the significance of the flatness of the ocean basin floor off the Antarctic coast, which we now know to represent an abyssal plain, but he cannot be faulted for not appreciating every nuance of *Schwabenland's* astounding and novel echo-sounding profiles. He was working at a time when nobody fully understood the shape of the deep, and Shepherd's first textbook on the topic had not even been contemplated - indeed it did not appear until 1948.

The unique photographs of the high mountains of Dronning Maud Land may still have something more to tell us. In them is a record of the snow-line in January 1939. A careful comparison with the snow-line in photographs taken today will show how this far off environment has responded to the several ensuing decades of climate change. There is no comparable source of data until the International Geophysical Year of 1957-58, and that was nothing like as comprehensive in its coverage. *Boreas* and *Passat* may still have their uses in the science of global warming - a realisation that was far from the minds of Alfred

Ritscher and his men when they set sail for the south.

Finally, we hope that this comprehensive and true account of the expedition, based on the archives of the participants and reputable publications, lays to rest the ghosts at the heart of the urban myths surrounding the expedition and its aftermath. The expedition did not create a German base of any kind on the Antarctic shore. There was no follow up to do so. And in any case, German submarines of World War II vintage could not have penetrated a 1000 km wide ring of sea ice to reach the coast of Dronning Maud Land in the southern winter of 1945 to deposit human or other relics of the Nazi regime. The myth of German occupation of Dronning Maud Land during the war years has no substance whatsoever.

Acknowledgements

Research for a book like his is impossible without the help of many people and for many different reasons. We would like to record our debt to whaling expert Klaus Barthelmess for contributing the chapter on biology and whaling, and his contribution to Chapter1. Sadly Klaus passed away shortly before the publication of this book. We are grateful to Bob Headland and Peter Clarkson (Scott Polar Research Institute – SPRI, UK), for advice on Antarctic science and history; Lisle Rose (USA) for advice on the 1939-1941 expedition of Admiral Richard E Byrd, for press cuttings from the New York Times, and for an unpublished manuscript by Richard (Dick) White; Carlos Mey (Argentina, Histamar), and Daniel Mesa (Argentina, www.elsnorkel.com) for providing U-Boat photos; Naomi Boneham (SPRI) for help with British press cuttings; Mark Gilbert and Shirley Sawtell (SPRI), for library assistance; Don Manning (Cambridge University), for reproducing some of the figures; Stein Tronstad (Norwegian Polar Institute, Norway) for the base map in the colour section; Susan Barr (Norway) for providing historical information on Norwegian claims; Hartwig Gernandt (Alfred-Wegener Institute – AWI, Bremerhaven, Germany) for photographs, satellite pictures, advice on maps, and the history of German research in Dronning Maud Land, as well as Hans Werner Schenke (AWI) for detailed maps from the General Bathymetric Chart of the Oceans and from the *Meteor* Expedition; Maike Thomsen (AWI) for a photo of the Neumayer III station; Kurt Brunner (Universität der Bundeswehr, München) for his detail scan of the map of the Wohlthat Massif; Laura Kissel (Byrd Polar Research Centre, USA) for advice on connections between the German and American expeditions of the period; Jane Stephenson (National Oceanography Centre Library, Southampton, UK) for help in tracking down documents and maps; Tillmann Mohr (Germany) for advice on Herbert Regula; Regine Damm (Zoologischer Garten, Berlin, Germany) for information on the arrival at the Berlin Zoo of penguins from the expedition; Frode Skarstein (University of Tromsø, Norway) for information about Adolf Hoel; Gwyn Griffiths (National Oceanography Centre, Southampton, UK) for information on horizontal echo-sounding and comparable modern expedition costs: Gerd Wegner (Johann Heinrich von Thünen-Institut Institut für Seefischerei, Hamburg, Germany) and Katrin Linse (British Antarctic Survey, UK), for information on the expedition's plankton samples; Hans-Werner Schencke (AWI) for reviewing the seabed chapter; David McNeill (Map Librarian, Royal Geographical Society, UK) for Antarctic information in the 1958 Times Atlas; Stella Duff (International Whaling Commission, Histon, UK) for providing a copy of the report of the International Whaling Conference of 17-20 July, 1939; Sarah Hartwell (Rauner Special Collections, Dartmouth, USA), Fred I. Presteng (Norwegian Polar Institute Library, Norway), Lynn Lay (Byrd Polar Research Center, USA), and

Hayley Thomas (British Antarctic Survey Library, UK) for help in tracking down the accession dates on Ritscher's 1939 report; Henk Brolsma (Australian Antarctic Division, Australia) for tracking down the source of German Antarctic data for the 1939 Australian map of Antarctica; Rosemary Nash, for help with typing and scanning; Karl-Heinz Pörtge (Geographical Institute, Göttingen, Germany) for informing us about the existence of Kosack's draft of a new Antarctic map; Olav Orheim (Norway) for helpful discussions; and Fred Roots (Canada) for sharing his memories of the Norwegian-British-Swedish Expedition with us. We apologise if we have inadvertently left anyone out.

Our special thanks go to Ritscher's youngest daughter Gertraude Hartman, who provided us with Ritscher's files of the *Schwabenland* expedition, which nearly completely survived the Second World War. We also thank Herrmann's daughter Barbara Ronte-Herrmann for the information from Herrmann's private files about the expedition. We were also happy that we were allowed to use Ritscher's and Herrmann's private pictures and diagrams from the expedition.

For gracefully tolerating our shared obsession in bringing this project to a conclusion, and putting up with our many absences – both physical and mental, CL thanks her husband Gerhard and daughters Sabine and Christine, and CS thanks his wife Diana.

APPENDICES

I
The German whaling fleets 1936/37 to 1938/39 in tabular overview

The German whaling fleets: ownership and management

Floating factory & home port	Owner / charterer		Managing company
Jan Wellem Wesermünde	Henkel & Cie, GmbH, Düsseldorf		Erste Deutsche Walfang Gesellschaft mbH, Hamburg
C.A. Larsen Sandefjord	Blaahval A/S, Oslo	Margarine-Rohstoff-Beschaffungs-Gesellschaft, Berlin	Hamburger Walfang-Kontor GmbH, Hamburg
Skytteren Tønsberg	Skytteren A/S, Finnhval A/S, Tønsberg	Margarine-Rohstoff-Beschaffungs-Gesellschaft, Berlin	Hamburger Walfang-Kontor GmbH, Hamburg
Südmeer Hamburg	Deutsche Ölmühlen – Rohstoffe GmbH, Berlin		Hamburger Walfang-Kontor GmbH, Hamburg
Walter Rau Bremen	Walter Rau Neußer Ölwerke AG, Neuß		Walter Rau Neußer Ölwerke AG, Neuß
Unitas Bremen	Jurgens – Van den Bergh Margarine Verkaufs Union GmbH, Berlin		Unitas Deutsche Walfang-Gesellschaft mbH, Hamburg
Wikinger Hamburg	Ölmühlen-Walfang-Konsortium, Berlin		Hamburger Walfang-Kontor GmbH, Hamburg
[prospective]	?		Walfang-Kontor Bremen GmbH

The German whaling expeditions: captains, whaling managers and biologists

Floating factory / research vessel	Season	Captain	Expedition leader[1]	Biologist
Jan Wellem	36/37	R. Schönwald	Otto Kraul	Dr. Nicolaus Peters
Jan Wellem	37/38	R. Schönwald	Otto Kraul	Dr. Kurt Schubert
Jan Wellem	38/39	R. Schönwald	Hjalmar Christensen	Dr. Kurt Schubert
C.A. Larsen	36/37		H. Bjønness-Hansen	./.
C.A. Larsen	37/38		H. Bjønness-Hansen	cand. Erich Barkley
C.A. Larsen	38/39		H. Bjønness-Hansen	Dr. Johann Schwanitz
Skytteren	36/37		Søren Berntsen	./.
Skytteren	37/38		Søren Berntsen	Dr. Hans Peters
Skytteren	38/39		Edvard Skontorp	Dr. Wilhelm Windecker
Südmeer	37/38	Jahrs[2]	Carl (?) Bjercke	Christian Hennings
Südmeer	38/39	Jahrs	[German manager]	Dr. Hans Peters
Walter Rau	37/38	H. Petersen	Lars Andersen	K.-J. Lamby
Walter Rau	38/39	Harzmeyer	Lars Andersen	cand. Fr. Zeller
Unitas	37/38	Sauerbier	Arnt Karlsen	cand. G. Herrmann

[1] Expedition leaders (or whaling managers, Norwegian: *bestyrere*) identified after *Norsk Hvalfangst-Tidende* 27 (1), Jan 1938; 27 (12), Dec 1938; 28 (1), Jan 1939; 29 (1), Jan 1940.
[2] Ian Hart (in e-litt 17 Dec 2008) suggests an alternative master's name, viz. Feddersen. This may be Hans-Peter Feddersen, who actually sailed on *Südmeer*, but it is unclear in what capacity. Could he have been the German whaling manager of the 1938/39 season?

Unitas	38/39	Sauerbier	Støkken Nilssen	Dr. Nicolaus Peters
Wikinger	38/39	Karl Kircheiss	C[arl?] Bjer[c]ke	Dr. F.H. Karcher
Schwabenland	38/39	Alfred Kottas	Alfred Ritscher	Erich Barkley

The German whaling fleets: technical details[3]

Vessel * = on charter	GRT	L (m)	B (m)	iHP	knots	crew	year built	builder's shipyard
Jan Wellem	11776	147	21.70	4500	11.5	250	1921	Bremer Vulkan, Vegesack
Treff I	331	38.90	8.00	1260	12	15	1936	H.C. Stülcken Sohn, Hamburg
Treff II	331	38.90	8.00	1260	12	15	1936	H.C. Stülcken Sohn, Hamburg
Treff III	331	38.90	8.00	1260	12	15	1936	H.C. Stülcken Sohn, Hamburg
Treff IV	330	38.90	8.00	1450	13	15	1936	Seebeck, Wesermünde
Treff V	330	38.90	8.00	1450	13	15	1936	Seebeck, Wesermünde
Treff VI	331	38.90	8.00	1260	12	15	1936	H.C. Stülcken Sohn, Hamburg
Treff VII	356	40.70	8.00	1700	14.5	15	1937	H.C. Stülcken Sohn, Hamburg
Treff VIII	356	40.70	8.00	1700	14.5	15	1937	H.C. Stülcken Sohn, Hamburg
C.A. Larsen *	13246	160	20.30	4000	11	200	1913	Swan, Hunter, Wigham & Richardson, Wallsend-on-Tyne
Wal 1	226	33.90	7.00	700	11.5	13	1925	Jarlsø Vaerft, Tønsberg
Hval II *	224	33.90	7.00	700	11.5	13	1927	Jarlsø Vaerft, Tønsberg
Hval III *	246	35.10	7.10	700	11.5	13	1928	Nylands Vaerksted, Oslo
Hval IV *	248	35.10	7.10	700	11.5	13	1929	Nylands Vaerksted, Oslo
Hval V *	248	35.10	7.10	700	11.5	13	1929	Nylands Vaerksted, Oslo
Hval VI *	248	35.10	7.20	700	11.5	13	1929	Nylands Vaerksted, Oslo
Hval VII *	249	35.40	7.20	700	11.5	13	1930	Akers Mek Verksted, Oslo
Wal 8	348	40.40	8.00	1550	14	15	1938	Seebeck, Wesermünde
Wal 9	348	40.40	8.00	1550	14	15	1938	Seebeck, Wesermünde
Skytteren *	12358	183	21.00	5000	13.5	235	1901	Harland & Wolff, Belfast
Skudd 1 *	247	35.20	7.00	800	12	15	1929	Kaldnaes M.V., Tønsberg
Skudd 2 *	247	35.20	7.00	800	12	15	1929	Kaldnaes M.V., Tønsberg
Skudd 3 *	245	35.10	7.00	800	12	15	1929	Nylands Vaerksted, Oslo
Skudd 4 *	245	35.10	7.00	800	12	15	1929	Nylands Vaerksted, Oslo
Skudd 5 *	265	36.10	7.20	800	12	15	1930	Nylands Vaerksted, Oslo
Skudd 6 *	323	38.90	7.60	1250	13.5	15	1930	Kaldnaes M.V., Tønsberg
Wal 10[4]	376	40.40	8.10	1700	14	15	1939	Seebeck, Wesermünde
Wal 11[5]	376	40.40	8.10	1700	14	15	1939	Seebeck, Wesermünde
Südmeer	8133	167	19	4900	13	170	1902	Wigham, Richardson & Co. Newcastle
Shera *	253	35.40	7.40	850	12	15	1929	Smith's Dock Co., Middlesbro
Stefa *	253	35.40	7.40	850	12	15	1929	Smith's Dock Co., Middlesbro

---

[3] After Peters, 1938, and Winterhoff, 1974. [Winterhoff, E., 1974, Walfang in der Antarktis. Stalling AG, Oldenburg, 234 pp]

[4] Not launched in time for the last German whaling season.

[5] Ditto.

Süd I	220	33.30	6.60	700	11.5	15	1925	Framnes M.V., Sandefjord
Süd II	219	33.30	6.60	700	11.5	15	1925	Framnes M.V., Sandefjord
Süd III	201	33.70	6.60	700	11.5	15	1924	Akers M.V., Oslo
Süd IV	201	33.70	6.60	700	11.5	15	1924	Akers M.V., Oslo
Süd V	220	33.30	6.60	700	11.5	15	1924	Framnes M.V., Sandefjord
Süd VI (1)[6]	248	35.30	7.35	900	12.75	15	1929	Smith's Dock Co., Middlesbro
Süd VI (2)[7]	381	40.40	8.10	1700	14	15	1939	Seebeck, Wesermünde
Süd VII[8]	381	40.40	8.10	1700	14	15	1939	Seebeck, Wesermünde
Walter Rau	13750	175	22.60	6000	12	270	1937	Deutsche Werft AG, Hamburg
Rau I	354	40.50	8.00	1550	14	15	1937	Seebeck, Wesermünde
Rau II	354	40.50	8.00	1550	14	15	1937	Seebeck, Wesermünde
Rau III	354	40.50	8.00	1550	14	15	1937	Seebeck, Wesermünde
Rau IV	354	40.50	8.00	1550	14	15	1937	Seebeck, Wesermünde
Rau V	354	40.50	8.00	1550	14	15	1937	Seebeck, Wesermünde
Rau VI	354	40.50	8.00	1550	14	15	1937	Seebeck, Wesermünde
Rau VII	354	40.50	8.00	1550	14	15	1937	Seebeck, Wesermünde
Rau VIII	354	40.50	8.00	1550	14	15	1937	Seebeck, Wesermünde
Rau IX[9]	387	40.40	8.10	1550	14	15	1939	Seebeck, Wesermünde
Rau X[10]	387	40.40	8.10	1550	14	15	1939	Seebeck, Wesermünde
Rau XI[11]	273	35.90	7.60	850	12	15	1927	Kaldnaes M.V., Tønsberg
Rau XII[12]	262	35.40	7.30	700	11.5	15	1925	Kaldnaes M.V., Tønsberg
Unitas	21846	193	24	6000	12	294	1937	Deutsche Schiff- & Maschinenbau AG, „Weser" shipyard, Bremen
Unitas 1	591	48.90	9.50	3000	16	20	1937	Bremer Vulkan, Vegesack
Unitas 2	341	41.10	7.90	1700	14	15	1937	Bremer Vulkan, Vegesack
Unitas 3	341	41.10	7.90	1700	14	15	1937	Bremer Vulkan, Vegesack
Unitas 4	341	41.10	7.90	1700	14	15	1937	Bremer Vulkan, Vegesack
Unitas 5	341	41.10	7.90	1700	14	15	1937	Bremer Vulkan, Vegesack
Unitas 6	341	41.10	7.90	1700	14	15	1937	Bremer Vulkan, Vegesack
Unitas 7	341	41.10	7.90	1700	14	15	1937	Bremer Vulkan, Vegesack
Unitas 8	341	41.10	7.90	1700	14	15	1937	Bremer Vulkan, Vegesack
Unitas 9	244	35.10	7.00	800	11	15	1927	Nylands Vaerksted, Oslo
Unitas 10	339	41.10	7.90	1700	14	15	1938	F. Schichau, Danzig
Wikinger	14526	149	21.50	4300	12	200	1929	Swan, Hunter, Wigham & Richardson, Wallsend-on-Tyne
Vestfold IV *	273	35.80	7.40	850	12	15	1927	Kaldnaes M.V., Tønsberg
Vikingen VI *	299	38.90	7.60	1300	13	15	1935	Smith's Dock Co., Middlesbro

---

[6] Ex *Kos III*, bought from Norway in 1937 and re-named. Sunk off the Canary Islands after the 1937-38 season on 12 April 1938. Thanks to Ulf Wiggo Gustafsen for pointing the existence of two *Süd VI* catchers out to me.

[7] Launched as *Süd VI* and re-named *Wiking 9* in 1939 after the last German whaling season.

[8] Launched as *Süd VII* and re-named *Wiking 10* in 1939 after the last German whaling season.

[9] Commissioned and delivered before the war, but not used for whaling by the *Walter Rau* fleet.

[10] Ditto.

[11] Purchased or chartered before the war, but not used for whaling by the *Walter Rau* fleet.

[12] Ditto.

Vikingen VII *	355	40.10	8.00	1400	13	15	1936	Smith's Dock Co., Middlesbro
Wiking 1	250	35.40	7.40	850	12	15	1929	Smith's Dock Co., Middlesbro
Wiking 2	250	35.40	7.40	850	12	15	1929	Smith's Dock Co., Middlesbro
Wiking 3	250	35.40	7.40	850	12	15	1929	Smith's Dock Co., Middlesbro
Wiking 4	250	35.40	7.40	850	12	15	1929	Smith's Dock Co., Middlesbro
Wiking 5	250	35.40	7.40	850	12	15	1929	Smith's Dock Co., Middlesbro
Wiking 6 [13]	381	40.40	8.10	1700	14	15	1939	Seebeck, Wesermünde
Wiking 7 [14]	381	40.40	8.10	1700	14	15	1939	Seebeck, Wesermünde
Wiking 8 [15]	381	40.40	8.10	1700	14	15	1939	Seebeck, Wesermünde
Wiking 9	ex *Süd VI*							Seebeck, Wesermünde
Wiking 10	ex *Süd VII*							Seebeck, Wesermünde

---

[13] Delivered after the last German whaling season.
[14] Ditto.
[15] Ditto.

The German whaling expeditions: seasons and catch[16]

Floating factory	season	whaling grounds	Catch[17]						Total
			Blue	Fin	Sei	Hum	Sperm	O	
Jan Wellem	36/37	N. Weddell Sea	297	691	7	63	22		1,080
Jan Wellem	37/38	N. Weddell Sea	306	755	-	26	37		1,124
Jan Wellem	38/39	Peru / Ecuador N. Weddell Sea W. Indian Ocean	330	810	-	-	749		1,889
C.A. Larsen	36/37	?	373	246	-	37	16		672
C.A. Larsen	37/38	ca. 80-160° E	423	533		39	69		1,064
C.A. Larsen	38/39	ca. 10-30° E	288	393	-	-	61		742
Skytteren	36/37	?	466	281	-	214	122		1,083
Skytteren	37/38	ca. 10-30° E	463	533	-	28	69		1,093
Skytteren	38/39	ca. 10-30° E	335	486	-	-	96		917
Südmeer	37/38	ca. 20-50° W	225	563	-	20	4		812
Südmeer	38/39	ca. 15-65° W	114	388	-	-	25		527
Walter Rau	37/38	N. Weddell Sea	390	1,213	5	71	22		1,701
Walter Rau	38/39	N. Weddell Sea	423	758	3	-	146	1[18]	1,331
Unitas	37/38	ca. 20-40° E	823	827	-	58	7		1,715
Unitas	38/39	ca. 20-45° E	724	578	-	-	113		1,415
Wikinger	38/39	N. Weddell Sea	220	468	-	-	27		715
Total catch			6,200	9,523	15	556	1,585	1	17,880

---

[16] Revised catch figures after Kock, K.-H., 1996, Validation of Catch Data from German Whaling in the Southern Ocean before World War II., In: International Whaling Commission (ed.): *Reports of the International Whaling Commission* 46, 649-651.

[17] "Hum" means humpback whale, "O" means other whale species.

[18] Southern right whale, erroneously taken by *Rau V* on 1 March 1939 some 400 km SSW of the South Orkney Islands. Barthelmess, K., 2008, Die Walstatt des Südkapers der *Walter Rau*, In: *Fluke* 15, 2008, p. 9.

II

Names of Expedition Participants (based on data from Ritscher, 1939)

No.	Category	Name	Organisation
	SCIENCE STAFF		
1	Expedition leader	Capt. Alfred Ritscher	Oberkommando der Kriegsmarine
2	Meteorologist	Dr. Herbert Regula	Deutsche Seewarte, Hamburg
3	Meteorologist (graduate teacher)	Heinz Lange	Reichsamt für Wetterdienst, Berlin
4	Technical assistant to meteorologist	Walter Krüger	Reichsamt für Wetterdienst, Berlin
5	Technical assistant to meteorologist	Wilhelm Gockel	Marine Observatorium, Wilhelmshafen
6	Biologist; student teacher	Erich Barkley	Reichstelle für Fischerei (Institut für Walforschung), Hamburg
7	Final year geophysics PhD student	Leo Gburek	Erdmagnetisches Institut, Leipzig
8	Geographer	Dr. Ernst Herrmann	Secondary School Teacher, Berlin
9	PhD student of oceanography	Karl-Heinz Paulsen	Universität Hamburg
	FLYING CREW		
1	Flight Captain (*Passat* pilot)	Rudolf Mayr	Deutsche Lufthansa
2	Flight Mechanic	Franz Preuschoff	Deutsche Lufthansa
3	Flight Radio Operator	Herbert Ruhnke	Deutsche Lufthansa
4	Aerial Photographer	Max Bundermann	Hansa Luftbild
5	Flight Captain (*Boreas* pilot)	Richardheinrich Schirmacher	Deutsche Lufthansa
6	Flight Mechanic	Kurt Loesener	Deutsche Lufthansa
7	Flight Radio Operator	Erich Gruber	Deutsche Lufthansa
8	Aerial Photographer	Siegfried Sauter	Hansa Luftbild
	SHIP'S CREW		
1	Ship's Captain	Alfred Kottas	Deutsche Lufthansa
2	Ice Pilot	Capt. Otto Kraul	Hamburg (no institution)
3	Ship's Doctor	Dr. Josef Bludau	Norddeutscher Lloyd
4	First Officer	Herbert Amelang	Norddeutscher

			Lloyd
5	Second Officer	Karl-Heinz Ropke	Norddeutscher Lloyd
6	Third Officer	Hans Werner Viereck	Norddeutscher Lloyd
7	Fourth Officer	Vincent Grisar	Norddeutscher Lloyd
8	Ship's Radio Leader	Erich Harmsen	Deutsche Lufthansa
9	Ship's Radio Officer	Kurt Bojahr	Deutsche Lufthansa
10	Ship's Radio Officer	Ludwig Müllermerstadt	Deutsche Lufthansa
11	Chief Engineer	Karl Uhlig	Norddeutscher Lloyd
12	Second Engineer	Robert Schulz	Norddeutscher Lloyd
13	Third Engineer	Henry Maas	Norddeutscher Lloyd
14	Fourth Engineer	Edgar Gäng	Norddeutscher Lloyd
15	Fifth Engineer	Hans Nielsen	Norddeutscher Lloyd
16	Assistant Engineer	Johann Frey	Norddeutscher Lloyd
17	Assistant Engineer	Georg Jelschen	Norddeutscher Lloyd
18	Assistant Engineer	Heinz Siewert	Norddeutscher Lloyd
19	Electrical Engineer	Herbert Bruns	Atlas Werke
20	Electrician	Karl-Heinz Bode	Norddeutscher Lloyd
21	Catapult Overseer	Herbert Bolle	Deutsche Lufthansa
22	Catapult Leader	Wilhelm Hartmann	Deutsche Lufthansa
23	Flight Storekeeper	Alfred Rücker	Deutsche Lufthansa
24	Flight Mechanic	Franz Weiland	Deutsche Lufthansa
25	Flight Mechanic	Axel Mylius	Deutsche Lufthansa
26	Flight Mechanic	Wilhelm Lender	Deutsche Lufthansa
27	Boatswain	Willy Stein	Norddeutscher Lloyd
28	First Carpenter	Richard Wehrend	Norddeutscher Lloyd
29	Second Carpenter	Alfons Schäfer	Norddeutscher Lloyd
30	Seaman	Heinz Hoek	Norddeutscher Lloyd
31	Seaman	Jürgen Ulpts	Norddeutscher Lloyd
32	Seaman	Albert Weber	Norddeutscher Lloyd
33	Seaman	Adolf Kunze	Norddeutscher Lloyd

34	Seaman	Karl Hedden	Norddeutscher Lloyd
35	Seaman	Eugen Klenk	Norddeutscher Lloyd
36	Seaman	Fritz Jedamezyk	Norddeutscher Lloyd
37	Seaman	Emil Brandt	Norddeutscher Lloyd
38	Seaman	Kurt Ohnemüller	Norddeutscher Lloyd
39	Ordinary seaman	Alfred Peters	Norddeutscher Lloyd
40	Deck Boy	Alex Burtscheid	Norddeutscher Lloyd
41	Cabin Boy	Karl-Heinz Meyer	Norddeutscher Lloyd
42	Storekeeper	Walter Brinkmann	Norddeutscher Lloyd
43	Motor attendant	Dietrich Witte	Norddeutscher Lloyd
44	ditto	Erich Kubacki	Norddeutscher Lloyd
45	ditto	Walter Dräger	Norddeutscher Lloyd
46	Boiler attendant	Karl Oelbrich	Norddeutscher Lloyd
47	ditto	Georg Niemüller	Norddeutscher Lloyd
48	Cleaner	Friedrich Mathwig	Norddeutscher Lloyd
49	ditto	Ferdinand Dunekamp	Norddeutscher Lloyd
50	ditto	Erwin Steinmetz	Norddeutscher Lloyd
51	ditto	Herbert Callies	Norddeutscher Lloyd
52	Kitchen Hand	Helmut Dulatschow	Norddeutscher Lloyd
53	First Cook	Otto Siedland	Norddeutscher Lloyd
54	Second Cook	Fritz Troe	Norddeutscher Lloyd
55	Cook's Mate and Baker	Gottfried Thole	Norddeutscher Lloyd
56	Cooks Mate and Butcher	Ferdinand Wolf	Norddeutscher Lloyd
57	Cook's Boy	Hans Büttner	Norddeutscher Lloyd
58	Chief Steward	Willi Reeps	Norddeutscher

			Lloyd
59	Steward	Wilhelm Malyska	Norddeutscher Lloyd
60	Steward	Rudolf Stawicki	Norddeutscher Lloyd
61	Mess Steward	Willi Fröhling	Norddeutscher Lloyd
62	Mess Steward	Johann von de Logt	Norddeutscher Lloyd
63	Mess Steward	Rudolf Burghard	Norddeutscher Lloyd
64	Mess Boy	Rolf Oswald	Norddeutscher Lloyd
65	Mess Boy	Johann Bates	Norddeutscher Lloyd

III

Compilation of costs for the German Antarctic Expedition 1938-39
(compiled by by Ilse Uhlmann on 10.10.40)
(Source Ritscher's estate, Bh2)

In 1938 there were 12.4 RM to £1, and UK inflation since then has been x 50. Given the overall cost of the operation as RM 2,440,018, and the current UK equivalent as being £9,838,750 the conversion to £ sterling for any figure in the financial report of the expedition, below, is roughly x 4, as shown.

- - - - - - - - -

I. Ship M.S. Schwabenland   – Remodelling and overhaul:

a)	Ship remodelling and engine construction works	RM	1.619.471,96	
b)	Personnel costs:			
	Salaries and social insurance	"	7.831,03	
	Travel costs	"	6.153,20	
c)	Miscellaneous:			
	Mail charges		254,91	
	Freight costs	"	1.197,90	
		"		1.634.909.--

II. Deck material and engine equipment		RM		18.161.52

III. Scientific equipment

a)	Instrument equipment	RM	2.794,38	
b)	Movie and photo equipment	"	24.141,55	
c)	Ship library and journals	"	632,86	
		"		27.568,79

IV. Operating fluid and water for the ship		"		67.583,70

V. Crew complements:

a)	Salaries, wages, pay, and social insurance	RM	161.340,92	
b)	Flight option money for radio operator	"	3.233,18	
c)	Travel costs and board money	"	10.979,18	
d)	Equipment	"	20.328,77	
e)	Honorarium for preventive examination	"	111,--	
		"		195.993,05

VI. Aircraft:

a)	Remodelling and various supplies	RM	30.027,88	
b)	Transportation costs	"	1.969,15	
d)	Personnel costs:			
	Salaries and social insurance	"	51.666,45	
	Flight option money	"	21.544,16	
	Travel costs and board money	"	6.482,25	
	Equipment	"	8.493,84	
		"	120.183,73	
		RM		1.944.216,06

	Balance	RM	120.183,73	1.944.216,06
d)	D.L.H. administration costs ...."		17.500,--	
e)	Amortisation of aircraft ...."		37.609,03	
f)	Overhauling of aircraft and			
	maintenance ...."		106.914,08	
g)	Consumption of operating fluid ...."		4.083,28	
		"		286.290.12

VII. Provisions 23.817,75

VIII. Scientific crew:
a)	Personnel costs:		
	Salaries and social insurance ....RM	16.789,83	
	Travel costs and board money ...."	4.846,95	
	Equipment ...."	2.600.--	
b)	Instruments ...."	8.180,47	32.426,25

IX. Assistant of the expedition leader and office expenses
a)	Personnel costs:		
	Salaries and social insurance ....RM	2.252,60	
	Travel costs ...."	1.429,36	
b)	Office expenses................................."	5.504,64	9.178,60

X. Removal and overhaul of ship and engine ...."   46.667,85

XI. Liquidation and Analysis ...."   17.997,24

XII. Insurance ...."   42.850,18

XIII Miscellaneous ...."   36.575,29

RM 2.440.019,34

[NOTE: Due to miscalculations the total should be RM 2,440,018,34]

IV
Fitting out the Aircraft - Routine and Survival Equipment

The *Boreas* weighed 6336 kg, *Passat* 6318 kg [1]. Each machine included a set of sea equipment including: radio, 1 inflatable rubber boat and paddles for four persons, 1 drift anchor with lines; 1 drift anchor retrieval line; 1 swivel-shackle; 2 throwing lines; 1 axe; 1 tool box for repairs during flights; 1 first aid kit.

Additional loads came from the following:

4,200 litres of fuel for 15 hours	3150 kg
water reserve	60 kg
navigational equipment	20 kg
photographic equipment	190 kg
50 swastika darts and 10 swastika flags for territorial makers	36 kg
4 men with polar clothing	400 kg
polar survival equipment in case of accident	324 kg
2 serial cameras and film rolls	190 kg
Total	4380 kg

Boreas flying weight	10516 kg
Passat flying weight	10498 kg

Thus at the start each plane carried an excess weight of half a ton (1 ton = 10,000 kg).

The navigational equipment comprised the following [1,2]:

1 sextant	4,7 kg
1 drift meter	4,5 kg
1 sun compass	2,8 kg
1 sun pin	0,5 kg
1 pair binoculars	2,5
1 yearbook (ephemerides)	
1 nautical table, 1 map 1:1,250,000, 1 log-book	
1 compass, triangle, pencil, and eraser	4,2 kg
Total	19,2 kg

The polar survival equipment in case of a crash landing comprised [1,2]:

2 x 2-man tents (10 kg each)	20,0 kg
4 x sleeping bags with rubber mattresses (4,5 kg each)	18,0 kg
1 x sled with tarpaulin cover, 20 m pulling rope, and 2 pulling harness	15,3 kg
4 x pairs skis (5,7 kg each)	22,1 kg
1 x ice axe	1,0 kg
2 x primus stoves with 2 spare burners, cleaners,1 funnel for fuel, and 2 cooking pots (each set 2,12 kg)	4,3 kg
1 litre spirit	1,1 kg
10 x litres petrol for stoves	8,5 kg
1 x 3-barrelled rifle with telescopic sight	4,1 kg
rifle cleaning kit 100 lead cartridges shot and 50 rifle cartridges t	7,0 kg
2 x canister of coloured munitions (green, white and red) (4,45 kg each)	9,0 kg

1 litre spirit	1,1 kg
10 x litres petrol for stoves	8,5 kg
1 x 3-barrelled rifle with telescopic sight	4,1 kg
rifle cleaning kit 100 lead cartridges shot and	
50 rifle cartridges	7,0 kg
2 x canister of coloured munitions (green, white and red)	
(4,45 kg each)	9,0 kg
1 x portable shortwave radio	24,5 kg
1 x first aid kit	4,0 kg
4 x packed rucksacks (13 kg each)	52,0 kg
Total	190,9 kg

Each rucksack contained [2] :

1 knife; 1 sewing kit; 1 snow shovel for 2 men, 1 knife and fork, 1 rope (10 m); 1 spare ski binding; 1 pack macrobiotic; ski wax; 1 pair sealskins; 1 pair snow shoes; 1 pair leggings; 2 pairs of ski gloves; 1 long pants (wool); 1 vest (wool); 1 cup; 1 toothbrush.

Food supplies for the crew in case of accident comprised one food bag with known contents for two men per day [2]:

56 food bags	120 kg
1 side of bacon	7 kg
tobacco	1 kg
Total	128 kg

Provisions for two men per day (923 g per man per day) [3]:

255 g pemmican
250 g pumpernickel
115 g sugar
  56 g oat flour
  50 g chocolate
  50 g pease-flour sausage
  40 g bacon
  15 g tea
  25 g butter
  20 g dried milk
  15 g cacao
  20 g spices
  12 g cigarettes

Clothing for the Flight Crew [2]:

Woollen underwear (shirt and pants); long ski pants; linen shirt; pullover (hare-hair); wool socks; fur shoes; fur gloves; fur cap.
As an over-suit the pilot and radioman wore a sealskin combination; the mechanic and the photographer wore a fur/leather combination, but took a sealskin combination with the survival equipment.

Weight of clothing per person [2]:

Sealskin combination	6 kg
Leather combination	7 kg
Under-clothing	6 kg
Life vest	1 kg
Total	20 kg

Reference

1. Ritscher, A. 1942, Wissenschaftliche und fliegerische Ergebnisse der Deutschen Antarktischen Expedition 1938/39, Hrsg. im Auftrag der Deutschen Forschungsgemeinschaft, Koehler & Amelang, Leipzig, Vol. I, 22, 232-234.

2. Herrmann, E., 1941, Deutsche Forscher im Südpolarmeer. Safari Verlag, Berlin, 184 pp.

3. Schirmacher, R., and Mayr, R., 1942, Flüge über der unerforschten Antarktis. In: Ritscher, A., 1942, Wissenschaftliche und fliegerische Ergebnisse der Deutschen Antarktischen Expedition 1938/39, Hrsg. im Auftrag der Deutschen Forschungsgemeinschaft. Koehler & Amelang, Leipzig. Vol 1, 232-234.

V

Names given to geographic features in Neu-Schwabenland by the German Antarctic Expedition 1938/1939.

DAE Name	Named After Expedition Member	Origin of Other Names	Present Name	Origin of Present Name
Alexander-von-Humboldt-Gebirge		German geographer and initiator of earth magnetic research in Antarctica	Humboldtfjella, Humboldt Mountains	Norwegian
Altar		Flat-topped rock summit in the Alexander-von-Humboldt-Gebirge	Altaret The Altar	Norwegian
Amelangplatte	First Officer		Ladfjella	Norwegian
Am Überlauf		Pass in northern part of Alexander-von-Humboldt-Gebirge	Grautenna	Norwegian
Barkleyberge	Biologist			
Bastei		Buttress-type mountain in the central Wohlthat-Massif	Bastionen, Mount Bastei	Norwegian
Bludauberge	Ship's Doctor			
Bolleberg	Catapult Supervisor		Mount Bolle	
Boreas		Flying boat used during the expedition	Boreas Nunatak	
Brandtberg	Seaman		Mount Brandt	
Brunsberge	Electrical Engineer		Bruns Nunataks	
Buddenbrockkette		Aviation manager of Deutsche Lufthansa	Buddenbrock Range	
Bundermannketten	Flight Photographer		Bundermann Range	

Conradgebirge		Rear-Admiral; Director of the Meteorological Division of the Naval High Command	Conradfjella, Conrad Mountains	Norwegian
Dallmannberg		Whaling captain, explored the west coast of the Antarctic Pensinsula (1873/74)	Mount Dallmann	
Drygalskiberge		German geographer, Antarctic Explorer (1901-1903)	Drygalskifjella, Drygalski Mountains	Norwegian
Eckhörner		Mountain peaks in the northern part of the Alexander-von-Humboldt-Gebirge	Hjörnehorna, Eckhörner Peaks	Norwegian
Filchnerberge		German Antarctic Explorer (1911-12)	Filchnerfjella, Filchner Mountains	Norwegian
Gablenzrucken		Director of Deutsche Lufthansa	Gablenz Range	
Gburekspitzen	Earth Magnetician		Gbureck Peaks	
Geßnerspitze		Director of Hansa-Luftbild	Gessner Peak (Not: Gessnertind)	(Norwegian)
Gneiskopf		Mountain peak of gneiss in the southern part of the eastern Petermann-Kette	Gneiskopf Peak (Not: Gneisskolten)	(Norwegian)
Gockelkamm	Meteorology Technical Assistant		Gockel Ridge	
Graue Hörner		Grey peaks at south end of the northern part of	Gråhorna, Gråhorna Peaks (Not: Graue Hörner)	Norwegian

		Petermann-Kette		
Gruberberge	Flying Boat Radio Engineer		Gruber Mountains (Not: Gruberfjella, Otto von Gruberfjella, Gory Rikhtgofena)	(Norwegian)
Habermehlgipfel		President of the Reich Weather Service	Habermehl Peak (Not: Habermehltoppen)	(Norwegian)
Häderichberg		Procurator of Deutsche Lufthansa	Mount Häderich	
Heddenberg	Seaman		Mount Hedden	
Herrmannberge	Geographer		Herrmann Mountains (Not. Herrmannfjella)	(Norwegian)
Humboldt Graben		See above	(Not: Humboldtsökket)	(Norwegian)
In der Schüssel		West facing cirque in the north-central part of the Alexander-von-Humboldt-Gebirge	Schüssel Cirque (Not: Graufatet, Große Breischüssel, In der Schüssel)	(Norwegian)
Johannes- Müller-Kamm		Leader of Nautical Department of Norddeutscher Lloyd, Navigation Officer of Filchner's Antarctic expedition (1911-1912)	Müller Crest (Not: Müllerkammen, Johannes Müller Crest)	(Norwegian)
Kayekamm		Surveyor of German Lloyd	Kaye Crest	
Kleinschmidtgipfel		Head of main division (Hauptabtei-lungsleiter) of the German Maritime Observatory		
Kottasberge	Ship's Captain		Heimefront Range	

			(Not: Gory Kottas)	
Kraulberge	Ice Pilot		Kraul Mountains	
Krügerberg	Meteorology Technical Assistant		Krüger Mountain (Not: Krügerfjellet)	(Norwegian)
Kubus		Huge cube shaped mountain at the SE corner of the Mühlig-Hofmann-Gebirge	Kubus Mountain (Not: The Kubus)	
Kurzegerbirge		Vice Admiral; Director of the Nautical Division of the Naval High Command	Kurze Mountains	
Langeplatte	2nd Meteorologist			
Loessnerplatte	Flying Boat Mechanic			
Lose Platte		Plate shaped area W of the southern part of Alexander-von-Humboldt-Gebirge	Lausflaeet	Norwegian
Luzrücken		Commercial director of Deutsche Lufthansa	Luz Range	
Matterhorn		Colossal peaked mountain of about 4000 m, similar to Matterhorn in Switzerland	Ulvetanna (wolf tooth)	Norwegian
Mayrkette	Pilot		Mayr Range (Not: Mayr Ridge, Jutulsessen (giant's seat))	(Norwegian)
Mentzelberg		President of German Research Foundation	Mentzelfjellet, Mount Mentzel	Norwegian
Mühlig-Hofmann-Gebirge		Division Director of	Mühlig-Hofmann Mountains	

		Reich Air Ministry		
Neumayer-steilwand		Founder of German Naval Observatory, promoter of Antarctic research	Neumayerskarvet, Neumayer Cliffs (Not: Neumayersteilwand, Neumayer Escarpment)	Norwegian
Neuschwabenland		Expedition ship Schwabenland	New Schwabenland (Not: Neu-Schwabenland)	
Nordwestinsel		Island shaped mountain NW of Wohlthat-Gebirge	Nordwestliche Insel Mountains (Not: Nordwestöya)	(Norwegian)
Östliches Hochfeld		Plateau between the south ends of the eastern and western Petermann-Ketten	austre Högskeidet	Norwegian
Obersee		Lake at NE end of Central Wohlthat-Massif	Lake Ober-See (Not: Övresjöen)	(Norwegian)
Passat		Flying boat used during the expedition		
Paulsenberge	Oceanographer		Paulsen Mountains	
Payergruppe		Austrian polar researcher	Payerfjella, Payer Mountains (not Payer Group)	Norwegian
Penckmulde		German geographer	Penck Trough (Not: Penck-Mulde, Pencksökket,	(Norwegian)
Petermannketten		German cartographer, geographer, and promoter of Arctic research	Petermannkjeda, Petermann Ranges	Norwegian
Preuschoffrucken	Flying Boat Mechanic		Hochlinfjellet, Preuschoff Range	Norwegian
Regulakette	1st Meteorologist		Regula Range	
Ritschergipfel	Expedition leader		Ritschertind, Ritscher Peak	Norwegian

Ritscherland, Ritscherhochland	Expedition leader		Ritscher Upland (Not: Rischer-Land, Ritscher Flya)	American
Röbkeberg	2nd Officer		Isbrynet (ice rim)	Norwegian
Ruhnkeberg	Flying Boat Radio Engineer		Festninga (fortress), Mount Ruhnke	Norwegian
Sauterriegel	Flight Photographer		Terningskarvet (die mountain)	Norwegian
Schichtberge		stratified mountains SW of Central Wohlthat-Massif	Mount Schicht (Not: Sjiktberga)	(Norwegian)
Schirmacher-seengruppe	Pilot		Schirmacher Ponds or Schirmacher Oasis (Not: Schirmacher-Seengruppe, Schirmacheroasen, Vassfjellet)	(Norwegian)
Schneiderriegel		Head of department for equipment at Norddeutscher Lloyd		
Schubertgipfel		Head of nautical department at German Naval Observatory		
Schulzhöhen	Second Engineer		Lagfjella	Norwegian
Schwarze Hörner		Black horn shaped peaks S of the northern part in the middle of Petermann-Ketten	Svarthorna, Svarthorna Peaks (Not: Schwarze Hörner)	Norwegian
Seekopf		Cape at NE end of Central Wohlthat-Massif	Mount Seekopf (Not: Sjöhausen)	(Norwegian)
Seilkopfberge		Head of department of sea aviation	Seilkopf Peaks (Not: Seilkopffjella)	(Norwegian)
Sphinxkopf		Long rock	Sphinxkopf Peak	Norwegian

		island close to Humboldt-graben	(Not: Sfinksskolten	
Spießgipfel		Admiral and President of German Seewarte		
Steinkuppen	Boatswain		Stein Nunataks (Not: Steinkuppen, Straunsnutane)	
Todtriegel	Ritscher's assistant		Todt Ridge (Not: Todtriegel, Todtskota	(Norwegian)
Uhliggipfel	Leading Engineer		Urfjell (mountain with rock-strewn slopes)	Norwegian
Untersee		Lake N of Central Wohlthat-Massif	Unter-See Lake (Not: Nedresjöen)	(Norwegian)
Vorposten		Nunatak at the eastern border of Neu-Schwabenland	Vorposten Peak (Not: Forposten, The Outpost)	
Wegenerinlandeis		German meteorologist, Greenland researcher		
Westliches Hochfeld		Plateau between the south ends of Alexander-von-Humboldt Gebirge	yestre Högskeidet	Norwegian
Weyprecht-Berge		Polar researcher and initiator of the 1st International Polar Year	Weyprechtfjella, Weyprecht Mountains	Norwegian
Wittespitzen	Motor Mechanic		Witte Peaks	
Wohlthat-Massiv		Initiator and organiser of the Schwabenland expedition	Wohlthat Mountains (Not: Wohlthat-Massiv)	
Zimmermannberg		Vice President of German Research	Zimmermann-fjellet	Norwegian

		Foundation		
Zuckerhut		Peak in Central Wohlthat-Massif	Mount Zuckerhut (Not: Sukkertoppen)	(Norwegian)
Zwiesel		Highest (forked) mountain in SW Petermann-Ketten	Zwiesel Mountain (Not: Zwieselhöga)	(Norwegian)

References:

Alberts, F.G. (ed.), 1995, Geographic names of the Antarctic. 2nd ed., United States Board of Geographic Names, Reston, Virginia, 834 pp.

Alberts, F.G., (ed.), 1981 Geographic Names of the Antarctic. 1st ed., United States Board of Geographic Names. Washington D.C.

Hallstein, 1952 Bekanntmachung über die Bestätigung der bei der Entdeckung von "Neu-Schwabenland" im Atlantischen Sektor der Antarktis durch die Deutsche Antarktische Expedition 1938/39 erfolgten Benennungen geographischer Begriffe. Bundesanzeiger 4 (149), 5 August 1952, pp. 1-2.

Institut für Angewandte Geodäsie (Hrsg.), 1988, Digitale Namenbankbasis Antarktis, Frankfurt/Main, pp. 75 + 6 pp.

VI
Aerial Surveying, Cartography, Cameras and Film

Germany, with its unrivalled reputation for the precision manufacture of lenses, was in the forefront of the development of cameras for special uses like aerial photogrammetry, a technique becoming more and more important for exploration and the production of maps from unknown areas. Aerial photographic mapping was popular with the military, which had contributed to the development of state-of-the-art cameras for this purpose. Usually photogrammetry was based on the taking of overlapping photographs that could later be examined to produce stereo pictures from which distances and elevations could be calculated or estimated. German explorers had used aerial photogrammetry with a panoramic camera of Photogrammetrie GmbH of Munich, and a twofold aerial frame camera of Zeiss-Aerotopograph of Jena, during the flight of the German airship LZ 127 "Graf Zeppelin" over the Russian Arctic to Franz-Josef Land and Novaya Zemlya in July 1931. The results were published by Otto von Gruber (1884-1942) of Zeiss, the leading German expert for photogrammetry [1].The results showed that stereo photogrammetry is of the utmost importance in the geographical investigation of unknown regions from the air, because it provides a unique three-dimensional view [2]. Hansa Luftbild GmbH in Berlin provided the *Schwabenland* expedition with equipment for aerial photogrammetry in the shape of two aerial frame RMK 21 cameras from Zeiss-Aerophotograph, two hand-held cameras (FK 12,5 and FL 38004) for oblique photographs, and a 16 mm movie camera (Siemens D16) [3].

On the expedition they had 60 reels of Agfa-Aeropan B-aerial film 50 m long and 19 cm wide, 166 cassettes of 16 mm Agfa-Isopan FF negative film 15 m long, 33 cassettes of 16 mm Kodak chrome colour film, 25 reels of Agfa-Aeropna B film 3 m long and 80 mm wide, and, for experimental purposes, 5 reels of the new Agfa-Colour film 3 m long and 8 mm wide. Altogether they shot 11,600 oblique photographs in 18 x 18 cm frames. In addition 434 black and white and 90 colour pictures in 7 x 9 cm frames were taken with handheld cameras, as well as 1800 m of 16 mm black and white and 485 m of 16 mm colour movie film.

The expedition's maps contain all the information provided by thousands of pictures and observations. Each track of the seven long distance flights followed a polygonal pattern and used about six reels of around 360 m length in total, representing about 1800 pictures of 18 x 18 cm frame size [4]. The following information was available for the cartographic analysis:

1) the position of *Schwabenland*, determined astronomically,
2) 11,600 oblique photographs of 18 x 18 cm frame size,
3) radio communications giving the position of the aircraft, flying altitude above ground and above sea level, and observations of landmarks,
4) completed observation forms,
5) weather reports, and
6) positions of the shelf ice edge at selected locations, determined astronomically.

References

1. Gruber, O.v. 1933a Ferienkurs in Photogrammetrie. Eine Sammlung von Vorträgen und Aufsätzen. Konrad Wittwer, Stuttgart, 510 pp.

2. Gruber, O.v. 1933b Über die photogrammetrische Ausrüstung des "Graf Zeppelin" auf der Arktisfahrt 1931. Über die Auswertemethoden und die bisherigen Ergebnisse aus dem gewonnenen Aufnahmematerial. Petermanns Mitteilungen, Ergänzungsheft 216, 68-77.

3. Ritscher, A. 1942 Wissenschaftliche und fliegerische Ergebnisse der Deutschen Antarktischen Expedition 1938/39, Hrsg. im Auftrag der Deutschen Forschungsgemeinschaft, Koehler & Amelang, Leipzig, Vol. I , Bilder- und Kartenteil, 57 Tafeln mit Erläuterungen, 3 Karten.

4. Geßner, W. 1942. Die deutschen luftphotogrammetrischen Arbeiten in Neu-Schwabenland. In: A. Ritscher, Wissenschaftliche und fliegerische Ergebnisse der Deutschen Antarktischen Expedition 1938/39, Hrsg. in Auftrag der Deutschen Forschungsgemeinschaft, Koehler & Amelang, Leipzig, Vol. I , 115-125.

VII
Medical Report [1]

The ship carried a qualified Doctor, Josef Bludau, and a well-stocked medicine chest, and there were supplementary medicine kits on the aircraft, including ointment against frostbite, and dressing materials for wounds. Scurvy was not a problem given the plentiful supplies of fresh and frozen fish, fruit, and vegetables. Hygiene standards were high, with the ship toilets and bathrooms being disinfected every day. And Bludau gave lectures on how to stay healthy under Antarctic conditions. Probably as a result, while the ship was in the Antarctic there was only one case of slight frostbite to one man's feet. Most exposed to the cold were the aircrew, who spent hours sitting in a narrow unheated aircraft cabin at temperatures of -30 °C while flying 3500 m above the Antarctic ice; their leather and fur clothes proved perfect protection.

There were only a few injuries. Hermann broke the little toe of his right foot, which had to be set with a splint, but it did not stop him working. Gburek was not so lucky. Carelessly he stayed on deck too long with too little protection from the cold and came down with influenza that kept him in bed for 12 days. Krüger developed an abscess on his tonsils and could not work for 11 days.

Overall health was excellent. Food was plentiful and varied, and there was ample for the large appetites of men working in extreme cold. The food was kept in a cold store, which proved essential in the tropics. There was plenty of fish on the menu, along with fresh fruit like apples, oranges, lemons, grapes, and pears, as well as fresh vegetables, although these all tended to run out after a while and had to be replenished at port stops. There were fresh rolls, bread, and butter daily. Fresh water for the whole journey had been bunkered in Hamburg, and was still good enough to drink on their return. Sparkling water and beer never ran out. The men were pleased about that.

The doctor's main concern seemed to be ensuring that the crew avoided catching sexually transmitted diseases while on runs ashore en route to and from the ice. On both the outward and homeward journeys he gave a lecture on this topic to the whole crew, before the port stops in Cape Town for the night on 6 March 1939 and in Recife for the night of 22 March 1939. On those occasions the crew were provided with means of protection against sexually transmitted diseases. After each shore leave a prophylactic medical fluid (Prostargol solution) was available to all without questions being asked. That's life at sea for lonely seamen. Despite this precaution one sailor was infected by gonorrhoea during the stay in Recife, although he swore he had used protection. Dr Bludau knew what treatment to provide to him and to two sailors suffering from an advanced stage of syphilis.

That's all the ship's physician had to report when *Schwabenland* came home to Hamburg.

Reference:

1. Medical Report in Ritscher's estate file Bb1 (Medizin)

VIII

Whaling Information Tables

Table 1: Organisation of whale research in the major Antarctic whaling nations[1]

Whaling nation	Antarctic whaling since		Whales research institute / founded	Scientific periodical or publication series	Whaling handbook
	shore station	factory ship			
Norway	1904/05	1905/06	Hvalkomite, 1924; Hvalrådet, 1929; Statens Institutt for Hvalforskning, 1937	*Hvalrådets Skrifter*, 1:1931	Knudtzon, 1951
Great Britain	1907/08	1911/12[2]	Discovery Committee, 1918/19 - 1949	*Discovery Reports*, 1:1929	./.
USA		1930/31	de-central research at several institutions, but not pertaining to Antarctic whaling	no specialized periodical or publication series	./.
Japan		1934/35	Geirui Kenkyūsho [Whales Research Institute], 1947	*The Scientific Reports of the Whales Research Institute*, 1:1948	Omura & al., 1942
Germany		1936/37	Reichsstelle für Walforschung, 1937 Institut für Walforschung, 1939 - 1948	*Zeitschrift für Fischerei und deren Hilfswissenschaften*, 38, supplement 1: *Walforschung* part I, 1940; 40, supplement 2: *Walforschung* part II, 1942 [all published]	Peters, 1938 Willer 1942 Willer and Peters 1940
South Africa		1936/37	Fisheries Development Corporation of SA, 1962, & Division of Sea	no specialized periodical or publication series	./.

[1] Data were supplied or checked by Peter B. Best, D. Graham Burnett, Mike Dyer, Ray Gambell, Karl-Hermann Kock, Ed Mitchell, Seiji Ohsumi, Alexey Yablokov.

[2] Floating factory *Sobraon* from the British Dominion of Newfoundland operated in the Antarctic in the 1907/08 season.

		Fisheries (Department of Industries), 1969		
Soviet Union	1946/47[3]	Whale research branches (Kaliningrad, Odessa, Vladivostok) within pre-existing, de-central All-Union fisheries and ocean research institutes for the Pacific (TINRO), the North Atlantic, Arctic, and distant seas (VNIRO), etc.	no specialized periodical or publication series, studies appeared, eg. in: *Trudy VNIRO*, 1:1911; *Izvestiya TINRO*, 1:1912; *Zoologicheski Zhurnal*, 1:1921; *Trudy IMZh AN SSSR*, 1:1927	Golovliev, 1959
Netherlands	1946/47	Werkgroep Walvisonderzoek T.N.O. [Toegepast Natuurwetenschappelijk Onderzoek], 03 Oct 1947; housed in Zoological Laboratory, University of Amsterdam, 1952 – 1964. After the end of whaling general cetacean research by the Stichting Werkgroep Onderzoek Cetacea, 1966.	no specialized periodical or publication series, studies appeared, eg. in: *Proc. van de Koninklijke Nederlandse Akademie der Wetenschappen*; *Norsk Hvalfangst-Tidende*; *Hvalrådets Skrifter*, etc.	Feltman & al., 1949

[3] Conducted pelagic whaling in the North Pacific since the 1932/33 season. The All-Union ocean research institute in Vladivostok conducted whale research in 1935-1937. Alexey Yablokov, pers. comm. 22 Feb 2008.

Table 2: Chronology of the Institute for Whale Research, Hamburg

(after Lundbeck & al 1962; Willer 1942; Klatt 1950; contemporary news clippings in Barthelmess Whaling Archive)

1936-09-26 – 1937-05-10	German biologist Dr. Nicolaus Peters (10 Feb 1900 – 23 Sep 1940) despatched with floating factory JAN WELLEM. Also on board: meteorologist and oceanographer Werner Reichelt (1912 – 1995).
1937	Dr. Hans Peters on staff at designated whale research institute
1937-06	Dr. Kurt Schubert on staff at designated whale research institute
1937-10-07	Reichsstelle für Walforschung (RfW) formally instituted by the Reich Ministry for Food and Agriculture at the Hamburgisches Zoologisches Staatsinstitut und Museum, Steintorwall 1
1937-10-07	The institute's founding director is Dr. Nicolaus Peters, who was a biologist on board a German floating factory in the previous season and since had trained six other biologists for the coming season
1937-end	Whaling handbook commissioned by the Ministry to be edited by Dr. Nicolaus Peters
1937-fall – 1938-spring	RfW biologists despatched with floating factories JAN WELLEM, C.A. LARSEN, SKYTTEREN, WALTER RAU, SÜDMEER, UNITAS
1938-08	Whaling handbook „Der neue deutsche Walfang" published under the editorship of Dr. Nicolaus Peters
1938-09-01	Chemist Dr. Hans Lüneburg (1911-1990) on staff at RfW[22]
1938-fall – 1939-spring	RfW biologists despatched with floating factories JAN WELLEM, C.A. LARSEN, SKYTTEREN, WALTER RAU, SÜDMEER, UNITAS, WIKINGER, and Antarctic research vessel SCHWABENLAND
1939-04	name changed to Institut für Walforschung and incorporated into the Reichsanstalt für Fischerei
1939	moved from Steintorwall 1 to Kirchenallee 47
1939->04	Dr. Arno Meyer (1913 – 1982) on staff
1939-06	Dr. Hans Thiel on staff
1939-09	Preparations for the 1939/40 whaling season aborted due to the German invasion of Poland and the outbreak of WW II
1940-09-23	Dr. Nicolaus Peters †. Successor: Dr. Adolf Bückmann (1900 – 1993)
1940-09	first part of the results of German whale research published under the editorship of Dr. Alfred Willer (1889 – 1952) and Dr. Nicolaus Peters †
1942	second part of the results of German whale research published under the

---

[22] Dr. Reinhard Krause, AWI, in e-litt. 18 Jan 2008.

	editorship of Dr. Alfred Willer
1943-07-25	Institute, library (6,000 volumes[23]) & files destroyed in an air raid
1943-08?	moved to Lombardsbrücke 1
1945-05	building at Lombardsbrücke requisitioned by allied forces
1945	moved to private address of Dr. Werner Schnakenbeck (1887 – 1971), Maria-Louisen-Str. 92
1948	institute dissolved

---

[23] Combined libaries of the institutes for See- und Küstenfischerei and Walforschung.

Table 3: Whale biologists on board German floating factories (after Karcher 1940, p. 16)

Floating factory / research vessel	Season	Biologist	biogr data	Research diary extant[24]	contact print album extant[25]
JAN WELLEM	36/37	Dr. Nicolaus Peters	1900-1940		+
JAN WELLEM	37/38	Dr. Kurt Schubert		+	+
JAN WELLEM	38/39	Dr. Kurt Schubert & Dr. Hans Lüneburg, chemist	1911-1900	+	+
C.A. LARSEN	36/37	./.		-	-
C.A. LARSEN	37/38	cand. Erich Barkley	1912-1944	+	+
C.A. LARSEN	38/39	Dr. Johann Schwanitz			+
SKYTTEREN	36/37	./.		-	-
SKYTTEREN	37/38	Dr. Hans Peters		+	+
SKYTTEREN	38/39	Dr. Wilhelm Windecker	† 1979	+	
SÜDMEER	37/38	Christian Hennings		+	+
SÜDMEER	38/39	Dr. Hans Peters		+	+
WALTER RAU	37/38	K.-J. Lamby		+	+ (2 alb.)
WALTER RAU	38/39	cand. Fr. Zeller		+	+
UNITAS	37/38	cand. G. Herrmann		+	+
UNITAS	38/39	Dr. Nicolaus Peters			+
WIKINGER	38/39	Dr. F.H. Karcher			+
SCHWABENLAND	38/39	Erich Barkley			

[24] Nine research diaries were discovered at the Federal Fisheries Research Centre (Bundesforschungsanstalt für Fischerei), Hamburg and were transferred to the German Maritime Museum (Deutsches Schiffahrtsmuseum), Bremerhaven, in 1999. Correspondence in December 2007 and January 2008 with DSM staff disclosed the fact that the diaries could not be found back in the archives (Klaus-Peter Kiedel, pers. comm.). A 10th diary, of WALTER RAU 1938/39, was found at the BFA after that time, and is probably not to be transferred to the DSM in due course (Dr. Karl-Herrmann Kock, BfA, pers. comm. Dec. 2007).

[25] In the German Maritime Museum, Bremerhaven, presence confirmed (Klaus-Peter Kiedel, pers. comm.).

References (for Appendix VIII)

Feltmann, C.F., and Vervoort, W., 1949, *Walvisvaart. Biologische en technische grondslagen van de moderne, antarctische walvisvaart.* Gorinchem: Noordduijn & Zoon. The Dutch whaling handbook after Peters's prototype.

Golovliev, I. P., 1959, *Technika kitoboinogo promisla* [technology of whaling]. Moscow: Pishtshepromisdat. The Soviet whaling handbook after Peters's prototype.

Karcher, F.H., 1940, Über den Algenbewuchs auf südlichen Walen. In: *Zeitschrift für Fischerei und deren Hilfswissenschaften*, 38 (Beiheft 1: *Walforschung*, Teil I), pp. 13-36. Algae.

Klatt, B., 1950, Gedenken – Nikolaus Peters. In: *Mitteilungen aus dem Hamburgischen Zoologischen Museum und Institut* 50, pp. 1-2. Obituary.

Knudtzon, H. T., 1951, Hvalfangst – fangstnæring, part IV in: Jan Strøm (ed.): *Norsk fiskeri og fangst håndbok: Saltvannsfiskeriene, ferskvannsfiskeriene, ishavsfangsten, hvalfangsten.* Vol. 1 (of 2). Cammermeyers Oslo, 864-970. A handbook-like chapter, in part patterned after Peters's handbook.

Omura H., Matuura, Y., and Miyazaki, I., 1942, *Kujira. Sono kagaku to hogei no jiisai* [Whale. Its science and the practice of whaling]. Tokio: Suisansha. Japanese whaling handbook after Peters's prototype.

Lundbeck, J., Schubert, K., and Krefft, G., 1962, Die Geschichte der Institute: Institut für Seefischerei, in Paul-Friedrich Meyer-Waarden: *Festschrift zur Einweihung der Bundesforschungsanstalt für Fischerei am 1 Juni 1962 (= Archiv für Fischereiwissenschaft*, 13, Beiheft 1) pp 42-71. History of fisheries research institutes, i.a. the whales research institute.

Peters, N., 1938, *Der neue deutsche Walfang: Ein praktisches Handbuch seiner geschichtlichen, rechtlichen, naturwissenschaftlichen und technischen Grundlagen.* Hamburg: Hansa. The pioneering German whaling handbook.

Willer, A., 1942, *Walforschung, Teil II (= Zeitschrift für Fischerei und deren Hilfswissenschaften*, 40, Beiheft 2). Special issue on German whale research, part 2.

Willer, A., and Peters, N., 1940, *Walforschung, Teil I (= Zeitschrift für Fischerei und deren Hilfswissenschaften* 38, Beiheft 1). 1940. Special issue on German whale research, part 1.

PICTURE CREDITS

Dustjacket cover photo depicts Rudolf Mayr, Franz Preuschoff and Herbert Ruhnke (left to right), holding the German flag and standing on the Antarctic ice shelf at 69°55'S, 3°57'W on 18 February 1939, from Ritscher 1939 Tafel 1

248

aerial photographs of the *Schwabenland* expedition, from Brunk 1986, Satellitenbild 2

duced by kind permission.

Sea-floor spreading, Whitmarsh and al. 1996, Figure 8.7, 117, in Oceanography, © Man son Publishing, reproduced by kind permission.

152   Simplistic sketch map of the formation of a median rift valley at the crest of the Mid-ocean Ridge, from Open University 1998, Ocean Basins Volume Fig 4.5b source of material, © The Open University, reproduced by kind permission.

153   Herrmann's volcanic line, from Herrmann 1941, 164

156   *Schwabenland's* bathymetric map showing troughs and ridges, from Herrmann 1940, 431

158   Echo-sounding profile II across the deep Atlantic-Indian Antarctic Basin and its abyssal plain, from Schumacher 1958
Echo-sounding profile IIIa from the Atlantic-Indian Ridge near Bouvet (54°S) to Antarc tica, from Schumacher 1958
Echo-sounding profile IIIb from Alantic-Indian Ridge near Bouvet (54°S) across Schwa benland Seamount (near 46°S) and Discovery Bank (42°S), from Schumacher 1958

165   Pressure diagram of the Schwabenland expedition from 5 to 16 January 1939 with lowest pressure at about 725 mmHg (966,54 hPa) close to Bouvet Island on Saturday 15 January, from Herrmann's estate, permission given
Surface weather chart of 20 January 1939, and track of a depression from 20 to 24 January 1939, from Regula 1939, 34
Sketch of weather development (representing air pressure) at the coast of Neu-Schwaben land between 19 January and 6 February 1939, from Ritscher 1942, 83

169   Release of a radio-sonde from the quarterdeck of *Schwabenland*, from Stuttgarter Illustri erte Nr 37, 10 September 1939

170   Position and maximum height of radio-sonde ascents from *Schwabenland*, from Lange 1939, Tafel 6

172   Vertical movement of the air on a cross section between the Bay of Biscay and the Equa tor, from Regula 1949, 231
Meridional vertical section showing the distribution of temperature in the southern hemi sphere in summer, from Flohn 1950, 34 in Regula 1954, 29
Mean pressure chart from 20 to 26 December 1938, and weather observations of Schwa benland, from Regula 1949, 231

173   Components of upper atmosphere winds parallel to latitude in the southern hemisphere in summer, from Flohn 1950, 45 in Regula 1954, 31
Comparison of vertical temperature distribution in the Arctic and the Antarctic, from

Flohn 1950 in Regula 1954, 32

COLOUR PLATES (between pp96 and 97)

BLACK AND WHITE PLATES (between pp 144 and 145)

mayer II, 6 November 2004: (left, Henry Valentine [South Africa], right, Colin Summer hayes), courtesy of H Gernandt

4   *Boreas* moored to the ice edge, from Stuttgarter Illustrierte Nr. 37, 10. September 1939

5   An ice tunnel under the edge of the ice sheet bounding the south side of the Schirmacher Oasis, photograph by Wilfried Richter in Bormann and Fritzsche 1995; Fig. 8-7, permis sion given by D. Fritzsche

6   Expedition members on the return journey, from Ritscher's estate, permission given

7   *Schwabenland* run aground on a Norwegian beach close to Egersund, April 1944, from Nowak 26.1.1983 in Ritscher's estate, permission given

8   Alfred Ritscher, aged about 80, from Ritscher's estate, permission given
        Vignettes depicting the first three German Antarctic expeditions and Herrligkoffer's planned 4th expedition, from private possesion Lüdecke

INDEX